Lifers

Lifers

Barry Cummins

Gill & Macmillan

Gill & Macmillan Ltd
Hume Avenue, Park West, Dublin 12
with associated companies throughout the world
www.gillmacmillan.ie
© Barry Cummins 2004
0 7171 3765 1
Print origination by TypeIT, Dublin
Printed by AIT Nørhaven A/S, Denmark

This book is typeset in 10.5 pt Goudy on 14.5 pt.

*The paper used in this book comes from the wood pulp of managed
forests. For every tree felled, at least one tree is planted, thereby
renewing natural resources.*

A CIP catalogue record for this book is available
from the British Library.

1 3 5 4 2

For every victim

Contents

✧⟫∘⟪✧

Acknowledgments

This book would not have been possible without the assistance and support of a number of families of murder victims. Each family kindly gave of their time and often their hospitality, and spoke about the most upsetting of subjects. As well as recounting poignant memories of their lost loved ones, many families also have strong feelings about the criminal justice system, and their feelings are reflected in this book. The strength of each family in the face of such awful suffering was clearly evident during our meetings. To each and every family my heartfelt thanks.

In particular, thank you to the families of Katie Cooper, George A., Phyllis Murphy, Mary Kitt, Willie Mannion, Private Peter Burke, Corporal Gary Morrow, Denise Cox, Marilyn Rynn, Catherine Doyle, Paud Skehan, Brian Mulvaney and Nichola Sweeney.

Two very brave people recounted to me how they survived attacks by murderers. Sinéad O'Leary in Cork survived a knife attack that claimed the life of her friend Nichola. In a separate case Sinéad Smullen survived a knife attack in Newbridge that claimed the life of her baby, Leilah. The individual strength of both women in the face of such horrific events is truly admirable.

Many current and former members of An Garda Síochána gave me great assistance during my research. Not only were the Gardaí willing to talk about how they solved particular murders, they also readily spoke about lessons they learned during the investigations.

Thank you to Garda Commissioner Noel Conroy and staff at Garda Headquarters. Thank you to Superintendent John Farrelly and all the staff of the Garda Press Office for dealing so efficiently with my queries. A special word of thanks to Garda Damian Hogan in the Press Office for his continuous and invaluable assistance throughout the project. Around the country, thanks for assistance with historical research to Sergeant Luke Conlon, Sergeant Kevin Lavelle and Superintendent Tony Brislane.

There are many current and former Gardaí who kindly gave of their time during my research. It is apparent from my conversations with many of these officers that the violent scenes they have witnessed will remain with them. While they maintain an essential professional distance from any murder case, many officers continue to keep in contact with families of murder victims, and also keep track of the murderer's progress through the justice system.

During my research I met with Gardaí who investigated murder cases spanning over five decades. Many Gardaí are quoted by name in this book, and I take this opportunity to thank you all very much for your time and interest.

Due to the nature of the information other Gardaí imparted, these officers are not named in this book. Thank you to each and every one for your time and trust.

There are a number of prison officers who kindly gave of their time to offer an insight into what life is like in an Irish prison. Each officer outlined how they work in a dangerous environment but in a profession providing job satisfaction. Prison officers protect us from some of the most dangerous men and women this country has ever known. Thank you all for your time and trust.

I would also like to thank everyone in the Press Office of the Department of Justice, the Press Office of the Department of An

Taoiseach, the Irish Prison Service, and also the Prison Officers Association. Thank you also to the Defence Forces Press Office and PDFORRA. Thank you to Fr Liam Hickey and Fr Gerry Corcoran, and thank you to the staff at the ILAC Centre library and the library in Ennis. Thank you also to all at the Maxwell Photo Agency, and thank you especially to Courtpix.

Thank you to everyone at Gill & Macmillan, especially commissioning editor Fergal Tobin, and also D, Cliona, Nicki, Síofra, Lynn, Aoileann, Antoinette and Jaimee.

Thank you to my friends and colleagues in crime reporting and beyond for your continued encouragement and interest. Thank you to my fellow journalists and photographers and cameramen at the Four Courts for all your assistance throughout the years. Thanks especially to Brian, Ronan, Marc, Graham, Julian, Rocky, Diarmuid, Michael, Azra, Orla, Tomás, Seán, Mary, John and Paul. Thank you to the CCC agency, and the Ireland International agency, and thank you to Gerry Curran, Media Relations Advisor, the Courts Service. Thank you also to my former colleagues in Today FM for many happy years, and thanks as always to Barry Flynn for my break in Midlands Radio 3. Thank you also to my colleagues in the RTÉ Newsroom.

Thank you as always to the staff of St Mark's Primary School and St Mark's Community School in Tallaght.

On a personal note, I want to thank my family for everything. Thank you to my parents, Patricia O'Neill and Barry Cummins, and to my brother Mark for your constant support and interest. And thank you especially to Grace for all your encouragement, enthusiasm, guidance, suggestions and constant support, without which I could not have written this book.

Introduction

I f the mandatory sentence of life imprisonment for murder had any real meaning, Nancy Nolan might be alive today. Her killer, Thomas Murray, is a perfect example of everything that is wrong with the way the Irish State deals with its murderers. This man was already serving a life sentence for the murder of elderly farmer Willie Mannion, in Ballygar, Co. Galway, in 1981, when on 14 February 2000 he found the opportunity to strike again in the same village, beating Nancy Nolan to death with a lump hammer. Nancy was a widowed mother of six and a much-loved grandmother. She lived alone just across the road from the school where she and her late husband Tom had taught generations of local children. The attack she suffered in the hallway of her home in broad daylight was ferocious and frenzied. After murdering Nancy, Murray walked back out the front door, pulling it shut. It would be almost 24 hours before Nancy's body would be found. In the meantime, Murray hid the murder weapon, went home to visit his father, had his tea and then headed back to prison. It almost defies belief to think that Murray left Castlerea Prison on day release at 9 a.m. on 14 February 2000, murdered Nancy at around 2 p.m., and then returned to prison just before his 9 p.m. curfew to continue serving his life sentence for the first murder he had committed almost 19 years before.

Thomas Murray was just 17 years old when, on the Sunday evening of 19 July 1981, he called unannounced to the home of his 73-year-old neighbour, Willie Mannion, produced a knife and stabbed Willie over a dozen times in the head and neck. Like the murder of Nancy Nolan almost 19 years later, there was no motive for the frenzied attack on a well-liked bachelor farmer who had lived all his life in Ballygar. Murray would later tell the Gardaí how he had met Willie after Mass earlier that day and sometime during the afternoon decided to kill him. When Murray admitted the murder, he could give no reason for his desire to kill. Considering this random killer would later find himself in the position to murder another elderly person, one response he made to the Gardaí in 1981 is chilling: 'I killed Willie Mannion. ... I had it planned, but I hadn't it planned too long. ... I wouldn't do it again in a million years.'

The tragedy is that Murray did do it again, and that this country failed an 80-year-old woman who had dedicated her entire life to her family and her community. A further unsettling fact is that Murray had already reoffended, while out on temporary release from his life sentence, over a year before he murdered Nancy Nolan. In July 1998, Murray indecently exposed himself to young children playing close to the River Corrib in Galway city. He was given a six-month sentence, and his temporary release was halted. But by late 1999 he was being given further unescorted release from prison. When Murray was given his second life sentence for the murder of Nancy Nolan — to be served in addition to the life sentence for the murder of Willie Mannion — he was heard wondering how long a life sentence he'd have to serve this time. Murray's mentality is a result of allowing him out of prison less than 20 years after murdering Willie Mannion. Random killer Thomas Murray is one of the many lifers profiled in this book.

There is something wrong with the way this State deals with murderers. There is something wrong with a system where very few murderers will actually spend the rest of their lives behind bars. There is something wrong with a system where judges cannot make recommendations that killers like Thomas Murray serve minimum sentences of 25 years, or 40 years, or 60 years, or whatever the appropriate tariff is for the most brutal murders. There is also something wrong with the way the families of murder victims are treated by the Irish State. It is truly despicable that these families are rarely informed before their loved one's killer is released back into society. If rehabilitation is a central objective of the Irish prison system, common courtesy should be a primary objective of the State when dealing with the families of victims.

Over the next few years, some of Ireland's longest serving and most brutal and random killers will be released back into society. For decades, the practice of the Central Criminal Court, when a person pleaded guilty to murder, was to impose the mandatory life sentence without hearing any evidence of the crime. The Irish public was denied the opportunity to learn even the barest details about many murders and the background of those responsible. Justice was not administered in public, and the effect is that little is known of the life and crimes of some of this country's longest serving lifers. Two such killers who escaped much of the media glare and who feature in this book are Michael Holohan and Frank Daly. Both men have spent well over 20 years in prison for separate killings and both expect to be granted parole in the future. Both pleaded guilty to random murders; both already had a history of extreme violence; and both could have been stopped if violent men were tagged.

Another long serving lifer profiled in this book is triple killer Michael McAleavey who was less than a week into his first tour of United Nations peace-keeping duties in the Lebanon in October 1982, when he opened fire indiscriminately and murdered three members of the Irish Defence Forces. By 1996, after serving the equivalent of less than five years in prison for each of the lives he took, the Irish authorities saw fit to give McAleavey temporary release for a time. However, no one in authority had the courtesy to pick up the phone to inform the families of his victims, and it was left to journalists to break the news.

Sometimes justice has to wait a very long time. On the evening of 22 December 1979, 23-year-old Phyllis Murphy was abducted from a bus stop in Newbridge and taken to a location a few miles away in Co. Kildare, where she was raped and murdered. Her body was then hidden among trees over 20 miles away in a forested area of Co. Wicklow. It took four weeks before the Gardaí found Phyllis's naked body but, remarkably, semen found at the scene had been preserved. It would be another 20 years before advances in forensic science could match the semen with the DNA of married father of five, John Crerar, from Kildare town. The 23-year investigation into the murder of Phyllis Murphy is outlined in this book.

Forensic science has proved an invaluable tool in tracking many of the country's most dangerous men. As well as solving the murder of Phyllis Murphy, DNA evidence also led to a seemingly happily married man being caught for the murder of 41-year-old Marilyn Rynn, who was attacked while walking home in west Dublin in December 1995. It took over two weeks to find Marilyn's body, but freezing temperatures preserved semen found at the scene, which was later matched with 32-year-old David Lawler, who is now serving a life sentence for the random attack. Bodily fluids are not the only identifiers that can place a killer at a murder scene. Career criminal William Campion will forever rue the day he wore a particular pair of runners during a house robbery in Co. Clare, where he and an accomplice tortured and murdered 68-

year-old farmer, Paud Skehan, in April 1998. As Campion and his fellow murderer tied Paud's hands and legs, doused him with lighter fluid and beat him repeatedly, Campion stood in Paud's blood and left a distinct footprint on the timber floor. Today he is serving a life sentence for murder.

Campion was already known as an incredibly violent character before he murdered Paud Skehan. But despite his previous convictions, the lack of a violent offenders register or a tagging system meant that he found the opportunity to torture and kill. As judges have no discretion to impose a mandatory minimum sentence for particularly heinous murders, it is a sobering fact that over the coming years a number of dangerous killers, including Campion, will be entitled to apply for parole.

Another killer who should never have been in a position to take a life is Brian Willoughby. In the early hours of 11 March 2000, Willoughby led a gang that beat 19-year-old Brian Mulvaney to death on a road in Templeogue in south Dublin. Brian Mulvaney didn't know any of the young men who attacked him; he had only met Willoughby a short time earlier at a house-party. One of the most disturbing aspects of Brian's murder is that Willoughby was actually out on bail at the time of the murder. He was waiting to be sentenced for three horrific random attacks on men in Dublin city, one of whom lost the sight in one of his eyes after Willoughby stabbed him in the face.

Mark Nash from Yorkshire in north-east England is one of the most violent men to have ever set foot in Ireland. In August 1997, while visiting his girlfriend's sister and her family in Co. Roscommon, he turned from a seemingly friendly 'charmer' to a deranged and brutal killer. He first stabbed his girlfriend's brother-in-law, Carl Doyle, as he sat sleeping on a couch. Nash then crept upstairs and beat his girlfriend with an iron bar while telling her,

'You must die.' He then chased Carl's wife Catherine downstairs and stabbed her to death in the kitchen. When he was later arrested he made a statement relating to the murders of two other women repeatedly stabbed as they slept in a house in Grangegorman in Dublin the previous March, but he has since retracted that statement. The crimes of Mark Nash are profiled in this book.

One family who have taken a leading role in campaigning for a life sentence to have its proper meaning is the family of Nichola Sweeney, who was just 20 years old when she was stabbed to death by an intruder who broke into her Cork home in April 2002. Nineteen-year-old Peter Whelan didn't utter a word as he repeatedly stabbed Nichola and her friend, Sinéad O'Leary, in a random motiveless attack. Miraculously, Sinéad survived the assault and displayed remarkable presence of mind to raise the alarm before collapsing unconscious. Whelan, who lived close by, was arrested a short time later and eventually pleaded guilty to the murder of Nichola and the attempted murder of Sinéad. Judges are normally powerless to recommend that a murderer serve a particular length of time in prison, but Mr Justice Paul Carney found himself with a unique opportunity to ensure that Whelan would remain in prison for a long time. Whelan was given a 15-year sentence for the attempted murder of Sinéad and a life sentence for Nichola's murder, but the sentences were to be consecutive. Whelan will therefore not begin his life sentence until 2017, but even so, he will only be in his late forties when in the 2030s he will be entitled to apply for parole.

The fear of every family of a murder victim — that their loved one's killer will not serve a full life sentence — is entirely understandable when you consider that the longest serving prisoner in Ireland is only still behind bars because he wants to be.

Now in his seventies, Jimmy Ennis has been in prison since 1964 for murdering a Co. Cork farmer during a house robbery. Ennis has now spent more time in prison than the 40-year maximum term for murdering a Garda. He has served more than twice the average length of time a life sentence prisoner spends in jail. If he applied for parole he would get it immediately, but he is now institutionalised and happy to live out his days in Shelton Abbey Prison in Co. Wicklow. It is worth noting that Ennis committed the murder shortly after leaving Portlaoise Prison, where he had served a sentence for repeatedly stabbing a woman during another robbery. Like many other murderers profiled in this book, if Ennis had been tagged or monitored on his release from prison after the first attack, he might never have had the chance to commit murder and would not now be the longest serving prisoner in Ireland.

But this book begins with the case of the last Irish murderer who never had a chance to be a lifer.

1

Last Man Hanged

'I will tell you all. Drink was the cause of it.' Michael Manning rested on one elbow, a wall on one side of his bed, and four Gardaí on the other. It was 2.30 on the morning of Saturday, 19 November 1953. Manning lit up a cigarette one of the Gardaí had given him, and he paused. From a distance of two or three feet, the officers could smell the stale stench of alcohol from his breath. One garda sat on a chair beside the bed, ready to write down anything their murder suspect might say. In the next room, Manning's heavily pregnant wife was asking other Gardaí what all this was about. A detective told her about the body of the elderly woman found on the roadside just a few hours before, and said they needed to ask her husband some questions. The Gardaí had already found Manning's muddied and bloodstained overcoat and boots in the kitchen, and now as they stood in his bedroom, they looked at him and waited. Having taken some moments to think back over his random murderous assault, and as the rest of Limerick city slept soundly, 25-year-old Michael Manning began making the confession that would lead to him becoming the last man hanged in Ireland.

Five hours before his bedside confession, Manning crept up behind Nurse Katie Cooper as she walked on a quiet roadside less than two miles outside Limerick city. The first the 65-year-old woman knew of the danger she faced was when Manning put his arms around her from behind, knocking her yellow beret off her head and her glasses from her face. Within seconds he dragged her off the roadside towards a grass verge and began to subject her to a ferocious assault. He stuffed grass in her mouth to stifle her cries for help. He knocked out five teeth from her lower jaw, one of which she swallowed as he stuffed more grass into her mouth. He tried to rape Katie, but she fought him. Medical results would later show that she suffered bruising to her legs consistent with attempted rape but that no rape had occurred. As well as punching her in the face, causing extensive bleeding in her mouth, Manning fractured three of her ribs. Her tongue was severely bruised, most likely by his hands trying to stop her screams. Katie was five foot tall and slight. Her killer was five foot three but strong. At some stage during the attack Katie choked to death.

On the day he murdered Katie Cooper, Manning had earlier been working at Limerick docks where he earned an average of 25 shillings a day. It was welcome money for a young man with a pregnant wife. Sometimes he could get work with CIÉ as a carter and could earn even more. He came from a large family of 13 children, had left school early and had been put to work by his father. He had never been in trouble with the law and he was regarded as an honest and industrious man, a hard worker. But he also had a drink problem.

At the time of the murder, Manning and his wife of 14 months were living in a two-room single-storey house at Moore's Place, off Lelia Street in Limerick. His wife was expecting their second child. Their first baby had died. At around 2.30 p.m. on Friday, 18

November 1953, he arrived back from working at the docks. He and his wife sat down in the kitchen and ate their dinner. Within 12 hours, in the same house, he would be making a murder confession that would send him to his own death.

Katie Cooper was a woman ahead of her time. As well as dedicating her life to nursing the sick, she was also a keen photographer. In the 1920s, 30s and 40s, she was taking photographs of a professional standard that serve as a fascinating documentary of a time in Irish life before cameras were commonplace. She kept hundreds of photos in special albums, images of her nursing colleagues, friends, and her family in Co. Clare. She also kept photos of herself holidaying in the west of Ireland, horse riding and hill walking. The photo albums also served as scrapbooks where she wrote musings and pasted jokes or handy tips from newspapers. From some of the more serious notes, it is clear Katie was deeply affected by the amount of suffering she saw during her four decades as a nurse in both Ireland and England. When I meet her nephew Pierce in Katie's home village of Killimer in Co. Clare, he remembers how the albums arrived with the rest of Katie's belongings shortly after her murder.

I was 7 years old when Aunt Katie was murdered. I can remember when she used to visit us from Limerick, she'd bring us sweets, Liquorice Allsorts. And I remember the box camera; Aunt Katie showed me how she'd put the film into it, and then how she'd used chemicals with it. She took photographs of us all here. I was one of eight children, and as well as my mother and father, Katie's brother Willie and her sister Florrie were living with us too. And she'd take all these photos with this great camera. And I remember after she was murdered her trunk arrived and all her belongings were in it, including her photos.

Katie Cooper dedicated her life to helping others. Born in 1889 at the family farm at Donail in Killimer, she was one of a family of five boys and five girls. At an early age she witnessed her older sister Helena dying from consumption. This may have had a large bearing on her decision to become a nurse. It was a decision that would eventually take her from Co. Clare to Kidderminster Hospital in London, where she worked through the 1920s and 30s. In the aftermath of the First World War, she witnessed all types of horrific injuries suffered by both young and old. She was a good carer, both firm and friendly with patients, and was a popular nurse and later a matron at the busy hospital. By the late 1930s, as Britain prepared for war with Germany, Katie returned to Ireland, becoming the matron at Barrington's Hospital in Limerick city. She never married, but had a wide circle of friends in Limerick and a large extended family in Killimer. She was walking back to Barrington's Hospital on the night Manning grabbed her from behind and dragged her to her death.

After finishing his dinner at 3.30 p.m., Manning said goodbye to his wife and left his home off Lelia Street in the north of Limerick city. He drove his horse and cart to a store on nearby William Street, where he collected cement and lime and loaded them on to his cart. He was due to bring the goods out to his father on the Newport road, east of the city, but he had time to spare. He went into one pub and had two pints of stout. He met a friend, Michael Flaherty, and the two of them went on to another pub and had two more pints. The pair then tried to get more drink at two other pubs, but they were refused by bar staff who told them they had had enough already. But they tried a third pub, where Flaherty knew the barman, and they had a fifth pint of stout. It was now early evening.

At around 6 p.m., while Manning was out drinking, Katie

Cooper put on her brown overcoat, yellow beret and matching scarf, and headed out the door of Barrington's Hospital at George's Quay. Elizabeth Williams, a maid at the hospital, saw the matron to the door. It was a clear moonlit night as Katie set off towards Newcastle, just a few miles outside the city. She arrived at her friend's house before 7 p.m. and stayed chatting with her until around 9.20 p.m. She said goodnight and set off back towards Limerick.

After finishing his fifth pint, Manning left the pub with Michael Flaherty and they got up on the horse and cart. Manning dropped his friend off at a nearby corner and wished him goodnight. He drove his horse and cart out of the city to his brother Paddy's house, where he unloaded empty coal sacks. He then went on to his father's farm on the Newport road, where he delivered the cement and lime. John Manning spoke with his son for half an hour discussing the work prospects at Limerick docks. John asked Michael if he would have some tea, but Michael said no. At around 8 p.m. Manning left his father and headed back towards Limerick. He went into a pub at Annacotty and had a pint and a half. He had now drunk six and a half pints. He started to make his way home, but first he needed to leave his horse and cart in a field at Newcastle, near the old castle ruins, as he always did. Just a few hundred yards away Katie Cooper was walking back towards Limerick city. It was shortly after 9.30 p.m..

In the early 1950s there was an average of four or five murders in Ireland every year. Many of those murders were the result of domestic disputes, and random roadside attacks were quite rare. November 1953 was a time when people in the countryside left their backdoors open. It was a time when women felt safe walking along country roads, especially so close to a city. All that was about to be shattered.

There was no lighting along the roadside as Manning left the field and turned to walk home towards the city. But there was a full moon, and by the moonlight Manning saw a woman walking ahead of him in the same direction on the left-hand side of the road. There were no houses for a few hundred yards, no other pedestrians and no traffic on the quiet country road, which is now the N7, the main road between Limerick and Dublin. He later recounted to Gardaí how he pounced on Katie Cooper from behind.

I walked along behind her for a few minutes. I suddenly lost control of myself and jumped on her because I saw her alone. I pulled her into the grass. She struggled … She let out a few screams. I knocked her down on the grass and stuffed grass in her mouth to keep or stop her from roaring. … I tried to get at her, but I couldn't. … I had one hand in her mouth and the other under her back. She got quiet after about five minutes, but she began to struggle again and asked me to stop. … She just said 'Stop, stop.' The next thing I knew a motorcar with lights on stopped beside me. I got up and jumped over the ditch.

That car was driven by John McCormack who, along with his wife Anne, had walked by the scene just moments earlier. Both had seen what they thought was a courting couple lying on the grass verge of the roadside. But something wasn't right. Anne McCormack thought she had heard a muffled wail or some kind of distressing sound coming from the woman lying beside the man. The McCormacks walked on home, but Anne felt anxious about what she had seen and heard on the road. At around 10 o'clock they decided to drive back to the scene, and as their car pulled up they saw a man jump up and clamber over a wall by the side of the road. They stopped the car and saw the body of Katie Cooper.

Katie's skirt was still on her, but had been raised up around her upper body during the struggle. She was still wearing her brown camel hair overcoat buttoned and belted. Her yellow scarf was wound loosely around her neck. It was bloodstained and covered in grass. Her head was turned to the side and blood oozed from her mouth. There were cuts on her lips. Horrified, the McCormacks jumped back into their car and drove to a local priest to raise the alarm.

Meanwhile, Manning ran through the fields back to his brother Paddy's home. He wanted to borrow a bicycle that he often used to travel to and from his horse and cart. Despite having just committed a brutal murder, he spoke calmly to his brother, not giving away anything about what he had just done. His brother asked him to bring a horse down from up the road before heading home, and Michael did what he was asked. He then cycled home to Limerick, arriving at his home around half past eleven. His wife had prepared a supper for him, and they both ate before going to bed around midnight. Just 500 metres across a bridge, the staff of Barrington's Hospital were wondering where their matron was. Two miles away, a full-scale murder enquiry was already under way.

Pierce Cooper's older brother Seán tells me how it was their father Percy who had to travel to Limerick in the early hours of 19 November 1953 to identify the body of his sister.

Our father was the youngest of the ten, but it fell to him to identify Katie. They knew Katie was from Killimer, so this is where they came to find the next of kin. The Gardaí in Kilrush had been alerted and two Gardaí had to travel up the hill to find Percy Cooper. They arrived up on their bikes. I remember our father left Killimer for Limerick in the early hours of the morning, just hours after the murder. I remember him dressing himself to make the journey, and I remember, some time later, Aunt Katie's bicycle being brought to the family home in Killimer. Our father never really spoke about the murder in the years afterwards, or what he had to do that night.

Manning's distinctive cowboy hat was to be his undoing. As Garda Maurice Jones cycled from Limerick to the murder scene, he spotted two young men wearing odd-looking hats standing close to a garage. One was wearing a yellow beret, while the other was wearing a brown cowboy hat. Upon arriving at the scene, and with other Gardaí sealing off the area around Katie's body, Jones decided to go back and find the two men wearing the odd hats. Someone told him one of the men was Edward Tobin, a young man living a short distance away. He called to Tobin's house and Tobin produced both the yellow beret and the cowboy hat. He told the garda he and his friend John McNamara had found the hats out on the roadside at Newcastle that evening. The brown cowboy hat with three dints was particularly distinctive. It was a familiar sight on the head of Michael Manning as he drove his horse and cart around the city.

Anne McCormack had actually spotted the beret and the cowboy hat on the roadside when she and her husband found Katie's body. But the hats were gone when the couple returned to the scene with a priest. In the meantime, Edward Tobin and John McNamara had walked by the scene and found the hats lying on the road. They had playfully put them on their heads and continued walking, unaware that the body of Katie Cooper was lying only a few yards away on the grass verge. McNamara donned the yellow beret and Tobin wore the cowboy hat. The young men were totally oblivious to the fact that they were wearing crucial evidence linking a murderer and his victim. Within minutes of Garda Jones finding the hats at Tobin's home, a team of Gardaí was *en route* to Michael Manning's house in Limerick city.

As well as finding the two hats that night, Maurice Jones was one of the Gardaí who travelled to 7 Moore's Place at around 2.30 a.m. Over 50 years since that night, the now retired garda tells me he clearly remembers entering the home of the man who murdered Katie Cooper.

It was his wife who opened the door to us. The house was small, just a boarded partition between the kitchen and the bedroom. Manning was asleep when we arrived. I saw a grey tweed overcoat in the kitchen. It was wet and muddied, and bloodstained. Near the fireplace there was a pair of gent's boots with mud and grass stuck to them, also bloodstained. I remember Manning being in a kind of stupor after waking up. There was a mug of cold tea on a small table beside the bed. When he was asked about the incident out at Newcastle, I remember he propelled himself up by his elbows and asked, 'Is she dead?'

It took a few minutes for Manning's wife to wake up and open the door to the Gardaí. However, once the door was opened, half a dozen Gardaí, led by Inspectors Patrick Pender and Timothy Griffin, entered the house. Four of them went through the kitchen to the bedroom, where they found Manning lying in a double bed. As Manning rubbed his eyes to focus on the Gardaí, Timothy Griffin asked him, 'Were you out the road tonight?'

'I was,' Manning replied.

'Will you give an account of your movements. There was a woman attacked out the road.'

At that moment, the Gardaí noticed the bloodstains on Manning's hands. Griffin immediately cautioned Manning that anything he said would be taken down and might be used in evidence.

Manning stared ahead for a few moments in total silence. He then began twisting around in the bed, as if looking for something, and asked, 'Where are my cigarettes?'

A garda gave him a cigarette from across the room. He lit it, looked into the distance and after a long pause said, 'I will tell you all. Drink was the cause of it.'

Inspector Pender said to the other Gardaí, 'You better get me some paper.'

Over the next 70 minutes Manning outlined how he had attacked Katie Cooper and choked her to death. Pender sat on a chair beside the bed, resting his writing paper on a pane of glass on his knees and writing the statement that Manning's defence team would later contest because of the circumstances in which it was taken. Manning remained sitting up in bed with a wall to one side of him and four Gardaí effectively surrounding the rest of the bed. He spoke calmly but quickly, and a number of times the inspector had to get him to slow down. While taking the statement Patrick Pender could get the smell of stale liquor from Manning's breath. Manning told the Gardaí he thought his victim was still alive when he left her. He said the blood on his hands 'must have come from the lady's mouth'. Once the statement was completed, and with dawn still a few hours away, the Gardaí prepared to arrest Manning and charge him with the murder of Katie Cooper. As his young wife anxiously waited in the next room, wondering why all these Gardaí were in her home, Manning turned to Sergeant John Hanrahan and asked him, 'Will I have to come with you?'

On the evening of Wednesday, 17 February 1954, Michael

Manning was found guilty of the murder of Katie Cooper. After a three-day trial, the all-male jury at the Central Criminal Court in Dublin took less than three hours to convict him. Mr Justice George D. Murnaghan, who had only been appointed to the Central Criminal Court the previous month, told the jury: 'If it is any consolation, I agree with your verdict, gentlemen.' The only issue upon which the jury had to decide was whether Manning had been guilty of murder or manslaughter, or if he was guilty but insane. His defence team argued that the amount of drink he had taken that day rendered him incapable of being aware of his actions. The defence also outlined to the court that three of Manning's extended family had been treated in mental hospitals. However, the jury did not believe the suggestion that Manning himself had mental health difficulties and the defence that 'drink was the cause of it' was not accepted by the jury. After the verdict was read out, the registrar of the court asked Manning if he had anything to say. After a pause he replied 'Nothing to say, sir'.

Mr Justice Murnaghan then donned the black cap to pronounce sentence:

It is ordered and adjudged that you Michael Manning be taken from the bar of the court where you now stand to the prison whence you last came, and that on Wednesday the 10th of March in the year of Our Lord one thousand nine hundred and fifty four you be taken to the common place of execution in the prison in which you shall be then confined and that you be then and there hanged by the neck until you be dead, and that your body be buried within the walls of the prison in which the aforesaid judgment of death shall be executed on you.

Maurice Jones was one of the many Gardaí to travel from

Limerick to Dublin for the three-day trial. He remembers that Manning stood to attention as the death sentence was pronounced.

> I remember when Judge Murnaghan handed down the sentence, complete with black cap that had been ceremoniously handed to him by the court crier. Manning took it bravely; he stood firmly to attention, clasping the railing of the dock with both hands. I got to know him well during the course of the trial, and after the sentence was handed down he said to me, 'I was expecting that. I deserved it.' I've often passed by the scene of the murder, and I think about Nurse Cooper, and I think about Michael Manning and I say a prayer.

One week after Manning was found guilty of murder and sentenced to death, a 39-year-old Cork man, who had allegedly killed his wife by cutting her throat, walked free from the Central Criminal Court after being found not guilty of murder. The court had heard evidence of how the man's 21-year-old wife had been blatantly having an affair with a man with whom she had had a relationship before her marriage. Despite her husband's pleadings, the court was told she continued to keep company with the other man. The jury was not given the option of finding the accused guilty of manslaughter, and faced with effectively condemning him to death or setting him free, they found him not guilty of murder. While this man walked free from the Central Criminal Court back to his home in Cork to rebuild his life, Manning was sitting in the death cell in Mountjoy, busily writing a last-ditch petition for his life to be spared.

Despite the sentence handed down by the Central Criminal Court, Manning wasn't hanged on 10 March. By then he had lodged an appeal on a number of grounds, including the circumstances of his bedside confession. His barristers argued that the jury should not have been allowed to hear a confession that was taken while Manning was sitting up in his bed with four Gardaí effectively surrounding him. His barristers also said the jury should have been allowed to consider the defence of 'insane impulse', whereby Manning might have been temporarily insane when he attacked Katie Cooper. In supporting this argument, his barristers pointed out that he had made no attempt to cover up his crime. He had left the bloodstained clothes in clear view in his kitchen before going to bed. Also the barristers highlighted the fact that shortly after he had confessed to the murder, Manning had asked Sergeant Hanrahan, 'Will I have to come with you?' They argued that this question was very odd, coming from a man supposedly responsible for his actions and in control of all his faculties.

In an incredible act of compassion and decency, Katie Cooper's brothers and her sister were among those who signed a petition for a presidential reprieve to be granted to save Manning from the death penalty. It is a sobering fact that the last man hanged in the Irish Republic was executed against the wishes of his victim's family. Pierce Cooper says the feeling was that his aunt's killer was a simple character.

My family didn't hate Manning for what he did. They learned that he 'wasn't the full shilling' and that he used to drink a lot. They were willing to allow the sentence of death to be commuted. I think the correct sentence for Michael Manning should have been imprisonment for life, not hanging. When my father signed a petition for Manning not to be hanged, he would have considered the fact that Manning wasn't of sound mind and that he drank too much. I believe the correct sentence should have been life, but life with no parole.

From the time Ireland achieved independence in 1922 up to Michael Manning's murder conviction in 1954, the Irish State executed 34 people including one woman — Annie Walsh from Limerick, who was executed in Mountjoy Jail in 1925 for the murder of her husband. During the Irish Civil War over 100 people had been executed, and upon the foundation of the Irish State the use of capital punishment for civilian murders also became an accepted part of Irish life. Ironically, for a country trying to assert its new-found independence, an English executioner conducted every hanging carried out in the Irish State. But by the late 1940s there was a growing unease about the State's right to take life. The last person hanged before Manning was William Gambon, executed on 24 November 1948 after the Fine Gael-led five-party coalition government decided not to intervene. In the five and a half years since that execution, at least three other people had been given a presidential reprieve upon the recommendation of the government. However, despite petitions from members of the public, including Katie Cooper's family, and a plea from the condemned man himself directly from his death cell, the Fianna Fáil government of 1954 chose not to intervene in the Manning case.

On Friday, 3 April 1954, the Court of Criminal Appeal rejected Manning's appeal against his murder conviction. The three-judge court set the date of Tuesday, 20 April 1954, as the new date for his execution at Mountjoy Jail. Manning remained in the death cell at Mountjoy, a small room on the ground floor at the end of what is now D Wing in the eastern part of the prison. The cell where condemned prisoners were once housed is not in use today. It remains locked — a cold room where convicted killers spent their last hours playing cards with prison officers, drinking stout, writing messages to their families, and writing last-minute pleas to the politicians who held the power to save their lives.

While Manning wrote his petition to the government from his death cell, other people were making efforts to have his life spared. As well as Katie Cooper's family voicing their objections to the intended execution, Manning's own wife, expecting the birth of their child at any moment, visited members of the clergy in Limerick to try and save her husband. Her views were passed on to the government and were considered at a Cabinet meeting on Tuesday, 13 April, a week before the execution. The Cabinet also read Manning's petition. For the next 50 years Michael Manning's petition would remain locked away at the Department of An Taoiseach. Only in 2004 was the file deemed suitable for public viewing. From his death cell Manning wrote:

I am almost seven weeks under the death sentence and it is a hard sentence to be under for such a long time. ... It seems no matter what I do the punishment will have to be carried out so this is my last chance and I ask you to show mercy. ... As I was passing out the woman that night I suddenly lost my head and jumped on the woman and remember no more until the lights of the car shone on me. ... I was never in trouble in my life before that day. ... I am married eighteen months and my wife is expecting a baby within the next fortnight and it is a hard strain worrying how I am going to get on. We were always happy until this trouble happened. My wife says she will never hold anything against me no matter how long we will be apart. I am truly and heartily sorry for having committed such an offence against God and the Law of man. ... I have asked God to have mercy on me on account of my wife and my parents. My wife is only 22 years of age, and I am 25 years of age. So now as I send in this petition I ask you to show mercy upon me as it is so near Easter and Good Friday. ... I am not afraid to die as I am fully prepared to go before my God but it is on behalf of my wife as she is so young and so near the birth of the baby ... so I would be grateful to you if you showed your mercy toward my wife and me. I remain, your humble servant, Michael Manning.

The government also considered pleas for clemency made by members of the public. One person appealed directly to the Taoiseach, Éamon de Valera, noting that the execution was scheduled for the Tuesday of Easter week. The letter referred to the significance of Easter week for Irish people since 1916, and begged the government not to bring in an English hangman during this time.

The government also debated the issue of whether mental illness played a part in Manning's crime. It had emerged that an uncle and a granduncle of Manning's had both died in mental hospitals. Also a first cousin was a patient in the Central Mental Hospital in Dublin. However, a medical report sent to the government stated that Manning had shown no evidence of mental disorder. The report stated:

He has an average standard of education for his age and class. ... His behaviour has been quite normal during his imprisonment and he has taken part in social activities [in prison]. ... He is quite rational in speech and behaviour. He shows no evidence of depression or anxiety since his trial and appears to be taking his sentence in calm spirit.

On 13 April 1954, the government decided not to advise the President to grant a reprieve for Manning. Taoiseach Éamon de Valera phoned President Seán T. O'Kelly immediately after the

Cabinet meeting ended to inform him of the decision. Prison officials contacted the English executioner, Albert Pierrepoint, who made arrangements to travel to Dublin.

From the many photographs she took of her colleagues and her patients, it is clear that Nurse Katie Cooper dedicated much of her life to trying to save the lives of others. She witnessed the pain and suffering of people on a scale most do not. On an inner page of one of the scrapbooks there is a short stanza written by Katie which describes an ideal world, the pursuit of which makes for a decent society. Considering the terrible fate that later befell Katie, the five lines she composed are haunting.

So many gods
So many creeds
So many paths that wind and wind
When just the art of being kind
Is all this sad world needs

On the morning of Tuesday, 20 April 1954, Manning was brought the short distance from his death cell to the top floor of the two-storey Hanging House in Mountjoy Jail. Today the Hanging House is normally locked, just like the death cell. There is a coolness about the air inside this building, which lies in the part of the prison closest to Drumcondra. A long rusty lever serves as a reminder of the way the release of a wooden trapdoor sent dozens of convicted killers to their deaths.

Manning stood quietly as a sheet was placed over his head and a thick rope around his neck. A short time later the trapdoor below his feet gave way. His neck was broken, and the 25-year-old Limerick man became the last man hanged in Ireland. Within minutes prison officers in the room below the trapdoor used a stepladder to remove his body from the rope. With his work completed, Pierrepoint prepared to make his return journey to Britain. Outside the prison a small group of protestors recited the Rosary. A notice was posted on to the front gate of the prison stating that the sentence of death had been carried out at 8 a.m. Meanwhile, a post-mortem examination was performed. The cause of death was logged in the Prison Death Book as cardiac and respiratory failure following dislocation of the third vertebrae. Just over four hours after the hanging, Manning's body was placed in a coffin which was brought to a location at the north end of the prison, close to the Royal Canal. And there he was buried in an unmarked grave within the grounds of Mountjoy Jail, close to the unmarked graves of other murderers executed by the Irish State.

In the second half of the twentieth century, more and more of the ground of Mountjoy Jail was covered by concrete and tarmac. Although the general area is known where the executed prisoners are buried, there are no headstones, no markings whatsoever to indicate human remains lie within the grounds of Mountjoy. The prison's governor, John Lonergan, believes the situation is a scandal.

The system at that time was such that there was a total disregard for human life. I am personally opposed to the death penalty, and believe the State never had the right to take a life. And the other terrible wrong was that the families of these prisoners were denied the right to give their loved ones a proper burial. There is a basic humanity to uphold and to just dump bodies in the ground like that was, and is, a scandal. Those executed prisoners had mothers and fathers, and some had wives and children.

The growing unease about the use of the death penalty in the new Irish Republic came just too late for Michael Manning. Another man convicted of murdering a woman in Dublin city later that same year had his death sentence commuted to life imprisonment. Robert James Stephenson, from Scotland, was convicted of the murder of 24-year-old Mary Nolan from Crumlin. Stephenson, who was also 24 years old, was a crewmember of an oil tanker that had docked in Dublin. He went drinking in the city and later followed Mary Nolan out of a pub, punched her in the face and strangled her to death in a laneway off Gardiner Street in the north of the city. He was given a presidential reprieve from the death penalty just months after Manning's execution. Over the next ten years another six murderers would face the death penalty, only to be saved by a presidential reprieve. These convicted murderers ranged from a man who strangled a 6-year-old boy in a random attack in Co. Carlow, to Nurse Mary Cadden who was convicted of murdering a woman on whom she was carrying out an abortion in Dublin city. Ten years after Manning's execution, the Criminal Justice Act of 1964 removed the death penalty as the sentence for 'ordinary' murders. While the death penalty remained until 1990 as the sentence for the capital murder of a garda, from 1964 a new sentence of 'life imprisonment' was the punishment for most murderers. However, over the following decades it would become clear that very few murderers would actually spend the whole of their lives in prison.

While the jury in Manning's trial did not accept alcohol as an excuse for a random roadside attack, it is interesting to note the totally different verdict of a jury in another case that had some similarities. Thirty years after Manning was put to death, 23-year-old Michael Murphy of Ballsgrove in Drogheda was found not guilty of murder but guilty of the manslaughter of a woman he attacked at random. Murphy attacked a 65-year-old woman, Kitty Carroll, as she was walking home from a bingo hall in Drogheda on the night of 20 October 1983. Like Manning, Murphy choked his victim to death. While Manning stuffed grass in his victim's mouth, Murphy put his thumbs into Kitty Carroll's mouth, pressing down on her tongue, causing her to choke. Like Manning, Murphy blamed alcohol for his crime, claiming he had drunk at least ten pints that day. Unlike the Manning case, there was no evidence of any sexual assault in Murphy's crime, and in the absence of a motive for the killing the jury found him guilty of manslaughter. He was jailed for 12 years but was released from prison in the early 1990s, having served less than ten. However, his random violent ways were to resurface with similar devastating effect.

In February 2004, convicted killer Michael Murphy was found guilty by a jury of the murder of 28-year-old German journalist, Bettina Poeschel, who was abducted and murdered close to the village of Donore in Co. Meath. Bettina was on the last day of a holiday in Ireland in September 2001, and was walking towards the historic Newgrange site when she was attacked. Her body lay hidden in undergrowth for 23 days. The Gardaí believe her killer's motive was a sexual assault and that he most likely strangled Bettina. Because her body lay exposed to the elements for over three weeks, it proved impossible to determine an exact cause of death. However, 20 years after he was convicted of the unlawful killing of Kitty Carroll, Murphy received his second conviction for taking a life, but this time a jury said it was murder.

Murphy had the opportunity to take a second life because those convicted of manslaughter are not tagged when they finish their prison sentences. The Gardaí were therefore unable to monitor the movements of this very dangerous man. As Bettina Poeschel walked along the quiet roadside she would have had no idea that the man approaching her had previously choked a 65-year-old woman to death. Murphy is now serving a life sentence, but under the current laws he will be entitled to apply for parole in 2011.

The murder conviction and subsequent execution of Michael Manning in 1954 meant of course that he never had an opportunity like Michael Murphy to kill again. But witnessing Manning face the ultimate sanction left a sour taste in the mouths of those who dealt with the case. The accepted view is that the correct sentence should have been life imprisonment with no parole. Under such a sentence society would have been protected, Manning would have been punished for his crime, and could have been put to work within the prison, giving something back to society.

Katie Cooper's brother Percy was 84 years old when he passed away in 1981. In his latter years he spoke to his children about the objections there had been to Manning's execution. He didn't discuss much of the detail of his sister's murder, or how he had to travel to Limerick in the early hours of a November morning to identify her body. Instead, he remembered the happier times when she would visit her old family home in Killimer where Percy raised his own family.

His son Pierce says that hanging was never the right way to deal with murderers.

My argument against hanging is simply, who is to say we have the right to do that? I'm happy all references to the death penalty have been removed from the Constitution. People have been hanged in the past when they may not have been even guilty. The correct sentence for Michael Manning should have been life imprisonment and not hanging. But life should mean life. Nowadays it's gone a bit crazy. People are losing faith in the justice system when they see criminals getting sentences but not serving them. There's now too much leniency towards the perpetrator.

In September 2001, the remains of ten republican prisoners, executed by the British Government during the War of Independence (1919–1921), were exhumed from the grounds of Mountjoy Jail. These men were executed in the same hanging room that the Irish State would itself later use to execute 35 murderers, including Michael Manning. A record had been kept of where Kevin Barry and his nine republican colleagues were buried, and over 80 years after their executions their remains were exhumed and the ten men were given State funerals. Shortly afterwards, a relative of one of the other people hanged and buried in Mountjoy contacted the prison enquiring if their loved one's remains might also be returned to them for a proper burial. The authorities told this person that it was not known exactly where the bodies of dozens of prisoners executed in Mountjoy were actually buried. It is known that the bodies lie somewhere to the north end of the prison, at the end of B and C Wing and close to the hospital section of the prison. But major excavation work would have to be carried out to find the remains of the many prisoners, like Michael Manning, who were treated so shabbily by the State after their executions by being buried in unmarked graves. If proposals to close Mountjoy Prison are ever followed through, any building work at the site must be mindful that part of the prison is a burial ground.

The area where Michael Manning choked 65-year-old Katie Cooper to death in 1953 has changed greatly through the years. The lonely country road where Katie walked back towards

Limerick is now a national primary road, busy with heavy traffic between Dublin and Limerick. A motor company is now located close to the spot. Across the road detached houses are situated where once there were green fields. There are also many more pedestrians in the area, including students at the nearby University of Limerick. There is no memorial to signify the exact location where Katie Cooper was attacked and murdered. In garda photographs of the crime scene taken the day after Katie's murder, heavy rope and thick wooden sticks served as the only way to cordon off the crime scene lying in the shadow of the ruins of an old castle known as New Castle. The only identifiable landmark still in place today is that castle.

In one of Katie Cooper's photo scrapbooks I find another quotation that at some stage captured her attention. It reads: 'It is better to give an account to God for too much mercy than for too much severity.' Her phrases, so prophetic in light of the violent death she suffered, prove that she, like her family, might not have supported the execution of her murderer. Sitting with Pierce Cooper and looking through Katie's scrapbooks, it is clear her whole life's work was about saving the lives of others and enriching those of her family and friends. Her murder served as a watershed in how this country deals with random murderers. Throughout the rest of the 1950s and on through to the next century, many more men would attack women at random and murder them in the course of attempting to carry out sexual assaults. There would also be other random murderers who committed attacks during the course of robberies, or sometimes for no reason other than to kill. No matter what the circumstances, no other murderer would ever face the same fate as Michael Manning. Indeed, in time, killers would come to realise that the new sentence of life imprisonment, introduced in 1964, didn't really mean what it said. Considering that many convicted killers now expect to be given parole after serving 12 or perhaps 15 years, for example, it is interesting to note how times have changed. In the more than 50 years since the Irish State decided to press ahead with Manning's execution, it could be argued that we have gone from dispensing too much severity against murderers to showing too much mercy.

Katie lies buried in the old Cooper family plot at Burrane Lower in Killimer, close to the land where she grew up in the late 1890s and early 1900s. The grave lies within the ruin of an old church, which is centuries old and is a protected heritage site. Heavy foliage acts as a roof over Katie Cooper's grave. Coming out of the old doorway of the church ruin, just across a winding road can be seen a newer graveyard beside the wide expanse of the River Shannon. All is quiet as in the near distance the Killimer to Tarbert ferry gently glides back and forth across the river, linking south Co. Clare and north Co. Kerry. It's a calming and scenic sight that Katie, with her photographer's eye, would well appreciate. Nurse Katie Cooper is at peace.

2

The Longest Lifer

For Jimmy Ennis prison is home. He is by far Ireland's longest serving prisoner. He has already spent over 50 years in State institutions: first in Artane Industrial School, later in Portlaoise and Mountjoy Prisons, and more recently in the scenic and open surroundings of Shelton Abbey Prison in Co. Wicklow. If Jimmy Ennis applied for parole tomorrow he would get it. But he won't apply; he is institutionalised. He is more than happy with his surroundings at Shelton Abbey, doing gardening and odd jobs for locals and returning to prison at night. Regarded as a likeable fellow, a hard worker, an 'old school' prisoner, folklore has it that Jimmy even has his own key to the prison. Compared to other convicted murderers, Ennis has served more time than his life sentence should warrant. He has spent longer behind bars than even the maximum 40-year mandatory sentence handed down to killers who murder Gardaí. But despite the perhaps justified feeling that he may have paid his debt to society, there is also the legacy of two horrific random attacks he carried out during apparent robberies. Since 1964 he has been imprisoned for beating a Cork farmer to death in his own bed with an iron bar. Four years prior to that murder, he subjected a woman to a sustained knife attack at her Co. Kildare home, leaving her for dead. Now in his mid-seventies, the hands of time have passed quite happily for prisoner Jimmy Ennis. But he was lucky. The judge who sentenced him to life imprisonment for the Cork murder in 1964 lamented the fact that the death penalty had been abolished only months before.

The iron bar that Ennis used to relentlessly beat his victim around the head was one and a half feet long. George A. never had a chance.* We will never know if he saw his killer in the seconds before the bar crushed the left side of his face. If he did he would have recognised his former employee, Jimmy Ennis. They hadn't seen each other in well over five years. They couldn't have; Ennis had been in Portlaoise Prison since 1960 after repeatedly stabbing a woman during a robbery in Co. Kildare. But now he was out, only two days out in fact, and he was standing in the bedroom of his former employer in a village outside Cork city repeatedly swinging an iron bar down on his victim's head. George never had time to put up his hands to fend off the blows. He never even had a chance to warn his wife Annie to run from the bed. All he had time to do, before the first blow hit, was call out, 'Who's there?' After that, George was unconscious. Within minutes he was dead.

Annie never saw their attacker either. As Ennis swung the iron bar down on her husband's head, the weapon also hit her. She suffered three deep wounds to her forehead and skull and was knocked unconscious. She fell from the bed and for hours, as night turned to day, she lay on her bedroom floor close to her husband's body.

George and Annie farmed over 260 acres of land in Co. Cork. She was 49 and George was two years older. Their two sons, aged

---

* Surname withheld at request of George's family.

22 and 25, helped them run the farm. A farmhand also lived with the family in their 11-room two-storey farmhouse set close to a village in the east of the county. George and Annie had employed a number of farmhands in the past; running a sizeable farm meant they sometimes needed extra workers, men who could put in long hours during particular farm seasons. They had employed a young farmhand from Kildare named Jimmy Ennis in 1957 and 58. He had been a hard worker and they had paid him well, practically double what other farmers might pay travelling labourers. Ennis had gone back to Kildare when the work dried up and they hadn't seen him since. George and Annie had no idea that Ennis was coming back unannounced.

Shortly after 10.30 p.m. on Friday, 24 April 1964, George and Annie's younger son said goodnight to his parents and went to bed. The three had spent the evening watching television in the living room. The couple's other son and the farmhand had gone to a dance in Bandon and would not arrive home until 5 a.m. Shortly after going to his bedroom, the younger son was in bed and sleeping soundly. He never heard Ennis break into the house in the early hours of the morning. He didn't hear Ennis creeping up the stairs, having removed his shoes to silence his movements on the stairs. He didn't hear Ennis going into George and Annie's room, and never heard his parents being attacked. And he never heard his father's killer creeping back downstairs and making his escape.

Less than two days before murdering George and leaving Annie severely injured, Ennis had walked out of the gates of Portlaoise Prison. It was just after 7.30 a.m. on Thursday, 23 April 1964, when he packed his suitcase and left his cell, saying goodbye to other prisoners. Having served three years and four months of a four-year sentence for randomly attacking a woman with a knife, he was getting out early — for good behaviour.

A prison officer handed Ennis £11. 2. 2 — eleven pounds, two shillings and two pence — the balance of money he was due from the State following his three years in prison. He signed two receipts for the money and placed the cash in his suit pocket. He also accepted a train ticket from the prison officer, a one-way ticket from Portlaoise to Cork, just as Ennis had requested. Although he wasn't from Cork, he told prison staff that he knew people there, that he had worked there before, and it was where he might settle for a while. He had just over 20 minutes to make it to the 7.57 a.m. Cork-bound train. He said goodbye to the prison officer and set off with his small brown suitcase. As he got his bearings, he decided not to rush for the morning train; he'd get the midday one instead. He wandered around Portlaoise, gently swinging his suitcase and savouring the spring air and his new-found freedom. It had been almost three and a half years since he could walk where he wanted and move at his own pace. In less than 48 hours the 32-year old was to commit a murder that would see him return to prison for the rest of his life.

Ennis was a travelling farmhand without any real roots or responsibilities. He was from Kilmeague, just outside Naas in Co. Kildare, but he never settled in the locality. He was born in 1932, the youngest of a family of two boys and two girls. His father died when he was 2 and his mother later remarried. He was only 4 years old when he was placed in the Industrial School in Artane, where he stayed until his late teens. When he left Artane he found himself alone without any support structures. He travelled wherever he could get seasonal work on farms, and in the late 1950s his job-hunting brought him to Co. Cork. He met George A. and got work on George's extensive farm. He was a hard worker, only five feet three and ten stone, but he was strong and well used to long hours working outdoors in all kinds of weather. He was paid well by George for his work, and when the seasonal work finished in 1958, he said goodbye to George and Annie and their family and headed back towards Co. Kildare.

Unbeknownst to George A. and other farmers who employed Ennis in the late 1950s, the travelling farmhand had four criminal convictions for petty crimes including larceny and malicious damage dating from between 1950 and 1954. His longest prison sentence during this time was in 1954 when he received six months at Edenderry District Court for stealing a bicycle. He was 22 years old when he completed that sentence, and for the next six years he kept his criminal past a secret while travelling around the country seeking work on farms. During the time he worked for George in Co. Cork he was a seemingly law-abiding citizen, and there was no hint of the petty criminal instincts he had, or the extremely violent tendencies that would emerge just a few years later. For a few years Ennis was happy living and working with families on their farms. He often felt he was not so much an employee but almost part of a family unit, something he didn't have himself throughout his childhood. By December 1960 Ennis was back doing casual work in his native Co. Kildare, and on the surface it appeared the 28-year old might have found his feet and could be a decent member of society. But there was something wrong; there was some kind of silent rage within Jimmy Ennis that was about to see him moving beyond stealing bicycles; he was about to commit his first random violent attack.

Thirty-nine-year-old Mary Reynolds lived with her husband Joseph at Richardstown near Clane in Co. Kildare. Originally from Co. Tipperary, the couple had been married 15 years and led a happy life in their adopted county. Joseph was out working on the afternoon of Monday, 12 December 1960. The Reynolds had no children, and Mary was alone in their bungalow when she heard a knock at the door. She opened the door to find a man she didn't know standing a few feet back from the doorway. Ennis told her he was working in a field a short distance away but was a little cold and thirsty. He asked her if she'd mind boiling some water for him so he could have a cup of tea. Mary saw that Ennis was holding a billycan, a drinking cup used by outdoor workers. It wasn't unusual in rural areas to find travelling labourers looking for clean drinking water. She agreed to boil some water for the thirsty farmworker and told him to come back in ten minutes. She closed the door over and went back inside. Within moments Ennis was standing behind her in the house.

In one hand Ennis held a long cleaver type knife — a beet crowner — normally used to cut the stalks off beet. He held it up towards Mary and told her to give him any money that was in the house. Terrified, she tried to flee to the other room, but he ran after her, swinging the knife down on her head. She managed to reach another room, but Ennis stormed in after her, shouting at her again to give him money. Mary found a purse and threw it at him. Ennis caught up with her and continued striking her repeatedly on the head with the beet knife. Mary Reynolds suffered 14 wounds to her head during the attack, as well as a number of puncture wounds to her arms and hands which she received trying to protect her head from the long knife.

As Ennis repeatedly hit Mary on the head with the knife, the handle of the weapon broke in two, and the knife fell to the ground. He grabbed the purse Mary had thrown at him and took £5 out of it. He saw a man's watch and took that too, and then ran from the house. Suffering serious head injuries, Mary managed to stumble to her bed, where she collapsed. A doctor would later say that the manner in which she curled up on the bed probably saved her life, because she stemmed the loss of blood from her head.

Shortly after 3 p.m. Joseph Reynolds arrived home to find a scene that would stay with him for ever. He found the kitchen in disarray and blood on the floor. The back door was open and the couple's cocker spaniel Trixie was whimpering near by. He went into the bedroom and found his wife lying unconscious on the bed; there was blood all around her head and her scalp was a mass of deep cuts.

At the time, Mary's brother, Tony Ryan, was a Garda Sergeant in Castledermot in south Co. Kildare. Now retired many years, he clearly recalls the attack on his sister.

I remember when I arrived up at the house that day, a fellow garda advised me not to go into the house. My sister suffered a dreadful attack carried out by someone she didn't know; but she came through it, she recovered. Mary survived. She and Joseph left Clane shortly after the attack, and moved to Naas. They went on to live for another 35 years in Co. Kildare. Mary never remembered a thing about the attack she suffered. It was never discussed afterwards, and it was perhaps a blessing that she couldn't remember being attacked with the knife. The rest of her memory was fine after she came out of hospital, but she had no memory of the events of that particular afternoon.

While Mary Reynolds was being rushed to the Richmond Hospital in Dublin on the afternoon of 12 December 1960, and as the Gardaí were sealing off the scene of the attack, Ennis was already on his way to Cork. He had furiously cycled his bike for over five miles until he reached a point known as Young's Cross, between Celbridge and Lucan. He dumped the bike and got a bus into Dublin. He got off the bus near Heuston Station and took the train to Cork, arriving there in the early evening. He then got another bus heading east of Cork city and got off at Carrigtwohill, about five miles outside the city. But having fled Clane by such a circuitous route, he suddenly didn't want to run any more. He was about to make life very easy for the Gardaí. Just minutes after arriving in Carrigtwohill, he found the village's garda station and approached the front desk.

It was just after 7 o'clock when Inspector Eamonn Doherty received the telephone call at Clane Garda Station. Less than four hours after Mary Reynolds had been found lying injured, Doherty had begun to chair a conference of Gardaí to review the evidence they had found at the scene and from neighbours. Suddenly there was a message for the inspector: it was a sergeant calling from Carrigtwohill in Co. Cork. A man had turned himself in to the Carrigtwohill Gardaí claiming he had attacked Mary Reynolds in Clane that afternoon. From the information given to him over the phone, Doherty knew they had a potential suspect. He tells me he was hopeful but still a little doubtful as he set off from Clane for Co. Cork that December night.

It's a long way from Clane to Carrigtwohill and we knew there was no direct bus or train route from one to the other. You could imagine that we were slightly dubious, hoping we weren't going on a wild goose chase all the way to Cork. But naturally we had to check this lead out immediately and were hopeful this man admitting the attack was genuine. It was a very bad frosty night and myself and two other Gardaí arrived down in Carrigtwohill at a late hour. But once we met Jimmy Ennis at the garda station we knew we were on the right track. He readily agreed to go back to Naas Garda Station with us. So in the early hours of the morning we set off back for Kildare.

Eamonn Doherty later went on to become the Garda Commissioner. As an inspector in Co. Kildare in December 1960, he found himself in charge of his first serious criminal investigation. He remembers Ennis as being a very co-operative detainee.

Jimmy Ennis was a most amenable suspect; he answered all our questions. He was a quiet man, docile; his demeanour was in direct contrast to the very violent attack he had committed just hours earlier. He freely admitted how he had attacked Mrs Reynolds and how he had made his escape first to Dublin and then to Cork. He told us how he had taken the beet crowner from a farmer in Kildare some time before, how the handle had broken during the attack on Mrs Reynolds, and how he had thrown part of the handle away. I believe that if he was responsible for other crimes he would have admitted them to us too. In the hands of authority, Jimmy Ennis was totally co-operative.

For Ennis to give himself up after committing such a brutal attack was later to be a mitigating factor in the sentence he received for attacking Mary Reynolds. By making a full admission to the Gardaí, detectives did not have to interview Mary Reynolds, who was still in a serious condition in hospital after undergoing emergency surgery. Her physical scars would later heal, and by blanking the attack from her mind she had no lasting psychological scars. It would be many weeks before she was released from hospital, but by then Ennis had confessed to the attack. His candidness in freely admitting his crime saved Mary Reynolds from being compelled to enter the witness box, and the sentencing judge would later reward him for this fact. It is incredibly ironic to consider that less than four years later Ennis would again be turning himself in to the Gardaí and making another full confession — this time for murder.

In the early hours of Tuesday, 13 December 1960, as Mary Reynolds lay bandaged after emergency surgery in Dublin, Eamonn Doherty and Ennis arrived back at Naas Garda Station. As Ennis began to make his full confession, the Gardaí took his clothes for forensic testing to try and match them with evidence of the attack on Mary. This is a standard procedure which is done whether or not a person confesses to a crime. Officers in the station were asked to provide Ennis with any of their old clothes, to replace the ones they had taken from him. One young garda who gave a pair of black shoes was Tom Connolly. In later years he would become a member of the Garda Murder Squad, travelling around the country in the 1970s and 80s investigating dozens of cases. Tom Connolly remembers how the footwear he gave to Ennis would later resurface at the scene of the murder of George A.

I wore a size eight and a half shoe, and I gave Jimmy Ennis a pair of my old shoes that night in the garda station in 1960. Once Ennis went off to prison for attacking Mary Reynolds I thought nothing more of the shoes. It was only four years later, shortly after George A. was murdered in Cork, that I got a call from the Gardaí in Cork. Ennis had left a pair of shoes in the farmhouse when he was sneaking up the stairs to George and Annie's bedroom. He'd stolen a different pair of shoes as he made his escape, leaving his old ones downstairs. I checked this old pair out, and sure enough, they were the shoes I had given him back in December 1960.

James Ennis was charged with the attempted murder of Mary

Reynolds, and faced further charges of robbing £5 with violence, unlawful and malicious wounding, and stealing a watch belonging to Joseph Reynolds. As Ennis waited in prison for his trial to begin in April 1961, Mary Reynolds was making a slow but gradual recovery from the attack. She remained in hospital for a number of months, and like Annie A. who would later survive Ennis's iron bar attack in April 1964, she did not have to suffer flashbacks of the attack. Such was the terror Mary felt as Ennis chased her around her home, inflicting over a dozen knife wounds to her head, that she had erased it from her mind forever.

On Monday, 24 April 1961, Ennis pleaded guilty to all charges except the attempted murder charge which was suddenly dropped. The State was not obliged to give a reason for this; nor did it give a reason. Ennis had always denied he had intended to murder Mary Reynolds, and a *nolle prosequi* was entered in court whereby Ennis was not fully cleared of suspicion of attempted murder, but the State chose not to press ahead with the charge. As he approached his 30th birthday Ennis knew he was going to prison, but he didn't know for how long. He listened carefully as the judge first outlined that the court had the option of imposing a life sentence for the robbery charge. But no, the judge said he wouldn't do that. Ennis had to be given credit for turning himself in and making a full confession. The court also had to take note that Ennis had said he was sorry and had expressed his regret for attacking Mary Reynolds with the beet knife.

Ennis stood straight as the sentences were imposed. For robbery with violence he got four years; for malicious wounding he got three years; and for stealing the watch he got one month. Jimmy was confused for a moment. Did this mean he was going to prison for seven years and one month? The judge soon cleared up the matter for him. The sentences were to be concurrent, meaning that all the sentences were to be served at the same time, so he would spend just four years in prison. But of course four years didn't really mean four years. Ennis headed back to Portlaoise Prison, knowing that with good behaviour he'd be out in three years.

On Thursday, 23 April 1964, Ennis boarded the 11.55 a.m. train from Portlaoise to Cork. Having sauntered around Portlaoise that morning, enjoying the taste of freedom, he was now bound for his old stomping ground and he had robbery on his mind. As he settled into his seat for the journey, he thought of his old employer, George A., who always kept money in his farmhouse. Ennis knew the layout of the house, including where George kept his money stashed in the drawer of the roll-top desk close to the kitchen. Most importantly, he knew how to approach the house through surrounding fields without being seen. George had been good to him many years before, providing him with steady seasonal employment and good pay, better than many other farmers offered. But now Jimmy Ennis wanted more, he wanted to take more. He was going to rob his former boss.

Soon after arriving in Cork just after 3 p.m., Ennis found a guesthouse, where he had a meal and slept soundly until the following morning. Late that Friday morning he began to walk out towards his former employer's farm. It was a long journey; he walked by the main roads and then cut across fields to the outskirts of the farm. It was around 4 p.m. by the time he saw the farmhouse. He nestled down into a ditch and waited until it was dark.

Inside the house George and Annie said goodnight to their younger son. Aged just 22, it would be he and his older brother who would make the horrific discovery the following morning. He headed up to bed and was soon asleep. George and Annie turned off the television and went to bed. Their other son and a farmhand who lived with the family were still out at a dance in Bandon. George and Annie turned out the light and fell asleep.

When he saw the house was in darkness, Ennis began creeping up towards the front yard. It was now after midnight. He later recounted to the Gardaí how he entered the house.

> I stayed in the old ditch until it was dark. I went up to the house and I picked up an iron bar and a screwdriver in the front yard of the house. There were no lights on in the house and it was late. I then went to the back of the house and to the kitchen window. I tried to force one of the back kitchen windows but I could not open it with the bar. I then went to another window at the other end of the house and half of one of the panes of glass was broken and the glass missing. I knocked the rest of the glass out with my hand. I then climbed through the window and had the bar in my hand. I think the room I got into was the sitting room. I went from there to the kitchen and forced a drawer of a desk or sideboard and when I got it open I saw a wallet in the drawer.

Ennis took the wallet containing £10 and put it in his pocket. At this stage he could have left the house, taking the money and making a safe exit. Instead he paused, still gripping the iron bar in one hand; he wanted more. He decided to search upstairs. He took off his wet muddy shoes, the ones given to him by Garda Tom Connolly some years previously, and crept upstairs in his stockinged feet.

With the iron bar in his hand, Ennis first went to two of the bedrooms that were unoccupied, but he found nothing there of any value. He then crept into George and Annie's bedroom and in the darkness he started to look in a cupboard. As he was opening a press, George began to stir, and Ennis gripped the iron bar tight. With the intruder standing at George's side of the bed, the 51-year-old farmer only had time to ask, 'Who's there?' before the iron bar crushed his skull.

It would later be through Ennis's own words that much of the detail of the attack on George and Annie would emerge. In one statement to the Gardaí he described how he came to hit both with the iron bar as they lay side by side.

> When Mr A. shouted … he was in bed at the time, and I was beside him at the press. I struck him in the bed with the iron bar. … I struck at the head of the bed … I gave him a number of blows of the bar but I don't know exactly where I struck him. He was shouting for a while and then Mrs A. who was beside him in the same bed shouted. He was next to me and she was lying the other side of him. … I think that while I was striking Mr A., Mrs A. got struck with the iron bar. … I don't know how many times I struck Mrs A. as I was excited and nervous. For a few minutes I don't know what happened.

The attack on George and Annie was a sustained bout of extreme violence that lasted a matter of minutes. The State Pathologist, Professor Maurice Hickey, later concluded that there were no other injuries to George's body apart from his terrible head injuries. The left side of George's face had been crushed; he had suffered severe injuries to his skull, his nose and his left cheekbone. He had suffered between 4 and 12 blows to the head with the iron bar, but the exact number couldn't be established. The iron bar was in fact an old heavy gate hinge. Death, due to multiple head injuries, had been almost instant. Despite suffering three serious blows to her head Annie had tried to crawl towards her husband. She collapsed on the floor and for hours lay unconscious beside her husband until her sons found them both the next morning.

Ennis hadn't uttered a word as he repeatedly struck George and Annie with the iron bar. He would later claim he had been trying to get out of the bedroom door after waking George up, when George grabbed him by the shoulder and a struggle began. Ennis said he managed to push George back on to the bed and that he then panicked, raised his arm and struck George with the iron bar. Whether or not George did try to fight back, by the time Ennis dropped the iron bar on the bedroom floor he had swung it down on the couple up to a dozen times.

Before he left the bedroom Ennis looked around, ignoring his victims now lying on the ground. He saw a pair of gents' shoes and tried them on; they fitted so he kept them. He crept back down the stairs, leaving the murder weapon beside Annie on the bedroom floor. As he went to leave the house, he saw George's gabardine coat and a hat, and decided to steal these too. He picked up his own grey tweed coat and cap, and as he walked down the lane away from the farmhouse, he threw away his old coat and cap. He looked inside the wallet; there was about £10 in pound notes. He put the cash in his pocket and threw the wallet into a ditch. As night turned to dawn, he walked all the way to Cork city, arriving there at around 6.30 a.m. He knocked on the door of the guesthouse he was booked into, had breakfast and then went up to bed.

It was around 9 a.m. when George and Annie's two sons found their parents. The eldest son and the farmhand had arrived home from the dance at around 5 a.m. and had gone straight to bed. By that time Ennis had already broken into the house and carried out the attack. But neither of the young men had spotted anything out of the ordinary when they silently entered the house, keeping quiet so as not to waken anyone. It was only when their parents were not down in the kitchen the next morning that their sons looked around for them. At around 9 a.m. they went up to their parents' bedroom. There was blood all over the bed and a bloodstained iron bar on the ground. Annie was lying on the ground; she was semi-conscious, her eyes were closed and she was mumbling. George was also lying on the ground; he was dead.

Within moments of entering their parents' bedroom, the two young men raised the alarm, making urgent phone calls for an ambulance and the Gardaí. The two brothers carried their mother into a different room and tried to comfort her. Blood covered her head, she was moaning, but she was alive. A doctor who rushed to the scene would later describe how Annie's eyes were closed and she was mumbling something like 'Put on the light, put on the light.' She was rushed to the Victoria Hospital in Cork where she was put on the critical list. The couple's eldest son tells me how his mother eventually recovered from the attack.

My mother spent four months in hospital after the attack. And it took her nearly a year and a half before she started to get back to her old self. She never had any memory of the attack. She lived until the early 1990s, and by the time she passed away she was a proud grandmother.

When the Gardaí arrived at the scene of the murder, they quickly discovered the murder weapon lying on the bedroom floor beside George's body. The iron bar had been lying close to where Annie had collapsed while trying to reach her husband. George lay on his back, slightly turned on his right side. He had suffered massive and multiple head injuries. From looking at his wounds it was clear he never had a chance to protect himself from the blows. Downstairs the Gardaí found the wet muddy shoes lying beside the fire. The shoes looked out of place and after checking around it was discovered no one in the house owned them.

Back in Cork city the Gardaí considered who might be a prime suspect for the crime. It was obvious from the crime scene that after stealing items from the roll-up drawer in the kitchen the killer had made a decision to go upstairs to the main bedroom, where George and Annie would obviously have been. The killer had shown a total disregard for the suffering of his victims, and the degree of violence had been extreme. The Gardaí knew that George's former employee, Jimmy Ennis, had been convicted of a knife attack on a woman in Co. Kildare. He would definitely be capable of a frenzied attack such as this. Within a very short time detectives had confirmed that Ennis had been released from Portlaoise Prison only two days before, and with a one-way train ticket to Cork.

As every garda station in the country was notified and security personnel at all ports alerted to be on the lookout for Ennis, little did detectives know that their murder suspect was still in Cork city. After sleeping until early afternoon in the guesthouse, Ennis changed his clothes, putting the shoes and coat he had stolen from George A. into a suitcase. Late on the Saturday evening, he left the suitcase at the Bus Station at Parnell Place and checked into another guesthouse, where he slept until dawn on Sunday morning. And then he coolly walked past a team of detectives at Glanmire Station and got on the 8 a.m. train to Dublin.

How Ennis managed to slip through the Garda net to get on the train in Cork, and safely off at the other end in Dublin, would later be the subject of much debate within the Gardaí. Although detectives had a good description of him from his prison file —

32 years old, 5 feet 3$^{1}/_{2}$ inches tall, 10 stone, fair hair, blue eyes, brown eyebrows, scar on cheek — an old accompanying photograph did not bear a good likeness to the thin and more haggard features of the Jimmy Ennis of April 1964. More importantly, he chose to make his getaway from Cork on the morning that almost 5,000 sports fans travelled on five specially chartered trains from Cork to Dublin. The five trains travelled non-stop to Dublin's Amiens Street Station (now Connolly Station) ferrying supporters of Cork Celtic, playing in the FAI Cup soccer final at Dalymount Park, and supporters of the county's hurling team, playing in the National League semi-final at Croke Park. About 700 people were on the train Ennis travelled on and despite the Gardaí walking up and down the aisles during the three-hour journey and studying the faces of those on board, he evaded detection. When the train pulled into Dublin at 11 a.m., he again managed to slip through, hidden among the soccer and hurling fans. Intriguingly, having made a successful escape, something stirred within Ennis, just as it had when he fled from Clane to Carrigtwohill in December 1960. Again, suddenly he didn't want to run any more.

Ennis was only a short time out of the train station and standing on Dublin's Talbot Street when he saw the front page of a Sunday newspaper and realised George A. was dead and that a murder investigation was under way. He would later say, 'This was the first time I knew of the death, and I felt sorry for him and what I had done.' Just as he had walked into Carrigtwohill Garda Station over three years before to admit attacking Mary Reynolds, at around midday on Sunday, 26 April 1964, Jimmy Ennis walked into Store Street Garda Station in Dublin to turn himself in. He approached Sergeant Peter Sherlock at the front desk and said, 'I have seen in the papers the police want to see me. Here I am.'

But there was to be a short-lived twist to Ennis's desire to help the Gardaí. As they urgently contacted their superiors, alerting them that Ennis was at Store Street Garda Station, he suddenly felt he wanted to be free again. He wasn't going to run. He didn't like being on the run, but he didn't want to admit what he had done either. He started to make up a false story in his mind, one where he would be helping the Gardaí but he wouldn't be in trouble. When Detective Superintendent Bernard McShane, Superintendent John Coakley and Detective Inspector James Dempsey arrived to question him at around 1 p.m., they found a gentle and co-operative suspect who told them he knew nothing about the murder. Ennis accepted that he had been in Cork, but claimed he had met a young woman whom he didn't know and they had spent the Friday night together in an unoccupied house near Blackpool in Cork city. He said the woman was in her twenties, with long dark hair and had a Cork accent. The Gardaí wrote down everything Ennis said, although they had firm suspicions that the young woman was a figment of his imagination, and that he had been in George and Annie's bedroom at the time he claimed he was having a romantic night. However, for over seven hours he stuck to this fabricated story.

Shortly after 7 p.m. Ennis had tea with the Gardaí in a room at Store Street Garda Station. Although he had so far failed to tell the truth to the detectives, he had been very friendly towards them and he happily chatted away about general things as they sipped their tea. But as he sat with the detectives the enormity of what he had done was beginning to sink in. He thought of how his anger and rage had taken over again and how he had attacked his former boss, a man who had been good to him. Just like when he was arrested for attacking Mary Reynolds with a knife in 1960, he now wanted to co-operate with the Gardaí; he wanted to help them and he wanted help for himself. After Ennis and the officers finished their tea, he suddenly said, 'Tear up that statement and I will tell you the truth. I want to make a confession.' Over the following two hours Ennis made a detailed statement admitting attacking George and Annie with the iron bar. Neither he nor the Gardaí could have imagined it at the time, but as darkness fell outside Store Street Garda Station, Ennis was inside a small room making a statement that would later ensure he became the longest serving prisoner in Ireland.

Towards the end of the lengthy statement, outlining how he broke into George and Annie's home and beat them in their bed, Ennis spoke about his victims.

I came down to the garda station as I was after reading the newspaper and saw that Mr A. was dead. This was the first time I knew about his death and I felt very sorry for him, and what I had done. ... I had worked for Mr and Mrs A. for two to three years, and it is some years ago. I found them very decent people to work for and live with. ... I would like to say and express my sorrow to [their sons] for what I have done to their father and mother.

Ennis also told detectives where he had thrown George's wallet and where he had thrown the screwdriver he had picked up outside the house but hadn't used during his attack on George and Annie. More importantly, when the Gardaí went to the bus station in Parnell Place in Cork where he said he had left a suitcase, sure enough, in the case they found George's overcoat, hat and shoes that Ennis had stolen from the house. Coupled with the fact that Ennis had left his own shoes in the house, there was now ample circumstantial evidence to put him at the scene of the murder and back up his confession.

Ennis was detained in Mountjoy Jail to await trial for the murder of George A. During the summer of 1964 he made two attempts at self-harm, but both attempts were made in the presence of prison staff and were more attention-seeking than anything else. One doctor who examined him prior to the trial described him as a 'belligerent psychopath, a man of definite unstable personality, whose actions would be completely unreliable under stress'.

By the time the murder trial began in November 1964, Ennis had changed his story somewhat. He agreed he had broken into the farmhouse and had taken an iron bar into George and Annie's bedroom, but he was now suggesting that George had grabbed him and that he swung out with the iron bar during a scuffle. He said he could not remember striking George with the iron bar after delivering the first blow, and could not remember when he stopped hitting his victims. His defence team did not raise the question of insanity, but argued that the jury could find Ennis guilty of manslaughter because he hadn't brought a weapon to the farm, but had picked up the iron bar from an outside shed just before breaking into the farmhouse. The defence argued that Ennis had a 'hair-trigger' temper and when he 'exploded' in a temper he did not know that his actions were wrong.

The prosecution argued that Ennis could have simply left the house without being detected after robbing the wallet downstairs. The jury was asked to consider why, after finding £10 in the wallet, Ennis crept upstairs where he would surely know people were sleeping. If he had picked up the iron bar to break into the house, why did he keep hold of it going up the stairs? When Ennis was asked under cross-examination why he brought the weapon upstairs, he replied, 'Well, I don't know.'

During his evidence to the jury Ennis said that when he had been caught by George in the bedroom he had become very nervous and was in a daze.

> I tried to get away and get out the door. I could not see who was hitting me. I got another blow of some object on the shoulder. I took the bar out of my jacket pocket. I struck out with the bar. I shoved him back on the bed and struck him again. I cannot recall how many times. ... I was afraid and did not want to have any trouble with Mr A. or anybody else in the house. I never intended doing harm to Mr A. or Mrs A. I would not have wished harm to come to them in any circumstances. I have a life-long regret and sorrow for what happened that night.

The jury was faced with a choice of two verdicts — murder or manslaughter. The main question was — did Ennis intend to kill or cause serious injury when he repeatedly struck George with the iron bar? Ennis said he couldn't remember much after hitting George the first blow, and that he was in a daze.

Following a six-day trial and after considering its verdict for two and a half hours, the jury found Ennis guilty of murder. As Ennis stood in the dock of the Central Criminal Court, on the same spot where he had previously stood when being sentenced for the knife attack on Mary Reynolds, Mr Justice McLoughlin lamented the fact that the death penalty had only recently been abolished for 'ordinary' murders by the Criminal Justice Act of 1964. Ennis stood quietly as the judge said:

> As a lawyer and judge of some experience, I doubt the wisdom

of this new legislation. In my view, the lives of innocent citizens should have all possible safeguards, and now one of them is gone.

On Monday, 9 November 1964, Jimmy Ennis became one of the first convicted murderers to be given a mandatory sentence of life imprisonment. No one could have foretold that over the following decades the sentence of life imprisonment for countless other murderers would be shown up as a sham. No one in 1964 could have imagined that hundreds of other murderers who would receive a life sentence would simply walk out of prison on parole while Ennis, one of the first ever lifers, would opt to stay behind bars.

Ennis didn't settle into long-term prison life immediately. Although the defence team did not raise the possibility of insanity during the murder trial, he was later treated for a short time at the Central Mental Hospital. He returned to the mainstream prison population and settled into life in Mountjoy Jail. One garda who dealt with Ennis says he is not surprised that at some stage Ennis made a subconscious decision to remain in prison for the rest of his life.

Jimmy Ennis was never close to his family. He'd two sisters and a brother, but Jimmy had been away in Artane Industrial School, and he had no real roots. He then ended up working on farms from Monaghan to Cork, and lodged with his employers. So from Artane to the farms he always had someone looking after him, providing him with meals and a bed, and he had no real responsibilities, no family, and no bills. And then he ended up in Portlaoise Prison for attacking Mary Reynolds, where again all decisions about his life were taken away from him. By the time he murdered George A. in 1964 Jimmy was struggling to survive on the outside. As the years then went by on his life sentence, he came to settle down so that his fellow prisoners and some prison officers became his 'family'. Eventually, he simply came to see prison as home. He's now institutionalised. He's happy and he's never going anywhere else.

Annie A. didn't attend the murder trial of her husband's killer. Her sons did attend and gave evidence of the horrific sight that met them on the morning they entered their parents' bedroom in April 1964. Both men remained living in Co. Cork, but neither would ever forget seeing their parents lying on the floor that morning. Annie spent over a year in hospital recovering from the three blows of the iron bar to her head. She never remembered a thing about the attack.

The victim of Ennis's first attack, Mary Reynolds, took well over a year to fully recover from being repeatedly stabbed at her Co. Kildare home in 1960. While Ennis was beginning his life sentence for murdering George, Mary and her husband Joseph had moved from Clane to Naas, where they would live until Joseph passed away in the mid-1990s. Mary had many friends in Co. Kildare, but when she lost her husband she needed to be closer to her family. One of a family of six, Mary moved to a town in north Munster close to her brother Tony and other family members. In the more than 40 years since being stabbed repeatedly in the head, she never remembered a thing about the random attack. Her remarkable fighting spirit brought her through the physical injuries she suffered that day. She fought for her life and she won.

It costs just over €84,000 a year to keep Ennis at Shelton Abbey Prison in Co. Wicklow. He gets the standard €2.35 a day pocket money, but he gets much more cash from the odd jobs he does for local people around Arklow. He is still a hard worker and a familiar sight wheeling his barrow and tending to local gardens. A sociable man, he enjoys chatting with local people, including the Gardaí. He is very happy at the low-security prison that is set in an impressive former stately home surrounded by acres of scenic grassland. The prison can accommodate up to 56 prisoners in 13 dormitory-style rooms. Most of those who stay at the prison are nearing the end of their sentences and are being prepared for release back into the community. Ennis has seen dozens of fellow prisoners pass through Shelton and on into the outside world, but does not believe life 'on the outside' is for him.

Considering the time that Ennis spent in Artane Industrial School, and later in Portlaoise, Mountjoy and now Shelton Abbey Prison, the Kildare man has only spent around 15 years of his life outside State institutions. When Mr Justice McLoughlin imposed a sentence of mandatory life imprisonment on him for the murder of George A. in 1964, the State really got what it was looking for. If Ennis has his way, he'll remain in prison for the rest of his life. One senior garda says that's the way it should be.

Jimmy Ennis has all his friends down in Shelton Abbey, and he's settled in his ways there. Throwing him out on the street at his age now would be inhuman. Jimmy Ennis is fine as long as he feels secure, and society is fine as long as Jimmy is secure.

3

Justice Delayed

For 28 days and nights Phyllis Murphy lay at the edge of a pine forest in the Wicklow Gap. Her naked body was just 20 yards from the road that cuts through the Wicklow Mountains linking the west of the county with the east. From the night of 22 December 1979 until 18 January 1980, Phyllis lay hidden beneath a canopy of trees in the townland of Ballinagee. Her killer, having strangled her at a location in Co. Kildare, drove over 20 miles towards the Wicklow Mountains to hide her body. After parking his car on the side of the road, he took her body from the boot, carried her down an embankment and left her lying among the pine trees. For four weeks her distraught family in Kildare town waited for any news. They already knew Phyllis was dead, as her belongings had soon been found dumped at various locations around Co. Kildare in the days after her disappearance. It was obvious that she had been abducted while standing at a bus stop in Newbridge, waiting for the bus home to Kildare. And it was highly possible she knew her killer, because even though she had been carrying Christmas presents, there was no sign of a struggle at the bus stop. As a new decade dawned, detectives in Kildare were looking for the body of a young woman while the Murphy family prepared themselves for the worst. Throughout the Christmas period and into the new year of 1980, Phyllis Murphy's killer enjoyed the holiday season with his wife and children in Kildare town. But as Phyllis's body lay exposed in the Wicklow Mountains, something remarkable was happening that both her family and the Gardaí would later say must have been Phyllis herself looking down from above — the freezing temperatures of December 1979 and January 1980 conspired to preserve vital evidence her killer had left with her body. It would be another 23 years before dogged detective work and advances in forensic science would allow a jury to consider this crucial preserved evidence, and a married father of five was finally given a life sentence for the murder of Phyllis Murphy.

It was just after 6.30 p.m. on Saturday, 22 December 1979, when Phyllis was abducted at a bus stop opposite the Keadeen Hotel in Newbridge. She had just said goodbye to Margaret Luker, her friend's mother. The Lukers lived close to the bus stop at Ballymany, on the road to Kildare. Phyllis had dropped by looking for Margaret's daughter Barbara but she wasn't home, so Margaret and Phyllis had a brief chat at the front door. Phyllis had got a new hair-do that day. It was an Afro-style cut, giving her a funky new look for Christmas. She and Margaret chatted about her hair and about their respective plans for Christmas and the New Year. Phyllis said she was going to get the next bus home to Kildare which was due shortly, and asked Margaret to tell Barbara she'd see her in Kildare later that night, where they were due to go to a dance. Margaret walked Phyllis to the gate, they wished each other a happy Christmas, and Phyllis turned left to walk the 50 yards to the bus stop. Minutes later, as Margaret Luker was back inside her house, the bus for Kildare pulled up outside. One person got off, but no one got on. Phyllis Murphy had already been abducted.

The abduction, rape and murder of 23-year-old Phyllis Murphy would eventually lead to the longest investigation and prosecution in Irish criminal history to date. At the time of her disappearance, no one could have foreseen the 23-year investigation that would follow. No one could have known it would take two decades for advances in DNA technology to identify the killer, or for the person who gave the killer a false alibi to finally do the decent thing and tell the truth. It is through their remarkable collective strength that the Murphy family have survived the strain of their sister's murder. Phyllis was the third youngest of a family of seven girls and three boys. Phyllis's eldest sister, Barbara Turner, tells me how, very soon after Phyllis vanished, the family knew she wasn't coming back.

Phyllis worked in Newbridge, and she had lodgings there with friends, but she was coming home to Kildare that Friday night. She had spent the day shopping and had Christmas presents for everybody, and was bringing them home to Rowanville, where the family home was, here in Kildare. But next day, when we discovered she hadn't arrived at the house, and hadn't stayed with friends, we went to the Gardaí and we started searching ourselves. And all over Christmas we searched. The men went out searching; they weren't inclined to bring women out searching for fear they might find something awful. Once Phyllis's belongings were found, just days after she went missing, we knew she was dead. The waiting for weeks before she was found was just dreadful. You didn't know what to be doing. You'd go to bed at night and it was so cold at that time, and you'd be saying, 'Oh God, where is Phyllis? Where is she lying? She's lying in the frost and cold.' It was dreadful. Every night having to go to bed, not sleeping, and lying in a warm bed thinking about Phyllis lying somewhere. And dreaming about her, I always dreamt she was coming back.

For four weeks Phyllis was officially classified as a missing person, but the Gardaí knew they were dealing with something very sinister. Very soon after Phyllis disappeared, some of her clothing and her Christmas presents were found on open ground at locations north of Kildare town and at Brannockstown, eight miles east of Kildare. The investigation into her disappearance was very quickly a murder investigation in everything but name. The major difference between her abduction and murder, and the murders of missing women such as 26-year-old Annie McCarrick who vanished in Co. Wicklow in March 1993, or 21-year-old Jo Jo Dullard who disappeared in Co. Kildare in November 1995, is that Phyllis's killer dumped her belongings where they were easily found, and did not conceal the body of his victim effectively. While no trace has yet been found of clothing or possessions belonging to Annie or Jo Jo or other missing women, Phyllis's killer was not so careful. It is possible that perhaps in an effort to confuse the Gardaí, her murderer left her belongings at a number of locations. However, a more likely theory is that soon after her abduction Phyllis tried to escape from the car close to Kildare town and struggled with her attacker, where some of her clothing and Christmas presents fell to the ground. Her abductor caught up with her, raped her and strangled her to death, before driving to the Wicklow Gap where he left her body. Later, while driving home to Kildare, the killer noticed that some of Phyllis's Christmas presents were still on the back seat of his car. He panicked and dumped the presents behind a wall at Brannockstown. While detectives tried to piece together the mystery, one thing was very clear: Phyllis had been abducted within seconds from close to the bus stop. One of the first items found by the Gardaí as they searched for her were her black mittens with six ten pence pieces — her bus fare — still inside one of them.

John Crerar spent the early afternoon of 22 December 1979 doing errands with his wife. With less than three days to go to Christmas, they had lots to do. Married eight years by now, the couple had young children, and Santa would be due soon. The Crerars headed off from their home in Kildare for Newbridge at midday and did Christmas shopping until 2 p.m. They then drove back to Kildare, and on the way Crerar dropped off a portable television to his work colleagues at the security hut at the Black & Decker plant just outside Kildare. He gave them a tip for a horse running that afternoon and headed home, where he and his wife unpacked their purchases. Shortly afterwards Crerar headed down to McWey's pub in Kildare town and remained there until around 6.30 p.m. He was due in work at 8 p.m. No one knew it at the time, but Crerar would be late for work that night.

While Crerar was shopping with his wife in Newbridge, Phyllis Murphy was by chance very close by. She was looking in shop windows in the centre of the town thinking of last-minute gifts to buy. At 12.30 p.m. she went to Blake's Hairdressers on Main Street, where she told them she wanted a new look for Christmas. She left the salon with a distinctive new hairstyle, giving her dark hair more thickness and prominence. She was delighted with her hair and she was in great form. She was looking forward to going home to Kildare and spending the holiday with her Dad and her brothers and sisters, nieces and nephews. She went into a shoe shop and bought a pair of tan boots, a Christmas present to herself, and she then went to Dunnes Stores. She later set off to the nearby house where she lodged with family friends, the Martins. It was now late afternoon. She had a snack and a bath and then gathered her presents and belongings and headed for the bus that would bring her from Newbridge to Kildare. On the way she stopped off to say hello to her brother Gerry and his family who lived close by. She then began her ten-minute walk towards the bus stop at the southern end of Newbridge. She wanted to drop in on her friend, Barbara Luker, on the way to show off her new hairstyle and make arrangements for meeting at the dance in Kildare that night. It was now after 6 p.m.

Phyllis Murphy was very much a home bird. She loved living in Co. Kildare. After finishing school in the Presentation Convent in Kildare, she had worked in the nearby towns of Naas and Monasterevin before finding work at the Curragh Knitwear factory in Newbridge. She lodged in Newbridge during the week and would often visit her family home at Rowanville in Kildare town, just a few miles away. Phyllis was a quiet but sociable young woman who loved children and babysat for many families. She loved the closeness of her own family, and apart from one older sister Ann who was in Australia, her five other sisters and three brothers were living locally. One brother would later follow Ann to Australia some years after Phyllis's murder, but the rest of the Murphy family have stayed local. As I sit with Phyllis's eldest sister Barbara in her home in Kildare town, another sister, Claire, who lives next door, drops by. If Phyllis had not been abducted and murdered, she might well now be living close to her sisters, long married and having reared a family. Barbara tells me Phyllis would have made a wonderful mother.

Phyllis would have loved to eventually be married and to have children. She was a great carer and might even have got a job working with children later on. She was full of fun, but she was quieter than the rest of us, more of a settled type. The last time I spoke to her was a few days before her murder. Most of the conversation was about boyfriends. She had been engaged to a lad, but it had broken up because he wanted to go out socially more, but Phyllis liked staying in and babysitting. She was asking me about whether to get back in touch with him. I later learned that they had met and had made their peace. Phyllis, being a very caring person, went to Lourdes with a group from Newbridge and she helped sick people on the trip. She was great for helping sick people and she just loved children. At the time of her murder she and a friend had put down a deposit on a sun holiday to Spain. This was just when Irish people were starting to go on package deals to the sun, and she was really looking forward to it.

As Phyllis walked towards the Lukers' house in Newbridge shortly after 6 p.m. on 22 December 1979, less than four miles away in Kildare town, John Crerar was leaving McWey's pub. He had been there for a couple of hours chatting away to other customers and listening to the horse racing commentary. The horse he had tipped had come in second. He rang his two work colleagues in the security hut at Black & Decker and jokingly told them he was enjoying Christmas drinks and wasn't going in to work. He met a friend of his, Peter Rooney, and he agreed to drop Peter back home to Maryville, a short distance away. Having left Peter at his house, Crerar wished him a happy Christmas and drove off alone. His own house was just a short distance away, but he didn't go home. He drove four miles north to Newbridge.

There are still many unanswered questions about what happened to Phyllis Murphy in the minutes and hours after she was abducted in Newbridge. There are many theories as to whether or not she managed to escape from the car of her abductor, and if so, how far away she got. Why were her belongings dumped where they could be easily found? Why was her body left above ground in the Wicklow Gap? How soon after being abducted was she murdered? How long did she suffer?

Ultimately, it was a jury of six men and six women who unanimously accepted the State's evidence that John Crerar murdered Phyllis Murphy shortly after abducting her at around 6.30 p.m. that Friday night in December 1979. The jury accepted the prosecution case that he was almost an hour late for work, arriving at around 8.40 p.m. Although it is possible that he might have left Phyllis's body at the Wicklow Gap some days after murdering her, he had ample opportunity to hide her body on the evening he strangled her to death. The Gardaí later conducted a time trial, driving Crerar's most likely route that night. They concluded that without speeding he could have travelled the 24 miles to the Wicklow Gap, left Phyllis's body at the pine forest and returned to Kildare well within the space of one and a half hours. It is reasonable to assume that during the early hours of that Friday evening, Crerar abducted Phyllis in Newbridge and drove three or four miles south-west to the outskirts of Kildare town. Soon after abducting her, he gave her a ferocious beating, raped her and then strangled her. He put her body in the boot of his car and drove east, travelling through Kilcullen, Brannockstown and Ballymore Eustace in Co. Kildare, turning south through Hollywood in Co. Wicklow, and east again to the spot in the Wicklow Mountains where he left her naked body hidden among the trees. On the way back, at Lockstown Upper, close to Hollywood, he set fire to some of Phyllis's clothes. He then drove on, but suddenly remembered the Christmas presents in the back seat of his car. Beginning to panic, he threw the presents over a wall at Brannockstown. He would still have had time to get back to his home, arriving some time close to 8.30 p.m., where he had a quick cup of tea, changed into his security uniform, said goodnight to his wife and drove to work, thinking of what he had done and how well he had covered his tracks.

Crerar most likely murdered Phyllis Murphy at Colgan's Cut, a section of open ground close to the Curragh, just north of Kildare town. It is here that some of her belongings were found during planned searches. Because she didn't drop any of her Christmas presents when she was abducted at the bus stop in Newbridge, it is possible that she may have willingly accepted a lift from Crerar. To this day he maintains he cannot remember having ever even spoken to Phyllis, but says he would have known who she was because they both lived in Kildare. However, her family are adamant that she babysat for the Crerars when she was a teenager, as did some of her sisters. Even though Phyllis knew Crerar, she was a cautious young woman and may have politely declined the offer of a lift. However, when Crerar pulled up at the bus stop, Phyllis might not have sensed any real danger when she recognised the driver, a seemingly respectable married man with young children. Perhaps as she stood close to the car, telling him she'd be fine getting the bus, he suddenly grabbed her, or perhaps he punched her, immediately stunning her long enough to pull her into the car without anyone seeing a thing. Certainly, the evidence of State Pathologist Dr John Harbison is that Phyllis was severely beaten before being strangled.

In the first few hours that the Murphys searched for their sister, they became increasingly concerned. None of her friends had seen her. She had planned to meet Barbara Luker from the 9 p.m. bus from Newbridge, but when Barbara arrived in Kildare there was no sign of Phyllis. The last anyone had seen of her was when Barbara's mother saw her walking towards the bus stop opposite the Keadeen Hotel in Newbridge. As Christmas Eve, Christmas Day and St Stephen's Day came and went, Phyllis's brothers were searching fields, graveyards and outhouses, while her sisters knocked on doors in the Kildare area looking for help. One sister called to the door of a garda who at first told her not to worry and invited her in for a Christmas drink. This man would later be one of the large team that searched for Phyllis, but his initial reaction, like most people, was that she would turn up safe. In December 1979 few people imagined that a young woman could be abducted from a busy roadside on the outskirts of a large town.

Barbara Turner gives an example of how naturally preoccupied the whole family were in searching for their missing sister.

While the search was continuing, one of our sisters, Ann, arrived back from Australia where she had been living. Having heard about Phyllis's disappearance, Ann had immediately arranged to fly back to Ireland, but she didn't have time to tell any of us she was coming. I remember she arrived at the family home in Rowanville late one night, having got a bus down from Dublin. However, we were all in such a distracted state that when she knocked at the front door she was greeted like any other member of the family who lived in Kildare. It didn't immediately register with us that she had travelled from the other side of the world.

As Phyllis's family searched over the Christmas period and as the Gardaí began a full-scale search, enlisting the help of the army and Civil Defence, clues soon began to emerge about the terrible death Phyllis had endured. On St Stephen's Day, a man out shooting game at Brannockstown found her weekend case and some of her neatly wrapped Christmas presents which had been thrown over a wall. Within hours a young boy came forward in Kildare to hand over a pair of tan ladies' boots and a child's cardigan that he had found lying on the ground at Colgan's Cut near the Curragh. The boots were the ones Phyllis had bought as a treat for herself; the child's cardigan was a present for one of her nieces. Later, when going over Colgan's Cut once again, searchers found the belt of Phyllis's coat and her black mittens with her 60p bus fare. To this day there is still a mystery about the mittens and the coat belt. Those who carefully searched Colgan's Cut the first time did not find these items, yet when the area was searched a second time the coat belt was found hanging off the side of a bush and the mittens were quite visible on the ground. Were they simply missed by the first search team? Or were the items picked up by someone soon after Phyllis's murder and later left anonymously on open ground once they realised the items might belong to the missing woman? On the other hand, they could have been left there by the killer in a desperate effort to keep the search away from Co. Wicklow, where he had hidden the body. Whatever the case, this is just one of the unanswered questions about Phyllis's abduction and murder that perhaps someone could and should answer.

Although Phyllis's belongings were found in the days soon after her abduction and murder, it would be four weeks after her disappearance before her body was found. Hundreds of people had searched thousands of acres of land in Kildare and Wicklow. The discovery of her suitcase and Christmas presents at Brannockstown indicated that the killer had travelled to the east of Co. Kildare, and it was logical to assume he had continued on that road towards the remote Wicklow Gap. Amid freezing temperatures the Gardaí, the army and volunteers searched for miles in the Wicklow Mountains. For weeks there was nothing, and then on Friday, 18 January 1980, Gardaí drafted in from the Traffic Corps searched a particular section of forested land close to Turlough Hill in the Wicklow Gap.

Beneath the pine trees close to Ballinagee Bridge the body of Phyllis Murphy lay at the foot of a steep embankment. She was naked; she lay on her back with her left arm extended above her head and her right arm resting on her chest. Her left ankle rested on her right foot and twigs covered her lower body. Her body was totally frozen and completely intact.

Within minutes of Phyllis being found, the Forensic Science Laboratory and the State Pathologist were both alerted and the area sealed off. These standard procedures were to pay off 23 years later when forensic evidence taken at the scene would be used to convict Crerar of the murder of Phyllis Murphy. But on 18 January 1980 everyone's first thoughts were with Phyllis and what she had suffered.

Barbara Turner remembers the period after hearing her sister's body had been found.

I think someone arrived at my house here to tell me just a split second before it came on the radio that a body had been found. Or I could have heard it on the radio. I remember I ran straight down to the old family home at Rowanville. My brothers Gerry and Michael went to where Phyllis's body was found and they identified her. They were very upset. They told us that Phyllis was fully clothed; they were trying to spare us. But then it came on the 6 o'clock News that her naked body had been found. My brothers were very upset about that; they thought they could spare us knowing that detail. It's strange that we almost celebrated when Phyllis's body was found. We already knew she was dead, but now we had found her and could lay her to rest. But after the relief of finding Phyllis, very quickly you go back to mourning.

At 10 p.m. on the day Phyllis was found, the State Pathologist Dr John Harbison began a post-mortem examination at Naas General Hospital. Six Gardaí attended the post mortem which was carried out in almost total silence. A post-mortem examination is an upsetting invasion of a person's body, but it is essential in establishing an exact cause of death. As the post-mortem examination began, 12 cotton buds were used to take swabs from Phyllis's body. No one could have foretold that this would be the start of a process that over two decades later would catch her killer. The cotton buds were placed in sealed containers and later showed the presence of semen, confirming that Phyllis had been raped. The cotton buds would be locked away and kept secure by Gardaí, who were following good practice in keeping potential evidence safe. In 1980 few people could have dreamt that advances in forensic science would one day unmask the killer.

After the swabs were taken Dr Harbison examined Phyllis's body. He found that she had been severely beaten before being manually strangled to death. She suffered multiple blows to her head, both her eyes had severe bruising and she had suffered a blow to her lower lip. Her jaw and chin were also damaged. Her arms were bruised, indicating that someone had held her arms tightly during the attack, and her chest was also badly marked. Her thighs were also very bruised. All the injuries were consistent with a sexual assault. Detectives who attended the post mortem were stunned at the ferocity of the attack Phyllis had endured. As he completed his examination Dr Harbison, a professional of much experience, commented that he found it remarkable that her body had survived completely intact for 28 days on open ground. Nobody realised at the time just how remarkable the investigation into Phyllis's murder was going to be.

On the Saturday evening that Phyllis was removed to a church in Kildare, a soft blanket of snow fell on the mourners. If it had snowed earlier that week, her body would have been covered from view in the Wicklow Gap and she might not have been found. Her family would have been denied their sister's remains and the Gardaí would have lost vital evidence her killer had left with her body. While the snowfall that weekend aptly reflected the scene of silent heartache, detectives were relieved that the snow hadn't come a day or two sooner.

Phyllis Murphy's father Michael died in 1985. He never recovered from the murder of his daughter. In the weeks after her death, her brothers and sisters tried to hide the newspapers from him to spare him reading the most upsetting details of the case. For the six years from Phyllis's murder until his own death, Michael prayed that the person responsible for taking her would be found. Originally from Enniscorthy in Co. Wexford, Michael met his future wife Kathleen when he was a soldier at the Curragh in Kildare. Kathleen was a local woman, and the couple settled in Rowanville at her old family home. Kathleen was only 41 when she died in 1963. Michael lived for another 22 years surrounded by his sons and daughters and grandchildren. Some months after Phyllis's murder, Michael Murphy gave a tearful interview that was broadcast on RTÉ.

I'd say the person responsible could strike again. That's what I'm mostly worrying about, other girls, this fellow striking again. …

If he's not caught, he will strike again. It's just a matter of time. ... I wonder how would he feel if it happened to his mother or his sister. How would he feel? Or has he any conscience? ... If he's not got in this world, he'll be got in the next.

John Crerar was 31 years old when he murdered Phyllis Murphy. Originally from Cloughjordan in Co. Tipperary, he left school at the age of 14. He joined the Defence Forces in June 1966 and served for over 13 years, rising to the rank of army sergeant before leaving on 26 August 1979. He left at his own request and his army file notes that his service in the Defence Forces at the time of his discharge was 'exemplary'. He and his wife were married in Finglas in north Dublin in January 1971, and they went on to have three daughters and two sons. Some of his children were not born at the time of Phyllis Murphy's murder. Crerar had no previous convictions, and when he eventually faced trial at the Central Criminal Court in October 2002, his family would fully support his pleas of innocence. However, as early as January 1980 he was a suspect for Phyllis Murphy's murder.

Crerar's name was quickly circled as a candidate for questioning after a garda received confidential information during house-to-house enquiries in the days after Phyllis was found. A garda sergeant met a young woman who told of an incident alleged to have occurred in the early 1970s. No criminal complaint was ever made by the woman, and she never mentioned it to anyone until the Gardaí came knocking on her door. But the information, if it was true, was very relevant to the murder investigation. It is incredible that from almost day one of the murder investigation, Crerar was one of the men who had the words 'Treat this man as a suspect' written on his file. Detectives would soon be knocking on his door.

The two Gardaí who interviewed Crerar in early 1980 were detectives drafted in from the Kilkenny division. He told them he had been at work on the night in question from 8 p.m. until the following morning, and had been at home before that. He said he had no difficulty in giving a blood sample to the Gardaí, and arranged to drop into the garda station to do so. His wife told the detectives that her husband had indeed been at home before going to work. However, it was a work colleague who really threw the Gardaí off the scent by giving Crerar a false alibi for the night in question.

Paddy Bolger was also a former army man working for Provincial Security at the Black & Decker plant. He was friendly with Crerar. Not only did they work together, but they'd see each other out socially. He had been in McWey's pub early that Friday evening as well, and he and Crerar were due to start work together at 8 p.m. When the Gardaí came looking for everyone to account for their movements on 22 December 1979, Paddy Bolger told them that he and Crerar had started work at 8 p.m. and that neither had left their post. He said he hadn't seen anything suspicious. The Gardaí thanked Bolger for his time and went on to question others living locally. The lie had now been told, a lie that would stay in place until the Gardaí came knocking on Bolger's door again on 13 July 1999.

Paddy Bolger never thought his work colleague could have committed such a terrible crime. He believed Crerar had been down in a pub enjoying a Christmas drink. He had covered up for his colleague so that Crerar wouldn't get into trouble with his employer. It's the kind of thing friends do, and so for 19 years a white lie for a friend unwittingly became a false alibi for a murderer.

Ultimately, Paddy Bolger found the courage to tell the truth.

When he was arrested 19 years after the murder, he immediately realised the enormity of his long silence and admitted he had lied in his first statement. Crerar hadn't started work at 8 p.m. on 22 December 1979; he had arrived at the Black & Decker plant around 8.40 p.m., claiming something had been wrong with the battery in his car. And Crerar had only stayed in work a few minutes before heading out again, telling Bolger he was 'going down to O'Leary's pub to play darts'. Bolger had worked alone, guarding the premises until Crerar returned to work just after half past ten. After telling the Gardaí the truth early on the morning of 13 July 1999, Paddy Bolger sighed with relief.

There are dozens of people like Paddy Bolger who have given false alibis for people they couldn't imagine being responsible for murders or other serious crimes. The Gardaí firmly believe this case might prove to such people that they have nothing to fear and everything to gain from telling the truth. Bolger did not face any charges for admitting he originally lied to the Gardaí. Ultimately, he was a key witness in the prosecution case and later passed a message to the Murphy family, apologising for what had happened. The Murphys told him they bore no ill feeling towards him. One garda believes that this example will have a knock-on effect.

Of course Paddy should not have given a false alibi for Crerar in the first place, but he's made up for it. I wouldn't go so far as to call him a hero, but it's not easy to learn you unwittingly protected a murderer for two decades. But the minute we spoke to him in 1999, Paddy Bolger retracted his original statement. And by him telling the truth, we could begin to piece together John Crerar's movements. Naturally, the fresh DNA evidence was overwhelming proof linking Crerar and Phyllis, but smashing his alibi so quickly was an extremely important step in building the prosecution case. I think that following the Paddy Bolger case, other people who are keeping similar secrets will come forward to ease their conscience.

Within 48 hours of the murder, John Crerar washed out his car with boiling water. He was working a shift at the Black & Decker plant and parked his car about 100 yards away from the security hut. A fellow security guard, Seán Phelan, who was also a former soldier, told the Gardaí that Crerar said his wife had spilt cream or milk in the car and it was stinking. Crerar boiled water in a kettle in the security hut, put the water into a bucket and brought the bucket and a mop over to the car. He boiled the kettle a number of times and spent a long time cleaning his car.

The Gardaí have often considered what might have happened if Paddy Bolger had not given the false alibi for Crerar in 1980. Had detectives known that Crerar's movements were largely unaccounted for on the night Phyllis disappeared, added to the fact that he was spotted cleaning out his car soon after the murder, it is possible that they might well have built a case against him. However, back in 1980 the small amount of semen recovered from Phyllis's body could not be matched with any suspect. It would be another 19 years before advances in forensic science would allow for a one in one thousand million match. So, in 1980 the State might have brought a murder charge against John Crerar largely based on circumstantial evidence, and he might well have been found not guilty. While Paddy Bolger's 19-year silence cannot be condoned, it is of comfort to him and the Murphy family that when he did tell the truth, something positive resulted — a killer was caught.

The murder of Phyllis Murphy was a crime that traumatised

the communities of Newbridge and Kildare town throughout the 1980s and 90s. Phyllis was one of four young women who were originally classified as missing, but who were abducted and murdered in Ireland in a four-year period in the late 1970s and early 80s. But Phyllis's murder was the only case that wasn't solved quickly. The first disappearance was 23-year-old Elizabeth Plunkett, who was abducted, raped and murdered by English serial killers, John Shaw and Geoffrey Evans, in Brittas Bay, Co. Wicklow, in August 1976. After strangling Elizabeth to death, her killers tied a lawnmower to her body, rowed out to sea and threw her body overboard. The following month, before Elizabeth's body was washed up on the Co. Wexford shoreline, Shaw and Evans committed their second murder, abducting 23-year-old Mary Duffy as she walked along the roadside near Castlebar, Co. Mayo. They brought their victim to an isolated spot at Ballynahinch in Co. Galway, where they tied Mary to a tree and subjected her to repeated sexual assaults before they strangled her. The killers then tied a concrete block to Mary's body and rowed out to Lough Inagh, where they threw her body overboard. John Shaw and Geoffrey Evans were already serving life sentences for murdering Elizabeth Plunkett and Mary Duffy by the time Phyllis Murphy was murdered. The failure to catch Phyllis's killer as quickly led to a palpable sense of fear that her killer might strike again too.

When the body of a woman was found in a ditch in Clane in Co. Kildare in September 1980, the Gardaí immediately feared Phyllis's killer had struck again. In time it would emerge that 19-year-old Deborah Robinson from Belfast had been murdered at a factory in Dublin by fellow Belfast native, Richard O'Hara, and her body had then been driven to Co. Kildare and left in undergrowth. Deborah's killer was caught by fibre evidence and convicted in March 1982. As he began his life sentence, O'Hara was ruled out as a suspect for Phyllis's murder.

From 1980 to 1999 the investigation into the murder of Phyllis Murphy was privately very active. Over 50 men including John Crerar had given blood samples in the weeks after Phyllis's body was discovered. However, hopes of a quick breakthrough were to be dashed. The small amount of semen taken from Phyllis's body did not allow for any possible match. But forensic science was still developing and a match might be possible in the future. Detectives locked away the semen sample and also the blood samples they had taken from possible suspects. The samples remained in a sealed locker, first at Naas Garda Station and later in Kildare, gathering dust but waiting for a time when forensic medicine might move things forward. One garda, who worked on the investigation from day one right through to the conviction of John Crerar, told me how the case was never far from his mind.

I worked in Co. Kildare all through the investigation into Phyllis's murder. Naturally, there comes a time in any investigation when leads peter out and you hit a brick wall. And yes, there are cases where the official line is that 'the case remains open', but very little happens. But the murder of Phyllis Murphy was different. There could not be a more serious case, a young woman taken in such a vicious fashion, and her body callously left hidden like that. I never knew Phyllis, but it got personal. It was personal to all of us. And we knew the killer could be very local, and could do it again. Not a week went by throughout the 80s and 90s that we didn't talk about Phyllis. We kept her photo up on a wall of the garda station. For so long we didn't have anything new, but we could never forget what happened.

A detective who was also involved in the case from the beginning explained how he thought of Phyllis every Sunday.

When I'd go to Mass I'd say a prayer for Phyllis. I was one of the many Gardaí who were there the day Phyllis's body was found. And I remember her brothers there at the scene identifying their sister's body. It was a very sad sight. Every week I would say a Hail Mary for Phyllis, and I'd pray that there would be a breakthrough in the case. If I'm fully honest, I have to admit that I prayed not only that we would solve it, but if there was a breakthrough I prayed that I'd have a part in it.

The sun rose early on Tuesday, 13 July 1999. John Crerar left the family home at Woodside Park in Kildare and drove to a stud farm, arriving before 7 a.m. He parked and walked the short distance to the security control hut, where he settled in to begin his shift. He had been working as a security guard for almost 20 years now, beginning at the Black & Decker plant in Kildare town in late 1979, and then at other locations around Kildare. Having raised three daughters and two sons, he and his wife were still living in Kildare. He had turned 50 the previous September, and he had a good job guarding the stud farm from intruders. As he began his day's work he looked out of the window. There was hardly a cloud in the sky; it was going to be a nice day. As he began his work three detectives were in an unmarked patrol car heading his way.

Detective Inspector Brendan McArdle of the Ballistics section in the Garda Technical Bureau never forgot the murder of Phyllis Murphy. As a uniformed Garda in the Kildare division in 1980, he had assisted in the search for her body. Less than two months later he was promoted to the Ballistics section of the Garda Technical

Bureau in Dublin, where for more than two decades he specialised in examining crime scenes. His work meant he had to keep up to date on advances in forensic science. He attended conferences and read up on the latest international research. Early in 1997 he became aware of the great potential of a revolutionary new process by which a DNA profile could be extracted from a much smaller sample of semen or blood than had been required before. Known as the Polymerase Chain Reaction (PCR) method, the procedure allowed a semen or blood sample to be expanded or amplified under laboratory conditions. The sample was first heated to very high temperatures, cooled slightly and heated again. The procedure needed between 20 and 30 cycles before a sample could be amplified. The process, while slow, was to have an incredible impact on the world of forensic science. It meant that a full DNA profile could now be identified from the tiniest sample of semen or blood. The American biochemist, Dr Kary Muller, received the Nobel Prize for Chemistry in 1993 for his pioneering work on PCR, but it wasn't until a few years later that the PCR technique became widely available.

Having learned about this new process of analysing minute samples, McArdle remembers wondering if it might help solve the murder of Phyllis Murphy.

I had worked on the cases of missing women, Annie McCarrick and Jo Jo Dullard. In both cases we were dealing with very sinister disappearances of women, but in the absence of a body or a crime scene we had little to go on. Naturally, having been one of the Gardaí who searched for Phyllis in 1980, I never forgot about that abduction and murder, and the fact that such a killer might strike again. But what also stayed with me was the knowledge that the killer had left potential evidence that could advance the case and possibly assist in advancing the cases of other disappeared. Back then the best that could be done with the semen Phyllis's killer left on her body was to identify a blood group. So the difference between Annie and Jo Jo's disappearance and Phyllis's murder was that we had potentially crucial evidence from Phyllis's murder, though for years it could not be advanced. There is nothing as frustrating as having evidence but not being able to advance it anywhere. When I heard about the PCR technique, I remember wondering if it might work on the samples taken from Phyllis's body, if we might actually get a DNA profile of the killer after all this time. It was just a hunch, but I started making tentative enquiries.

Brendan McArdle first had to find out where the samples were and what condition they were in. Even if they were still in existence, they might have been damaged or deteriorated with the passage of time. However, luck was to be on his side. The samples had been kept safe by two Gardaí who had the foresight to follow the correct procedure. Christy Sheridan kept control of the samples in his locker at Naas Garda Station from 1980 until 1988, and then Finbarr McPaul kept the samples safe at Kildare Station until the day in 1997 when Brendan McArdle came calling. McPaul even kept the key to the locker on his own key ring. Detective McArdle remembers the excitement of meeting McPaul and finding the crucial samples.

On 17 July 1997 I travelled to Kildare Garda Station and met Finbarr. He brought me upstairs to an office and we went to a locked press. He opened the press and took out a large brown envelope, and to my astonishment all the 12 swabs taken from

Phyllis's body were there, still sealed in protective vials. But there was a real bonus in the locker too. Not only had the semen samples been preserved, but also right there in the same envelope were the stain cards containing the blood samples volunteered by 50 men in 1980. I said to Finbarr, 'Right, let's do this formally.'

As Brendan McArdle took possession of the swabs and the blood samples, he and Finbarr McPaul itemised everything they had removed from the locker. They noted down each of the 12 cotton bud swabs. They also wrote the names of each of the 50 men whose blood had been dried on to special cloths, known as stain cards, each one slightly bigger than the average business card. McPaul had kept the samples safe in the hope that a day like this would come. McArdle was relieved that the samples had remained in safe hands and had not been damaged. He didn't know if the PCR technique would even work with the 17-year-old semen swabs, but at least they now had a fighting chance of extracting a DNA profile. As McArdle put the swabs and the stain cards into his car for the journey back to Garda Headquarters, he hoped the answer to Phyllis's murder lay in the vials on the seat beside him. He knew the vials might hold the secret identity of the murderer, but could modern technology uncover that identity? As he drove back to Dublin, he didn't yet know the significance of one of the stain cards itemised — blood sample 4/80-6/3/80 — John Crerar.

Throughout the 1980s and 90s Phyllis Murphy's brothers and sisters kept their sister's memory alive. They spoke a lot about her, about what she had been like, about what she had done in her life and what she might have done if she were still alive. The nieces and nephews for whom Phyllis had been bringing home Christmas presents in December 1979 were all now grown up and all knew about their murdered aunt. They looked at photos of Phyllis laughing with her friends, smiling at the camera. They read newspaper articles from the time of the murder. Naturally they loved her, and from their parents' stories and memories they felt they knew her too. As many of Phyllis's brothers and sisters became grandparents themselves, none of them knew that events were quietly unfolding that would eventually see most of them being gathered together on a Tuesday morning in July 1999 to be told the most amazing news.

Initially, the renewed investigation into the murder of Phyllis Murphy was low key and confined to a small number of personnel based at Garda Headquarters. When Brendan McArdle arrived back with the samples in July 1997, he signed them over to Dr Maureen Smith, a senior DNA expert based in the State's Forensic Science Laboratory. She carried out a detailed assessment of the cotton bud semen samples. It was a slow process lasting a number of months, but it was to bear fruit. By January 1998, Dr Smith told the detective that there was sufficient material on 9 of the 12 samples to deem them suitable for the PCR treatment. However, at that time the State did not have the capability to carry out the actual PCR process itself. Contact was made with scientists at a laboratory in Oxfordshire that had such a facility.

On 24 March 1998, Brendan McArdle took nine of the vials and flew from Dublin to London, hired a car and drove to the Forensic Alliance Laboratory at Abingdon in Oxfordshire, where he handed the swabs directly to scientist Matthew Greenhalgh. McArdle flew home, knowing the future of the investigation now rested in the hands of British scientists. They had told him they had been able to use the PCR technique to extract full DNA profiles from many other tiny samples, but none had been as old as the samples he was bringing from Ireland. It would take a number of weeks to complete the testing, and they told the garda they would let him know if they found anything.

There are many people centrally involved in this case who believe Phyllis Murphy herself had a guiding hand in catching her killer. Her family have always felt she had an influence on their lives after her death, and that in a way she was still there with them. In 1980 the State Pathologist had been taken aback to discover that Phyllis's body had been preserved so well, despite being exposed on open ground for four weeks. In 1997 Brendan McArdle was surprised and delighted to discover that fellow Gardaí had had the foresight to keep safe for 17 years the samples taken from Phyllis's body. A slow momentum was building, a process that would eventually solve one of the most troubling murders in recent Irish criminal history. Detectives investigating the disappearance of other missing women believed murdered had long lamented the fact that the failure to find the bodies of these women not only caused terrible agony for their families, but denied Gardaí any evidence that the killer or killers might have left at the scene. Detectives so often said that if they could identify a precise murder scene and found even a speck of dandruff, they then had a chance of catching the killer. But now that theory was about to be put to the test. When Gardaí had such evidence, just what could they do with it? Could advances in forensic science really make such a difference? The small group of Gardaí who knew about the PCR test waited nervously, knowing an awful lot hinged on Matthew Greenhalgh and his colleagues in Oxfordshire. If a DNA profile could be extracted from the swabs almost two decades after Phyllis's murder, who could tell to what extent forensic science could help solve other 'cold cases'.

In April 1998 a very excited Matthew Greenhalgh phoned

Brendan McArdle. The PCR test had worked, a full DNA profile had been extracted from the semen swabs and the killer's DNA had been identified. McArdle says there was a great deal of satisfaction, but the investigation was really now only beginning.

> Naturally we were delighted when we heard the news. I think the English scientists were as excited as we were, because this was the oldest sample they had analysed where the PCR test had worked. We now had a full DNA profile, but there was a lot more to do. We were only as far as we would be with any such recent crime where a killer left their unique DNA. We now had to find that killer. Finding the DNA profile of the killer gave us a fighting chance, but we were going nowhere unless we could find the person whose DNA had lain on the cotton swabs all those years.

The first thing the Gardaí did was check the DNA profile with that of a Co. Kildare man who had been recently nominated as a suspect after fresh information emerged in 1998 about the case. However, this man was soon cleared of any suspicion of being the murderer. The Gardaí also checked the British DNA database to see if the killer was known to the British police, but they drew a blank there. Because of the lack of a DNA database in this country, there was no prospect of a quick trawl through the DNA records of convicted rapists and other violent men. But there were still the 50 stain cards containing the blood samples volunteered by 50 men in early 1980. The Gardaí knew that to send these stain cards to England for comparison with the DNA profile from the semen swabs would take many more months, but the key to solving the case might be within those stain cards. Perhaps the killer was one of those men who had volunteered their blood sample shortly after the murder. These samples simply had to be checked out. The cost of having all the blood samples tested at the lab in Oxford would reach a five-figure sum. Detective McArdle began seeking financial approval to bring the 50 stain cards to England.

On 28 July 1998, an 18-year-old woman vanished in broad daylight from the roadside outside her home in Newbridge. No trace of the teenager has ever been found. Her disappearance was totally out of character and it is feared that she was abducted from the quiet roadside. Her family still hold out the hope that she might return home safe. The young woman was studying in London to be a teacher but was home in Newbridge for the summer and had just left Newbridge town centre and was walking close to her home when she disappeared. She was the sixth young woman to vanish in Leinster in the 1990s and her disappearance led to renewed fear that a person or persons might be responsible for more than one of the disappearances. The Gardaí responded by setting up the unique Operation Trace initiative where six Gardaí were handpicked to examine if any of the disappearances might be linked. As the Gardaí in Newbridge investigated this latest case, they were mindful of the abduction and murder of Phyllis Murphy almost 20 years before. Both women had been standing or walking on a roadside just outside Newbridge town when they vanished. People who could remember back to 1979 naturally feared that the same person might have struck again in the same town.

At Garda Headquarters the following month, Brendan McArdle was given the financial approval to bring the stain cards to England. The detective still had to keep a proper chain of evidence link in the hope that someone might one day stand trial for Phyllis's murder. He would therefore only give the stain cards directly to Matthew Greenhalgh and to no one else. On 18 September 1998 he brought 23 stain cards over to Oxford and, due to the painfully slow examination process, it would take a number of months before negative results came back on all these samples. On 16 February 1999 McArdle brought the rest of the stain cards over, as well as the blood samples of 12 other people who had more recently emerged as suspects. One of the stain cards he brought on this occasion was a sample of blood given in early 1980 by a married man who had an alibi for the night of Phyllis's murder. But for some reason, a garda had written 'Treat this man as a suspect' on John Crerar's file, so he had been asked to give a blood sample even though he had an alibi. Now, 19 years later and almost two years since McArdle began his methodical investigation of the original samples, Crerar's blood sample was *en route* to a laboratory in England to be compared with the semen found in Phyllis Murphy's body. McArdle had no idea yet of the significance of one of the stain cards he was carrying. He once again personally delivered the stain cards to Matthew Greenhalgh, and he returned to Ireland and waited.

It was around 3.15 p.m. on Thursday, 24 June 1999, when McArdle got the call. He was working at Templeton beach in Co. Louth as part of the team searching for the remains of Jean McConville, shot dead by the IRA in 1972 and whose body was supposedly buried at the beach. It was a message from Garda Headquarters that a scientist from the lab in Oxford wanted to speak with him urgently. The detective took a note of the number in his notebook and rang straightaway. He got through to a colleague of Matthew Greenhalgh who sounded very excited. He told McArdle they had a match. The semen on a swab taken from Phyllis's body matched the blood sample volunteered by a man named John Crerar. They had their murder suspect. The detective thanked the scientist for the call and all the hard work they had done in Oxford, and he made three quick calls, one to his immediate boss, Superintendent Liam Coen, one to Dr Louise McKenna in the Forensic Science Laboratory and one to Assistant Commissioner Tony Hickey who had overall operational control of Operation Trace. As McArdle stood on Templeton beach, he thought about all the remarkable and converging aspects of the case — the vital evidence being preserved within Phyllis's body, the samples being kept safe all this time, the advances in forensic science only dreamed of back in 1979, and the foresight of a garda who wrote 'treat this man as a suspect' leading to John Crerar giving a blood sample that was only now proving so crucial. A fellow garda excitedly asked McArdle if Crerar might still be alive. At this stage McArdle had no idea where Crerar was, what he looked like, whether he was married or single, or anything about him. But events in this murder investigation had taken on a life of their own. The detective replied to his colleague, 'I've no doubt but that he is alive.'

The following day, after making very subtle enquiries, members of the Operation Trace team established that John Crerar was indeed alive and well, married with five children and living in Kildare. As the Gardaí began to go back over the statements made in 1980 by Crerar and his work colleagues, a small team of detectives began to quietly monitor Crerar, building up a profile of his movements and habits. Within three weeks the Gardaí would make their presence known.

Finbarr McPaul was the garda who was sent to give the news to the Murphys. He called to Barbara Turner at 8.30 a.m. on Tuesday, 13 July 1999. As the eldest in the family Barbara had for years acted as a mother figure for many of her younger brothers and sisters, including Phyllis, after their mother Kathleen died in 1963. Now on a bright summer's morning Barbara was hearing the most amazing news from a garda who was a good friend. The two-year investigation into the semen and blood samples had been top secret. Only a handful of Gardaí were aware of the research of Brendan McArdle, Dr Maureen Smith and the scientists in Oxford, but now it was time to tell Phyllis Murphy's family that there had been a breakthrough in the search for her killer. Barbara will never forget that morning.

I remember Finbarr called to the door and he told me that a man had just been arrested for Phyllis's murder. I couldn't believe it. After all these years, it was just a total shock. Finbarr offered to get Gardaí to tell the rest of the family for me, but I said I'd do it. I got two of my sisters out of work and got the others to call around to my house. They all just burst out crying. One of my brothers arrived back from work in Dublin, having heard on the radio that a man had been arrested for Phyllis's murder. We rang Australia and told Ann and Gerry. Finbarr McPaul stayed with us all day. We knew there was new evidence in the case, and then we learned that the person responsible was going to be charged with the murder. And when we heard who it was, I remember thinking, 'Oh my God, he was one of the first suspects', and the first thing one of my sisters said was, 'Oh my God, we used to babysit for him. Phyllis babysat for him and his wife.' Within a few hours there were loads of reporters here. There were so many tears that day.

The arrest of John Crerar was well planned but low key. There were no flashing lights or sirens, just three detectives in an unmarked patrol car that quietly drove through the gates of the stud farm near Kildare town. It was 7.25 a.m. on Tuesday, 13 July 1999. It was 20 days since the laboratory in Oxford had matched

Crerar's blood with the semen found in Phyllis's body. During that time detectives had been pouring over statements in the original murder file. Crerar had an alibi for the night of the murder. He had been at home and had started work at 8 p.m., and a work colleague had confirmed this. But the forensic science evidence was clear. Not only did the PCR test prove that the DNA profile from the semen was similar to Crerar's, but the likelihood of such a match was one in 17 million. It would later be advanced to a one in one billion chance of such a match.

John Crerar heard his name being called and he stepped outside the security hut. He wondered who could be looking for him at such an early hour. His eyes focused on a man standing just a few feet from the door. It was Mark Carroll, the detective from Newbridge. Behind him, a good few feet back, were two other plain-clothes detectives. In a split second Crerar knew what was happening and his head began to swim.

Detective Garda Mark Carroll placed one hand on Crerar's shoulder, but a much bigger weight was suddenly resting on Crerar, the weight of a 20-year-old murder investigation. 'John, I'm arresting you in connection with the murder of Phyllis Murphy on or about 22 December 1979 within the State.' Crerar's face drained of all colour. He didn't say a word but took a sharp intake of breath as if he'd been punched in the chest. He offered no resistance to Carroll as he was cautioned. He sat into the back of the patrol car, and then along with Carroll and Detectives Bernie Hanley and Dominic Hayes from the National Bureau of Criminal Investigations, headed for Naas Garda Station.

The three Gardaí and their suspect arrived at Naas at 7.45 a.m. and Crerar was taken to an interview room to be questioned by Hayes and Hanley. Perhaps he was wondering if other people had been arrested too. He had given a blood sample back in 1980 along with dozens of other men, but he had heard nothing. Perhaps he wondered if some of those men had also been taken in for questioning. After all, back in 1980 he had given an alibi for the night of the murder. Now, 20 years later, he was in a garda station shortly after being arrested at work. His employers would soon find out he had been arrested, and his wife would naturally be worried when she found out. Why had he been arrested now after all this time? Detective Carroll came into the interview room and asked Crerar if he would provide samples of his pubic hair, blood and saliva. He was advised by the garda that he did not have to provide the samples if he chose not to. Crerar looked at the consent form and signed it. At 8.50 a.m. a doctor came and took the samples. Less than two hours after the arrest of John Crerar, the Gardaí had a new blood sample which could be analysed relatively quickly at the State Forensic Science Laboratory in the Phoenix Park. The sample was dispatched to Dublin and it would be the next day before the sample would match perfectly with both the original blood sample and the semen. In the meantime, Crerar was sticking to his story of 20 years before, that he'd started work on time at 8 p.m. However, in another interview room his former workmate, Paddy Bolger, who had also been arrested, was now admitting he had lied back in 1980. Crerar hadn't started work until closer to 9 p.m., over two hours after Phyllis was abducted from the roadside. With the DNA results from England and Bolger's fresh statement, there was no doubt that Crerar was going to be charged with the murder of Phyllis Murphy. At 7.23 p.m. on 13 July 1999, twelve hours after being arrested, John Crerar was told he was being charged with murder. He replied, 'Not guilty.'

One detective says the events of that day were the result of careful planning.

The arrest of John Crerar was quick and quiet. There was never going to be another arrest like it. It had to be done right. He was in custody and in an interview room less than half an hour after being arrested, and by choosing to arrest him at work his family were saved that particular trauma, because we knew that this was going to cause great joy for the Murphy family but incredible shock and emotional turmoil for Crerar's family too. And there were other concerns. By the time it hit the media, we had already gone to the homes of other security men who had worked with Crerar that night in December 1979. It was all co-ordinated; we were only going to get one chance at the element of surprise, where stories couldn't be rehearsed, where the truth would emerge.

When the Murphy family received the news in July 1999 that a man had been charged with their sister's murder, they never imagined they might hear news as dramatic ever again. They began preparing themselves mentally for the murder trial, not knowing at that time that it would take over three years before the case would come before the Central Criminal Court. In the meantime, they visited Phyllis's grave where she lay with her parents, and they spent hours talking about this incredible news that had come after almost 20 years. Little did they know that before the murder trial would begin there would be a totally different type of surprise, news that would bring tears of happiness in the midst of all the worry about the forthcoming murder case. It was about to emerge that Phyllis Murphy, her six sisters and three brothers had an older brother they never knew existed.

In 1943 Kathleen Murphy gave birth to a baby boy named Paul in Co. Tipperary. She brought her baby back to Kildare, but at the time felt she had no option but to give her baby up. Kathleen later married Michael Murphy and went on to have ten more children. Paul had a happy upbringing with the Delaney family in Carlow, where he was the youngest of three children. He always knew he had been taken in as a baby, but for almost 60 years he chose not to make enquiries about his birth mother. Then in 2000 he heard a radio programme about a man who had sought out his birth mother, and on the spur of the moment he decided to make similar enquiries. He was eventually put in touch with a social worker in Co. Kildare, who brought him back news that his mother was Kathleen Murphy, who had lived in Kildare but who had passed away in 1963. The social worker told him he had seven sisters and three brothers. He learned that one sister named Phyllis had died tragically in 1979, that she had in fact been murdered. There was further dramatic news for Paul; after all this time a man was due to stand trial for the murder of the sister he never knew he had. The social worker felt it would be better to wait until after the trial was over to contact the Murphys. In the meantime Paul visited Phyllis and Kathleen's grave in Kildare.

However, Barbara Turner soon got wind that a social worker was making enquiries about her mother. She contacted the social worker, who wouldn't tell her over the phone what it was all about. She agreed to call around and talk to Barbara in person, and advised her to have someone there as support. The following day the Murphys discovered they had an older brother. The social worker said she had thought of waiting until after the trial to introduce them to Paul, but the Murphys wanted to meet him straightaway. Paul wanted to meet them too, and he readily agreed to call to Barbara's house in Kildare. On one incredible day in June 2001 he travelled with his wife Breda and met most of his new brothers and sisters. He was originally meant to meet just Barbara and one of his brothers, Patrick, but the rest of his new-found family were too curious and excited and couldn't help calling to the house, so he ended up meeting most of them on one emotional day. Ann and Gerry phoned from Australia to also greet their new brother. And when John Crerar faced trial at the Central Criminal Court in October 2002, Paul sat side by side with Barbara, Michael, Claire, Ann, Gerry, Patricia, Breda, Martina and Patrick to see justice being done for the one sister he never got to meet.

Early on the evening of Thursday, 31 October 2002, John Crerar was found guilty of the murder of Phyllis Murphy and was given the mandatory sentence of life imprisonment. The unanimous jury verdict came on the fourth week of a trial that had taken over three years to come before the Central Criminal Court. During that time Crerar was granted bail, and so was not taken into custody until shortly after the jury of six men and six women returned their verdict to a packed courtroom. Phyllis's brothers and sisters had attended every day of the trial, as had her nieces and nephews. When the jury returned its verdict, no one knew it was going to happen until just a second before. Many thought it was just another question from the jury about the case, but a garda got wind from a court official that a verdict was imminent. The garda had just enough time to tell Phyllis's family at the back of the court that a verdict was due any second, before the jury came back into the room.

One of Phyllis's nephews would have been a little boy when his auntie was murdered. As the guilty verdict was announced tears rolled down his cheeks. A niece who was a tiny baby in December 1979 hugged her mother and they both cried. Everyone cried, every one of Phyllis's brothers and sisters, nieces and nephews, and her friends. They all thought of Phyllis and of her father who never lived to see the day his daughter's killer was caught, and they thought of Phyllis's mother who passed away long before such random violence struck her family. And they hugged the Gardaí who had caught the killer and some looked up towards where John Crerar sat, his head down and his eyes closed.

John Crerar continuously maintained he was innocent of the murder. He told the jury it was 'absolutely impossible' that there was a DNA match between his blood and the semen found in Phyllis Murphy's body. He said he knew that Phyllis 'was one of the Murphy girls', but did not know her to speak to. He maintained he had started work at 8 p.m. that night in December 1979, and he hadn't been late as his former colleague Paddy Bolger now claimed. He agreed he had washed out the boot of his car with boiling water sometime after 22 December, but he said this was to get rid of the smell of spilt milk.

However, the jury accepted the prosecution evidence that there was a one in 1,000,000,000 match between Crerar's DNA and the DNA in the semen found on Phyllis's body. The jury also considered the evidence of the Murphy family that Crerar would have known Phyllis, because she and two of her sisters would have babysat for him in the 1970s. And the jury accepted Bolger's admission that he had lied in his original statement but now wanted to 'do the right thing'. The unanimous view of a jury of his peers was that John Crerar murdered Phyllis Murphy.

While the Murphy family left the court with some Gardaí and friends to gather in a hotel close to the Four Courts and share an emotional evening, Crerar's wife and five children sat with him in the courtroom. One of his daughters had cried out with shock when the guilty verdict was announced. Crerar had covered his face with his right hand when he heard his daughter. Some of his children were not born when Phyllis Murphy was abducted, raped and murdered, but now as young adults they fully supported their father's plea of innocence. The six of them sat crying and shaking their heads. It was dark outside by the time Crerar's wife said goodbye to her husband of 31 years and left the Four Courts clutching her three daughters. Crerar left the court a short time later, both hands handcuffed together and his right hand also handcuffed to a prison officer. To the very end he tried to conceal his face from the glare of the cameras, pulling a hat down over his head and wrapping a scarf around his mouth. His two sons walked with him to the prison van, their hands on his shoulders, and then he was gone.

The conviction of John Crerar for the murder of Phyllis Murphy finally lifted a cloud of suspicion from other men who had also been suspects for the murder. One garda says there were a number of men in Co. Kildare who could only now be put in the clear when the killer was finally convicted in October 2002.

> There were a number of men who were suspects purely because they had no alibi for the night Phyllis was murdered. They had faced lengthy questioning back in 1980 and could never officially be put in the clear. Looking back, it must have been dreadful for them. We always thought it had to be someone Phyllis knew, someone that she would have trusted to either accept a lift from, or to approach the car and talk to him if even just to decline the lift. So unfortunately we had men in Kildare and Newbridge and beyond who were classified as suspects for the murder. It's inevitable that anyone without an alibi is considered a suspect, but I'm sure having that weight on your shoulders for over 20 years is not pleasant. Ironically, when we caught the killer it was someone who seemingly had an alibi all that time.

Some days after Crerar's conviction, the grave of Phyllis Murphy sank. One of her brothers noticed it first. The level of the ground seemed to have been disturbed, and it had to be filled in. It was an unusual thing to happen, but with everything that had happened it didn't seem too surprising. One family member said, 'It was like Phyllis gave one last sigh of relief and could now rest in peace.'

In August 2003 the body of Jean McConville was discovered by chance at Shelling beach in Co. Louth. This beach lies close to Templeton beach, where Brendan McArdle and fellow Gardaí had carried out intensive searches for Jean's remains in 1999. The IRA had wrongly identified Templeton as the location where they had buried the mother of ten after abducting her in Belfast in March 1972 and shooting her once in the head. As McArdle had stood on Templeton beach in June 1999 and got the news about the breakthrough in the Phyllis Murphy murder investigation, there was a satisfaction in obtaining a positive outcome to a methodical and time-consuming search of evidence preserved all those years. There was to be no such good fortune in the painstaking search for Jean McConville's body at Templeton beach; her body lay at an entirely different location and was only discovered by a man out walking his dog. The chance discovery of her remains after 31 years was another incredible occurrence, different in many ways to the Phyllis Murphy murder investigation, but similar in giving credence to the eternal optimism of the Gardaí that a breakthrough in an investigation can come at any time.

Crerar took a number of weeks to settle into Dublin's Arbour Hill Prison. The prison houses some of the most dangerous prisoners in the country, including men who committed random murders or random rapes. One such prisoner is Larry Murphy from Baltinglass in Co. Wicklow who, like Crerar, was a seemingly happily married man with children and had never come to garda attention when he committed one of the most horrific crimes of recent times. Murphy was 36 years old when, on the night of 11 February 2000, he abducted a woman in Carlow town by punching her in the face. He forced his victim to remove her bra, tied her hands, put a gag in her mouth and then bundled her into the boot of his car. He drove nine miles to a secluded area near Athy in Co. Kildare, where he raped the woman. He then forced her back into the boot and drove 14 miles to a remote forested area at Kilranelagh in Co. Wicklow, where he raped her again. He was about to suffocate his victim with a plastic bag when two hunters stumbled on the scene and saved the woman's life. Murphy later pleaded guilty to charges of rape and attempted murder and was jailed for 15 years, with the last year suspended to reflect his guilty plea. It's a sobering and disturbing thought that, just like Crerar's abduction of Phyllis Murphy in Newbridge in 1979 and the disappearance of a number of young women believed murdered in Leinster in the 1990s, when Larry Murphy abducted his victim in a secluded car park in Carlow, no one saw a thing. Murphy has now adapted to life in prison and is looking forward to his release date sometime after 2010. He refuses to speak about his crime and has not spoken about what he planned to do with his victim's body once he murdered her. Like Crerar, Murphy is a quiet prisoner, who spends much of his time working in the carpentry shop, where both prisoners are meticulous in their work.

The Gardaí investigating the disappearance of a number of women in the Leinster area in the 1990s would dearly like to get into the minds of men like John Crerar and Larry Murphy. Detectives would like to know how well Crerar and Murphy planned their separate crimes. Did Crerar roam the streets of

Newbridge looking for a victim to abduct before he spotted Phyllis, or did he just happen to see her and act on a murderous impulse? Had he already chosen the Wicklow Gap as the location to leave Phyllis's body after strangling her? Likewise, did Murphy search around Carlow for a woman to abduct and rape? When he tried to suffocate his victim at Kilranelagh Forest in Co. Wicklow, did he have a location in mind to hide his victim's body? One detective who worked on both investigations says a lot could still be done with such men when they are in prison.

> I really think the Gardaí should have the power to go to Arbour Hill and say to John Crerar and to Larry Murphy, 'Right, it's time to go over your life stories.' And I don't care how long it takes. It could take months and months to outline everything they have ever done in their lives, every place they've ever visited, every person they've ever met. But these men have a lot to offer us if only in relation to their *modus operandi*. Here we have two men who have been caught in the act. Only for an extensive search and bad weather holding off, Phyllis Murphy might have remained as a missing person and John Crerar would not be in prison. And if Larry Murphy had not been disturbed as he tried to kill the woman he abducted, he might have hidden her body so that she would be yet another missing woman in Leinster. And remember, he attacked his victim in three counties on the one night. Who knows where he was going next. You'd almost feel like trying to hypnotise these fellas to get them to tell everything they know.

Soon after Crerar's arrival at Arbour Hill Prison in 2002, he faced the unnerving experience of being physically threatened by a convicted serial killer from Galway, who has since been moved to another prison. Crerar had initially been placed in a three-man cell and seemed extremely nervous during the first few nights of his life sentence. Having never been in prison before, he found it difficult to accept his fate. However, he settled down after Christmas 2002, and in the carpentry shop he was one of those who helped provide podiums and other items for the Special Olympics and more recently has made furniture including lockers and wardrobes for youth groups and children suffering ill-health. He has posed no problems for prison staff at Arbour Hill and is considered courteous and friendly. He continues to maintain his innocence of the murder of Phyllis Murphy. One prison officer says Crerar fits the profile of a model prisoner.

John Crerar is considered to be courteous and friendly. He is no trouble and I think his military background is a help to him. I'd liken him to another former soldier, Seán Courtney, who was convicted of the murder of Patricia O'Toole, whose body was found close to the Dublin Mountains in 1991. You could tell on first meeting both of these men that, although they were not used to being in prison, they were accustomed to following orders and living by certain rules. It gave them both a distinct advantage, maybe, compared to other convicted murderers who also have never been in prison before and who have 'lost it' and broken down. Crerar is a perfectionist in the work that occupies his time in prison, and he keeps the head down. I'd say he has his eye firmly on the bigger picture. He'd be mindful that someone like Seán Courtney has already applied for parole and is now a low-security prisoner. Crerar is probably hoping for something similar in a few years.

Based on the way this country treats the mandatory sentence of life imprisonment, it is quite possible that Crerar may be given parole at some stage in the future. He has no previous convictions, presents no trouble for prison officers, and continues to maintain his innocence — all issues the Parole Board will be asked to consider at some stage. Because the term 'mandatory life imprisonment' has no real meaning, it is worth considering that if Crerar had been convicted of the murder of Phyllis Murphy in the months after her murder in 1980 and given a life sentence, he might well have been released by now.

On 23 January 2003, Phyllis Murphy's family travelled to the Wicklow Gap. It was 23 years to the day since Gardaí found Phyllis's frozen body lying beneath a canopy of spruce trees. It was still less than three months since John Crerar had been convicted. With her killer having spent his first Christmas behind bars, now was the right time to mark the spot where Phyllis lay for 28 days. The spruce trees were long gone, replaced by a steep section of land covered by rocks. Just hours before the Murphy family arrived from Kildare to visit the scene, the garda who had found Phyllis's body went to the spot and arranged some of the rocks in a cross to mark the spot for the family. Phyllis's family brought an inscribed wooden cross which they placed at the scene, and they cried. A small number of Gardaí who had worked on the case from 1979 through to 2002 stood silently by, men who never had the pleasure of meeting Phyllis Murphy yet felt they knew her. The family said a decade of the Rosary and they felt Phyllis's presence. For 23 years it seemed as though Phyllis had been watching, keeping a guiding hand over the investigation. Now her murder was solved, and she could finally rest in peace.

4

Remembering Mary

Mary Kitt was in her bedroom when she heard a sound. It was the early hours of Tuesday, 3 June 1980. The 45-year old looked towards the bedroom door and saw a man approaching her. He shouted at her demanding money. Terrified and alone, Mary told the man her handbag was downstairs. As the intruder went down to the kitchen and took £10 from a purse, Mary's heart thumped as she listened, hoping to hear the robber leave her house. But instead of just stealing the cash and leaving, the man picked up a knife in the kitchen and went back upstairs. He approached Mary, who was now standing beside her bed, he put one hand on her throat and he stabbed her once in her lower back. Although the stab wound damaged Mary's kidney, it was not fatal and she would have survived this injury. But 25-year-old Michael Holohan, already known to the Gardaí as one of the most violent criminals in Galway city, was out of control once again. He picked up an ashtray and hit Mary a number of times on the head. As the ashtray broke, he cut his own hand and wiped it on Mary's bedspread. Holohan put his hands on Mary's throat and strangled her to death. After committing such a random and callous murder, he did not run immediately from Mary's house. Instead, he made Mary's bed and then put his victim underneath the bed, hiding her from view. He then left the house through the back door and walked the short distance to his own home, also on Grattan Road. Within 48 hours Michael Holohan would admit to the Gardaí what he had done, and in time would become one of the longest serving prisoners in Ireland.

Mary Kitt spent almost her entire adult life working for the *Connacht Tribune*. She first joined the Galway paper in 1954 and spent 26 happy years working as a secretary for the paper. For the six years before her death, she worked as the personal secretary to the managing director. An only child, Mary's parents had long since passed away and she lived alone in a two-storey house on Grattan Road on the Salthill side of the city overlooking Galway Bay. It was the home where she had grown up and in which she felt safe and secure. Although she never married, Mary had a wide circle of family, friends and neighbours, and it wasn't long before it was noticed that she was missing.

Michael Holohan should never have been in the position to take the life of Mary Kitt. He had already shown the capacity for extreme violence at least twice before, and Mary's murder is an example of what happens when violent repeat offenders are not tagged.

Holohan was 19 years old when, six years before he murdered Mary Kitt, he abducted a 14-year-old French male student and held him hostage for over two hours, subjecting him to repeated assaults. He accosted the boy at a remote location close to the railway line in Galway city on the afternoon of 31 July 1974. He would later plead guilty to the attack and receive a 12-month sentence to be served in St Patrick's Institution in Dublin, but not before he had found the opportunity to commit another violent attack.

Holohan was arrested shortly after the attack on the French boy, but instead of being kept in custody he was granted bail. His parents decided to commit him to a psychiatric hospital in Ballinasloe, but he absconded from there within hours. He returned to Galway city where he started to live rough, evading the Gardaí who were searching the city for the violent teenager. He managed to lie low for just over a week, and then on 10 August 1974 he committed another random attack along the same stretch of railway line in Galway. This time his victim was a 25-year-old woman whom he attacked from behind, grabbing her hair and knocking her to the ground. He tightened his hands around her neck and she lost consciousness. However, when some youths who saw the attack shouted out, he ran off and the woman soon recovered consciousness. The Gardaí caught him within hours of this attack and this time he was kept in custody. He pleaded guilty to the attack on the woman, but the court directed that the six-month sentence he received be served at the same time as the 12 months for attacking the French teenager. So, in effect Holohan only served 12 months in St Patrick's Institution. Upon his release he returned to Galway and dabbled in petty crime but eventually found himself a job with the Corporation.

One garda who knew Holohan from an early age tells me he wasn't surprised when he heard Holohan was the main suspect for the murder of Mary Kitt.

Holohan had been involved in criminal activity from his late teens. He wasn't a career criminal, like an armed robber. He was perhaps more dangerous — a reckless individual with a very violent streak. We first became aware of him in 1971 when he was 17 years old. He stole a car in Galway and knocked down two pedestrians, causing them serious injuries. He got six months for that. He carried out a few small robberies, petty stuff. But the attacks on the teenage boy and the woman along the railway track put him in a different league. The assaults were random; they were reckless. Remember he had his hands around the woman's throat, and later said his motive in attacking her was robbery. And then six years later he strangled Mary Kitt while robbing her home. Holohan targeted Mary; he knew she lived alone. I really think there should be some system of keeping track of random attackers, even making them sign on at a garda station every week for the rest of their lives — anything to let them know they are being watched. Just think how absurd it is to actually say you weren't surprised to hear a criminal you had dealt with before had finally committed murder, but you had been powerless to keep track of him.

Mary Kitt went to 7.30 p.m. Mass in Galway city on Monday, 2 June 1980. She left the church at 8.05 p.m. and was walking down Dominick Street towards Grattan Road when she met a neighbour and friend, Eamonn Fitzpatrick. She was very fond of the Fitzpatricks who lived just a few doors away from her. Eamonn's wife, Thérèse, was one of the circle of women with whom Mary socialised, and the Fitzpatrick children would often visit Mary in her house to keep her company. Only that day 14-year-old Yvonne had gone to visit her, and was still minding the house while Mary went to Mass. When Eamonn met Mary, he asked her to tell his wife he was going for a drink and would be home soon. Mary said she would phone Thérèse for him. They said goodnight and she walked on towards Grattan Road. Just over 24 hours later Eamonn and his wife would find Mary's body.

As Mary Kitt was walking home from Mass, Michael Holohan was out drinking in the docks area of Galway city. He had spent much of the weekend drinking in pubs around Galway after receiving a cheque the previous Thursday for £188.69 in wages and arrears from Galway Corporation, for whom he worked as a general labourer. By Monday, 2 June, just hours before he would become a killer, he found he still had a little bit of money left and he went to Delargy's Bar at around 4 o'clock in the afternoon, where he drank Smithwicks, and vodka and red lemonade. He then went to the Olympic Bar at around 7.30 p.m., later returning to Delargy's where he continued drinking both pints and vodka. As Mary Kitt was leaving the Augustinian Church and walking to her home, her killer was settling in for a night's drinking and playing pool with three other young men. His behaviour was becoming more erratic as the evening wore on. At one point he showed one of the men some pellets that could be used in an air gun and jokingly said to one of the men, 'If you beat me, I'll shoot something off.' The men laughed and they continued playing pool. Holohan's drinking buddies had no idea the 25-year old's seemingly playful threats of violence were hiding a darker desire to terrorise and to kill.

Mary Kitt arrived home at 8.20 p.m., where Yvonne Fitzpatrick was waiting for her. The teenager stayed with Mary for 20 minutes before saying goodnight and heading up to her own home. Yvonne was the last person to see Mary alive. Mary phoned Yvonne's mother, Thérèse, and relayed Eamonn's message. The women had a brief chat; they had already made arrangements to go out for a meal with one of Mary's cousins the following night. She called another friend, Bridie, and had a quick chat with her, and she phoned Thérèse again around 9.30 p.m. and they spoke for around two minutes, again about nothing in particular. This was a regular routine, good friends keeping in touch on a daily basis. Mary lived alone but was rarely alone. She would either have company or she would be on the phone to friends. Sometime late on Monday night Mary dressed for bed. She had recently moved into a front bedroom where a firmer mattress was helping her with a back problem. She turned out the lights and got into bed.

Holohan and his three friends left Delargy's Bar at around midnight. They turned in the direction of the Customs House and said goodnight to each other. Holohan began walking home alone over Wolfe Tone Bridge away from the city and turned left down Claddagh Quay which extends on to Grattan Road. It would still be an hour or two before he would break into Mary Kitt's house and murder her, but before he would commit that crime he was about to display the most bizarre threatening behaviour towards other people.

Holohan arrived home at Grattan Road at around 1 a.m. and got a pistol he had hidden in his house. He then cycled towards a scenic and quiet area known as South Park in the Claddagh, near Galway Bay. The park offers scenic views of Galway city and was well known as a spot where courting couples would park late at night. At around 1.30 a.m. he approached one car, where he could see a man and a woman. He tapped on the window with the black-coloured pistol. The man in the car, not realising what Holohan held in his hand, wound down the window to see what the problem was. The man thought perhaps he was a garda and that something was wrong. Just as the man wound down the window, Holohan stuck the pistol in the man's face and said, 'Move this f***ing car 30 or 40 yards down the road.' The couple were stunned, and the man started up the car immediately and drove off at speed, leaving Holohan still standing there with the gun in his hand, and a smile on his face.

Enjoying this power to force terrified couples to flee the area, Holohan approached another car where another couple were enjoying a romantic evening. He produced the gun once again and repeated his threat. Once this petrified couple had driven off, he dumped the pistol and headed home again, where he had a cup of tea. It was now after 2 a.m. His parents were away on holiday in England and the house was quiet. But he wanted to commit more crime, he wanted to steal money and he decided to break into a house. He thought of Mary Kitt who lived alone a few doors down. He set off out of his house once again and walked the short distance to Mary Kitt's house. He walked to the back of the house and climbed up a drainpipe to her bathroom window, pulled down at the top of the window frame and found he could open it easily. As Mary slept, he crawled through the window, knocking over a towel rail as he stepped inside. He then began to search the bedrooms.

The murder of Mary Kitt has left a hole in the lives of many people. Mary had enriched the lives of her friends and work colleagues as well as her extended family in Ireland and England. One of her closest friends, who still fears her killer might one day be released, says Mary's lonely death was in total contrast to the active life she led.

Mary had so many friends and enjoyed living life to the full. She was always out with 'the girls' and was the life and soul of the party. The Sunday night before her murder she was singing away in a hotel as one of her cousins played the piano. She was an attractive woman who was not shy but modest. A couple of men had designs on her, and only the night before her murder one man had asked her out to dinner, but Mary politely declined. She had gone out with a man about 20 years before, but it had ended and Mary never took up with anyone after that. She loved the company of her family and friends and was active in a musical society and local drama. The year before her murder she was at Knock assisting elderly and disabled people during the visit of the Pope. She was intelligent and full of fun and we all miss her. Mary was a beautiful person.

Thérèse Fitzpatrick and Mary Corbett were beginning to feel alarmed. It was the evening of Tuesday, 3 June. The two women had arranged to go for a meal with Mary Kitt that evening, but there was no sign of her. The two Marys were cousins and they were very close. Mary Corbett had called around to the Fitzpatricks before 9 p.m. to collect her cousin and Thérèse so that the three of them could go for a meal in Eyre House, where Mary Kitt had said she would book a table. Thérèse told Mary Corbett she hadn't seen the other Mary all day, so Mary Corbett walked the short distance to her cousin's house and knocked on the front door, but there was no reply. She and Thérèse thought that perhaps their friend had gone on to the restaurant without them. This would have been unusual, but they decided to head into Galway and check none the less. However, when they got to Eyre House, they found Mary wasn't there; nor had she booked a table. They headed back to the Fitzpatricks' house on Grattan Road, where Mary Corbett rang her own mother, but she hadn't heard from Mary Kitt either. They rang Mary's boss at the *Connacht Tribune*, John Hickey, and discovered she hadn't been to work that day and she hadn't phoned in. Something was very wrong.

It was Thérèse Fitzpatrick who found her friend's body. She and her husband Eamonn, their son Ian and Mary Corbett walked up to Mary Kitt's house at around 11 p.m. Thérèse had a key for Mary's house, but when they tried the front door it was bolted from the inside. The house was in darkness and they checked around the back. They saw the bathroom window open and Eamonn got a ladder which he propped against the back wall. Because he had a back injury, his wife climbed up the ladder and got in the bathroom window. As Thérèse stepped into the bathroom she saw the towel rail lying on the floor. She picked it up and put it standing properly. She turned on the lights and looked around the bedrooms but saw nothing suspicious. She heard sounds downstairs. It was Eamonn, who had checked the back door and found it was open. He walked through the hallway and opened the front door to let Ian and Mary Corbett in. Thérèse called down that she had found no sign of Mary upstairs. While Ian and Mary stood in the kitchen, Eamonn checked upstairs too and he also saw nothing. In the kitchen they found Mary's handbag. Both Mary Corbett and Thérèse knew that Mary would never go out without her bag. Eamonn came back downstairs and Thérèse went upstairs again to look around. Suddenly, she called her husband.

Under the bed in the front room lay the body of Mary Kitt. She was lying face down and Eamonn and Thérèse could only see her lower body. Thérèse managed to reach her hand in to feel for a pulse, but Mary was cold. She couldn't reach Mary's hands because they were under her body. Shocked at their discovery, Thérèse immediately left the bedroom and went downstairs to ring the Gardaí and a doctor. Mary Corbett was in the kitchen with Ian. They both knew from Thérèse's voice that something terrible had happened. Meanwhile, Eamonn remained in the bedroom, and minutes later when he heard the Gardaí arriving he ran down to direct them upstairs.

When Sergeant Dan McNulty and Gardaí Pat Keaney and Michael Shaughnessy arrived at the house, the full horror of Mary Kitt's death soon emerged. McNulty shone a flashlight under the bed and saw Mary's body lying underneath the centre part of the bed. As the Gardaí entered the room they also noticed fragments of glass near the door, which would later be identified as the ashtray Holohan used to strike Mary on the head. The Gardaí naturally wanted to get to Mary as soon as possible, in the vain hope that she might still be alive. Eamonn Fitzpatrick and Garda Keaney lifted a dressing table out of the way to the far side of the room. Although her bed was made, the Gardaí noticed a blood stain at the top right end of the bed. The three Gardaí and Eamonn then lifted the double bed to the right-hand side of the room, leaving Mary's body free. She lay face down with her hands tucked under her body. She was wearing a green nightdress and a brown dressing gown and she had what looked like a stab wound to her lower back. It was clear Mary had suffered extensive head injuries, and there was blood on the floor. McNulty felt Mary's body but she was cold. He asked Keaney to contact a priest.

As the three Gardaí examined the scene, word of the discovery spread very quickly and shocked neighbours and friends gathered at the house to comfort Mary Corbett, and to comfort each other. As the Gardaí set about preserving the murder scene in the bedroom, Thérèse Fitzpatrick told them about the towel rail that she had seen knocked over in the bathroom, and Eamonn told them how he had found the back door unlocked. As Mary's shocked and distraught friends and neighbours cried together in the sitting room, the Gardaí set about preserving the bathroom and back door area, the locations whereby the attacker had most likely entered and exited the house. Their quick thinking ensured that a fingerprint of Holohan's was later found on the window ledge in the bathroom. This evidence would have been crucial if Holohan had denied any involvement in the crime. But within a few days he would be confessing to the crime and wondering aloud how long a prison sentence he might get for the murder.

Less than nine hours after murdering Mary Kitt, Holohan was

back drinking in a pub in Galway. It was 10.45 a.m. and he was in Taylor's Bar, showing a friend three valuable coins he said he had 'bought from a wino'. The coins were two half-sovereigns and a Victorian five shilling piece dating from the late 1800s. Holohan sold two of the coins to a drinking companion for a few pounds. The new owner later got £120 for the coins from a jeweller in the city. While Holohan would later admit he stole £10 from Mary Kitt's purse, it is highly coincidental that just hours after breaking into Mary's house he was showing three valuable coins to his friends. None of Mary's friends could identify the coins, but they did remember her saying she had old coins that had been her mother's special 'wedding money' that had been passed on to her, and which she kept safe for sentimental reasons. It is particularly distasteful to think of Mary's valuable keepsake being passed around by Holohan to his drinking buddies.

While the Murder Squad was dispatched from Dublin to assist Galway detectives with the murder investigation, Holohan was still committing crime in Galway city. He spent the Tuesday afternoon playing slot machines near his home in Salthill, and then went back to a pub and drank vodka and played pool. Still keen to impress his friends with acts of bravado, he showed one man an air rifle and a box of pellets he had. They remained drinking until closing time, after which he and two friends headed back towards his house. The three were walking along Quay Street when Holohan decided to break into a pub. He kicked in the door of a pub and handed out two bottles of vodka, three bottles of other spirits and cigarettes to his friends. He also stole £46 from the pub. The three of them headed back to Holohan's home on Grattan Road, where just a few hundred yards away a crime scene was sealed off. But Holohan's two friends were too drunk to notice anything like that. The three of them divided the £46 and they fell asleep at around 4 a.m.

The three men went drinking again the following morning at around 10 a.m., going to Taylor's Bar, where Holohan's two friends heard other people talking about the murder of Mary Kitt. Holohan said in a surprised voice, 'She lives only a few doors from me.' The conversation moved on and Holohan took a guitar and began to sing. At around 1 p.m. Holohan and one of his friends went to the Harbour Bar, where he remained until around midnight. But the Gardaí were closing in, and the following day he would be confessing to the murder of Mary Kitt.

A standard appeal that the Gardaí make when any murder takes place is for anyone who saw anything suspicious in the area to come forward. It's an open-ended plea for help that can often mean the difference in catching a killer before they can strike again. In the case of Mary Kitt's murder, the Gardaí made it clear they wanted to know of anything untoward that had happened in Galway city or in Salthill on the same night. Within a few hours detectives received a call from a man who seemed to be very shaken. He told of how he was sitting in a car at South Park close to Grattan Road on the Monday night, when he and his girlfriend were threatened by a man armed with a pistol. The description given matched 25-year-old Michael Holohan, the trouble-maker from Grattan Road.

Eight years before Holohan murdered Mary Kitt, a judge in Galway warned him he was facing a life behind bars if he didn't change his ways. Holohan was just 17 years old when in June 1972 he was sentenced to three separate six-month sentences — for stealing a car and knocking down two pedestrians, for breaking into a shop and stealing £65, and for breaking into a school and damaging property. As the arresting garda outlined how Holohan also drove a stolen van into a wall in Carraroe outside Galway city while being chased by the Gardaí, he commented to the judge:

'One good thing about him [Holohan] is that he owns up immediately he is caught.' As he imposed sentence, the judge told Holohan: 'You will have to make up your mind whether you are going to spend the rest of your life in jail. ... Your next time here will mean a long stretch for you.'

In June 1980, just two days after Mary Kitt's murder, the Gardaí called to arrest Michael Holohan at his home on Grattan Road. He offered no resistance and, as always, he would shortly make a full confession to the detectives. But this time his crime would put him away for well over a quarter of a century.

Two detectives from the Murder Squad, Tom Connolly and Tom Dunne, interviewed Holohan soon after his arrest. Within a short time he admitted he had gone into Mary Kitt's house and attacked her. Because he would later plead guilty to the murder, his account of the crime was never outlined in court. If his statement were to be believed, Holohan thought Mary was dead when he was leaving the bedroom after stabbing her and hitting her repeatedly with the ashtray. He said he returned to the room and choked Mary to death after hearing her cough. His statement reads:

I decided to break into a house because I needed money. I picked out Mary Kitt's place because I knew she was living alone. ... I got in through a bathroom window and I went to a couple of rooms. ... I went into the front bedroom where Mary Kitt was sleeping and she woke up when she heard the noise of the door opening. She asked me what I wanted and I said money and she told me her handbag was downstairs. ... I went downstairs and took a £10 note out of a purse. I got a knife from a drawer in the kitchen and went back upstairs. Mary Kitt was out of bed and she had a nightgown on her. She said, 'I know you, you are a Holohan.' I had the knife in my hand and I went over to her and put my arm around her neck and we both fell to the ground. I stabbed her in the side with the knife. ... I picked up a glass ashtray and hit her with it a couple of times in the head. ... I got two cuts on the palm of my hand. ... I started to get frightened and was walking out the bedroom door when I heard her coughing and I went back over to her and I choked her. I pushed her underneath the bed. ... I made the bed and went downstairs. ... I threw the knife away on my way home.

Holohan's statement is important in gaining an insight into his murderous mind, but it must be treated with great caution. He tries to justify attacking Mary by saying she had recognised him, but living in the same area of Galway he would have known that was a distinct possibility when he entered the house in the first place. He would later claim he picked up a kitchen knife and went back upstairs to frighten her and warn her not to raise the alarm until he was gone, but this does not seem logical. If robbery was his only motive, he could have simply fled the house after stealing the £10. The fact that he went back upstairs armed with a knife implies he intended to harm her. We will never know if Mary did actually tell Holohan that she recognised him, or indeed if she did cough and alert him that she was still alive after he attacked her with the ashtray. What is clear from all the evidence is that Holohan stabbed Mary, struck her repeatedly with an ashtray, choked her to death and then hid her body under her bed. Anything he might claim Mary said is just speculation.

Shortly after Holohan confessed to the murder of Mary Kitt, two local detectives, Brendan Moran and Denis O'Shea, visited him in an interview room and had a long conversation with him. Both men knew Holohan from their previous dealings, and he had asked to see a local garda. They asked him if they could help him in any way and he replied:

> I don't think I got an hour's sleep since. I woke up in the middle of the night in the horrors. I started screaming. … I just went in to get money. I'd say I [will] get life or 15 years, maybe 30 or 40. … I didn't mean to kill her. I just went off my head. She said, 'I know you, you are Holohan.' That was the worst thing she [could have] said.

While Holohan's confession meant the murder was solved very quickly, the Gardaí still collected all the available evidence just in case he'd later dispute the confession. His blood was found on Mary's bedspread, where he had cut his hand while striking her with the ashtray. He had left his fingerprint on the inside of the bathroom window while breaking into the house. The knife he used to stab Mary was never found. He had thrown it into deep water near Galway Bay and it was presumably washed out to sea. However, there was enough circumstantial and direct evidence to prove the sad truth of his confession.

On the same day that Holohan made his murder confession, his victim was laid to rest amid heart-rending scenes after Mass at the Claddagh in the area she had lived all her life. Journalists and other members of staff of the *Connacht Tribune* formed a guard of honour as Mary's coffin was brought to the church. And next day when her remains were brought to the cemetery, the funeral halted for prayers outside the offices of the *Connacht Tribune* on Market Street. Mary loved her job. There was a buzz about the newspaper that she really enjoyed. Her loss is still felt by all there.

If Holohan was initially confused as to how long a sentence he would get for murder, he was left in no doubt when on Monday,

9 February 1981, he pleaded guilty to the crime and was jailed for life. The practice of the Central Criminal Court at that time was that no 'useful purpose' would be served by hearing any evidence of a murder when the person responsible pleaded guilty. Therefore, the general public did not hear how Holohan had a long list of convictions including two for random assaults. The public did not hear how the Gardaí were frustrated by their inability to keep track of violent random attackers like Holohan, and there was no debate about how in the absence of a Violent Offenders Register the State had failed Mary Kitt.

Mary's murder traumatised her friends and family, and the wider community in Galway. One of her friends tells me how she still smiles when she thinks of Mary.

Mary was always in good form, always had a smile. Although she lived alone she had so much going on in her life. She had her friends and her nights out and the singing and laughing, we'd have such fun. Some of her friends have since passed away, and I miss them also. Mary was like a Mammy figure for some of the local children, and I think for some of the younger people in the *Tribune*. She was always interested in what people were doing, and they'd talk to her about exams, jobs, relationships. She had a small immediate family that miss her greatly, but her loss has deeply affected so many other people too.

One garda says there was an understandable feeling of anger after it emerged who had murdered Mary.

It's a sad fact, but it is a fact that there will always be disturbed people, mostly young men, who appear to be normal people but who will suddenly attack their vulnerable neighbours. All we can do is be as vigilant as possible to stop this kind of violent person who may be living in our midst. But Mary's murder was different; it could have been prevented. Although she was murdered by such a neighbour who gave no real thought to hiding his tracks, her killer was already known as a violent person. Local people asked, and they still ask how he was allowed do what he did.

Some months after Holohan was charged with the murder of Mary Kitt, there was an afternoon of sheer panic in Galway city after the suspect escaped from the courthouse. Holohan had demanded to be brought to court as he attempted to get back some of his possessions that detectives had taken as part of the investigation. But while waiting for the case to be heard, Holohan slipped away from his escorts and fled. The Gardaí searched all over the city for him, fearing he would carry out another random attack. It wasn't until later that night that a detective found him hiding out in a graveyard close to his home on Grattan Road. Having escaped from custody, Holohan realised he didn't really have anywhere to run to.

Michael Holohan is now one of the longest serving prisoners in the State. He is currently housed at Castlerea Prison and is occasionally brought in the company of prison officers to Galway city to visit family members. Having spent the last quarter of a century behind bars and away from direct sunlight, his complexion is pale and he has aged visibly. He is still a notorious drinker and has often been caught with 'prison-brew', a concoction made with yeast and food flavouring. He is generally regarded as being courteous to staff, and although he does some work as a cleaner in the prison he doesn't stretch himself too much.

In April 2004 Holohan was moved to a medium security

section of Castlerea Prison known as the Grove. This part of the prison consists of houses rather than cells and is a much more relaxed prison environment than the prison landings. Those who are transferred there must be able to get along with fellow inmates, share cooking and cleaning responsibilities and generally keep good order in 'their homes'. His transfer to the Grove would be viewed as a first move towards possibly granting him some form of parole in the future. Having spent over 25 years of his life in prison, and having seen so many other lifers walk free, Holohan is very active in seeking temporary release. However, his time at the Grove was short-lived. The Provisional IRA prisoners who are housed there objected to his presence after he reportedly made a derogatory comment about their Easter Commemoration parade. Holohan returned to the cells in the prison shortly afterwards.

In June 1980 the murder of Mary Kitt was reported on the front page of the *Connacht Tribune*, the paper for which she worked for 26 years. Every year since then, the paper puts in a notice to honour her passing. From her family and friends, to staff at the *Tribune*, and to the Gardaí who caught her killer, there are many who will always remember Mary Kitt.

5

Random Killer

J ust after 9 a.m. on 14 February 2000, life-sentence prisoner Thomas Murray left the front gate of Castlerea Prison and walked the short distance to his father's car. As was the norm every Monday for the previous couple of months, his father was bringing him home to Co. Galway for a 12-hour visit. Despite being caught indecently exposing himself to children in Galway city in 1998, the authorities had agreed to give Murray further temporary release from his life sentence imposed for murder in 1981. They decided he should be permitted a 12-hour release every Monday starting at 9 a.m. He would not be accompanied by a prison officer and was warned he had to be back inside the prison gates by 9 p.m. or his release would be halted. Murray was only too happy to accept this new form of parole, and as he sat into the front passenger seat beside his father, he was looking forward to another day of freedom. As usual they were going to spend the day in the village of Ballygar, where Murray had grown up, where he had killed before, and where shortly he would kill again. CCTV footage from that February morning shows Murray wearing a beige jacket and a black knitted jumper. Fibres from both items would later be found in the hallway of the 80-year-old woman he would murder within hours.

Murray took his first life on Sunday, 19 July 1981, when he was just 17 years old. Seventy-three-year-old Willie Mannion was a bachelor farmer who lived alone a few miles outside Ballygar. A popular member of the local community, Willie was a hard worker who liked nothing better than spending an evening with friends discussing politics and current affairs. He was a sociable man, and when he heard a knock at his door that Sunday evening he did not sense any danger when he saw it was young Thomas Murray from the nearby townland of Cloonlyon. He didn't really know Murray well, but he thought the teenager seemed like a nice young man, so he invited him in for a chat and a cup of tea. Willie had no idea that Murray had a knife in his possession.

Just a few hours before Murray called to Willie Mannion's house in July 1981, he had made a conscious decision to kill him. The two had met by chance after half-eleven Mass and said hello to each other, and at some stage later that Sunday afternoon Thomas Murray decided Willie would be his first murder victim. As with the second murder he would commit in Ballygar almost 20 years later, Murray had absolutely no motive in wanting to kill Willie. But there was some kind of indiscriminate murderous rage building inside the teenager; shortly he would take his first life, and in time he would prove himself to be beyond rehabilitation.

Murray waited until it was dark and then he fetched a knife he had hidden in a field near his home. He had stolen this knife sometime before from another house and had hidden it until he randomly chose his first victim. Having retrieved the knife from the field, the teenager cycled two miles to Willie's house and knocked on the door, pretending he was passing by and was just dropping in to say hello.

By the time he murdered Willie, Murray was already known to the Gardaí as a very disturbed young man. Just two years before, when he was 15 years old, he had sent obscene letters to a female neighbour. The matter was due to go to court, but he apologised and the case was dropped. But even before that, he had been a trouble-maker in school, puncturing the tyres of fellow pupils' bikes and prodding other pupils with a compass. He only lasted one year in secondary school before leaving to work full time on his father's farm. He was the youngest of two boys, he had few friends, and those that knew him thought him very strange.

Willie Mannion brought his guest into the kitchen and the two had a brief chat about the Gaelic games that had been played that weekend. It was just after 10 p.m. when suddenly, as the two sat chatting, Murray produced the knife and began stabbing Willie in the face and neck. The murder was a frenzied attack of extreme violence that lasted several minutes. Willie suffered 13 stab wounds to his head and neck. Raising his hands to protect his face, he suffered four defensive stab wounds to his hands. Murray also picked up Willie's hatchet after carrying out the knife attack, but for some reason did not use this weapon. Willie suffered a large stab wound to his right jaw, and another wound to his left cheek. One of the most distressing aspects of this senseless killing is that Willie did not die immediately, but sat slumped in his kitchen and suffered for up to an hour before bleeding to death.

Almost 19 years later, on 14 February 2000, a now 36-year-old Thomas Murray sat chatting to his father as they drove from Castlerea Prison towards Ballygar. They stopped off at a shop near the village and bought chops to have for their dinner that afternoon. They reached home shortly afterwards, did some odd jobs around the house and had a cup of tea. This is the same house in which Murray was living when he cycled to Willie Mannion's home. Now Murray was about to leave his family home once again to commit another motiveless and shocking murder. After having tea with his father, he said he was borrowing the car to go into the village. At some stage before he drove off, he picked up a lump hammer and secretly put it in the car.

At around the same time as convicted murderer Thomas Murray was leaving the gates of Castlerea Prison earlier that day to begin his 12-hour unaccompanied release, 80-year-old Nancy Nolan was beginning her day at her home just outside Ballygar. Her husband Tom had passed away five years before, and she now lived alone at their two-storey detached house close to the Ballaghlea National School, where she and Tom had taught generations of local children. Nancy's own children were now living in various parts of the country, and at the time of her murder Nancy was both an adored mother and grandmother. She was also a popular member of the Ballygar community and a friendly and outgoing woman who loved to chat to people both young and old. At around 12.10 p.m. on 14 February 2000, Nancy left her home and headed for Ballygar village.

In July 1981 the body of Willie Mannion lay undiscovered until around 24 hours after his murder. It was late on the Monday night of 20 July of that year when a neighbour, Martin Kelly, became concerned when he noticed that the lights were on in Willie's home but the curtains had not been drawn. Just after 11 p.m. the Gardaí broke open the front door of Willie's home. Garda Dan Keane had looked through the letterbox and saw Willie sitting slumped in the kitchen between a table and the stove. The Gardaí found Willie dead, and it was clear he had suffered a number of stab wounds to his head.

Willie Mannion was one of a family of seven who grew up on a farm in Ballygar in the early 1900s. Three of his brothers emigrated to the United States, all marrying and settling around New York. His only sister and another brother eventually moved to other parts of Ireland, leaving him and his brother Tom to work on the farm. When Tom passed away, Willie was the only one left in the old family home. His closest surviving relative in Ireland, a nephew, Michael Geraghty, remembers hearing of the murder on the radio.

My mother Mary was Willie's only sister. She had already passed away when my uncle was murdered. At the time of the murder, Willie's closest relatives in Ireland were his brother Frank who worked as a teacher in Dublin and myself in Athlone. I remember in July 1981 I was on a day off and had headed to Sligo with a friend of mine who was getting married. We were driving along listening to some country music station when we switched over to get the news. The lunchtime news came on and there was a headline saying, 'A Willie Mannion has been found murdered in Ballygar in Co. Roscommon.' The headline should have read Co. Galway and not Roscommon, but all the other information was accurate. My friend Brendan asked me if that was my uncle and I remember sitting there shocked and just saying, 'It has to be.' This was long before the era of mobile phones, so we had to drive on to Tubbercurry, and Brendan went to a solicitor's office and rang a garda he knew in Ballygar and confirmed it was my uncle Willie. My other uncle Frank was totally shattered by the murder. He only passed away in the late 1990s aged 84. He had attended the whole of the murder trial back in 1982 and he found it all very upsetting.

Michael Geraghty tells me there was some satisfaction in knowing his uncle's murderer had been caught.

I grew up close to Ballygar but I didn't know Thomas Murray. He would have been younger than me. I didn't really recognise him when I saw him during the trial in 1982, but I would have known who his family were. I remember keeping uncle Frank company at the trial and we were happy that at least Murray had been caught and that he was given a life sentence. We thought that's what he deserved. We thought he would serve a full life sentence. I mean that's what the sentence was, and that's what we thought it meant. But I have to say when I heard about the murder of Nancy Nolan I immediately thought of Thomas Murray, and when I heard he'd been out of prison at the time I knew it had to be him. What happened to my uncle was tragic, but what happened to Mrs Nolan is truly despicable. I remember her husband Tom taught me in Ballaghlea School. He was a lovely man. I have to ask, after carrying out such a terrible and unprovoked attack on my uncle, how could Thomas Murray have ever been in a position to murder a second time?

The day after he stabbed Willie Mannion to death, Murray took an overdose of pills he found at home. He ended up in hospital, where he soon made his first admission of guilt to a young medical student named Pauline, who simply asked him why he had harmed himself by taking the pills. Murray told her, 'I killed a man. I killed a man with a knife.' The Gardaí were immediately informed of the admission Murray had made and when they came to ask him to account for his movements on the night of Willie's murder, the teenager blurted out, 'All right, I killed Willie Mannion. That's the truth. Now ye have it.' He went on to outline to the detectives how he had murdered Willie and then hidden the knife in a boggy area near his home, and how he had then cycled five miles to a dance at Ballinamore Bridge, where he stayed until 2.30 a.m. Garda John Durkan would later find the murder weapon hidden at the spot Murray had indicated and it was forensically matched to the murder scene.

Murray was very co-operative with the Gardaí in the aftermath of Willie Mannion's murder. The teenager told them everything he could about his movements and about how he had planned to kill Willie, but there was one thing he couldn't explain — why he had committed the crime. At one stage he made a comment to the detectives that seemed like a statement anyone confessing to a murder might make. But in hindsight the comment is truly disturbing. Nineteen years before he murdered Nancy Nolan in the hallway of her home, Murray confessed to killing Willie Mannion in his home by saying, 'I killed Willie Mannion. ... I had it planned, but I hadn't it planned too long. ... I wouldn't do it again in a million years.'

Murray arrived in Ballygar village at around midday on 14 February 2000. After parking his father's car he decided he wanted a haircut, but he found the barber shop was closed. He went to a vet shop and bought eye ointment for the cows, something his father had been seeking for the cattle. At some stage he went to the local graveyard, where his mother had been laid to rest just over a year before. His mother had supported him when he had been charged with the murder of Willie Mannion, and she had been there for him throughout the trial and for most of the nearly 19 years he'd been in prison. He had been allowed out of prison to attend her funeral, but he was escorted to and from the prison. And now, just over a year later, the authorities felt he was safe enough to be let out alone.

Murray's older brother had been living away for a number of years, so by February 2000 his father was living alone for six days of the week. His father always looked forward to Thomas getting out of prison each Monday and coming home to help on the farm. When he gave his son the keys to the car on that February morning, he thought Murray was going to Ballygar village simply to get supplies for the farm and do a bit of shopping. He had no idea his son was already planning to commit another random murder.

Nancy Nolan arrived in Ballygar village shortly after 12.15 p.m. Those who spoke to her would remember she was in great form. Nancy was a great conversationalist, and having spent decades teaching local schoolchildren, she was well known and highly regarded by all.

As it was St Valentine's Day the local Spar shop had an extra supply of flowers, and she commented to one person in the shop about how lovely the roses were. She then visited another shop a short distance away and chatted with other shoppers before putting her purchases into her car and beginning her journey home, just over two and half miles outside the village on the Galway road.

At the same time that Nancy was driving home with her shopping, Murray was in the Spar shop where Nancy had been standing less than an hour before. He bought tobacco for roll-up cigarettes and then walked to his car and drove out of the village towards his home. The journey would bring him out on the N63 heading for Galway.

One detective who investigated the murder of Nancy Nolan and identified Murray as the killer tells me of the immense frustration the Gardaí still feel.

There is usually a satisfaction in catching a killer. We had that kind of satisfaction when we caught Thomas Murray for the murder of Willie Mannion. It was a terrible crime, but we were at least happy to get justice for Willie, and you sometimes do 'celebrate', if that's the right word. But there were no smiles of satisfaction when we caught Murray for Nancy Nolan's murder. It's a murder that could have been prevented. When you look at the CCTV images, it's so frustrating watching Murray leaving Castlerea Prison at 9 a.m. and returning to the prison twelve hours later, having committed such an awful crime — a man we put away a long time ago, a life sentence prisoner who should never have been in a position to harm another decent person. It is simply heart-breaking.

One of the most disturbing facts about the murder of Nancy Nolan is that less than two years before the murder, Murray had already proven himself to still be a danger to people. Early on the evening of 15 July 1998, almost 17 years after he murdered Willie Mannion, life sentence prisoner Thomas Murray indecently exposed himself to children in Galway city. He approached children playing at an area known as Fisheries Field along the River Corrib close to St Nicholas's Cathedral and carried out the offence. A woman who was minding the children witnessed the incident and shouted for help. A number of teenagers who were passing by stopped when they saw what Murray was doing and they also shouted at him. He ran off towards the back of the cathedral, heading for the city centre. The youths followed him, and when Garda Peadar Brick arrived on the scene, the teenagers pointed out Murray as the culprit. Brick arrested Murray and brought him to the garda station. At this stage the Gardaí didn't know that the 'flasher' they had just arrested was a convicted murderer. Murray was in a distressed state and insisted on being allowed to make a phone call. He phoned his father and said, 'They have me in again.' When Brick heard this comment he went upstairs to a computer and began searching for Murray's criminal file and soon established that Murray was on temporary release from Castlerea Prison. Within hours Murray was back inside Castlerea, but amazingly he would be allowed back out within a few months.

Murray spent the last few months of 1997 and the early part of 1998 effectively 'at large' in Galway city. He was out of Castlerea on temporary release and only had to return to prison once a month to 'sign on'. The authorities got him a job on a building site near Merlin Park in the city, and he lived in sheltered accommodation nearby, where he was supposed to be home by midnight each night. He did not come to the attention of the Gardaí until he exposed himself to the children in July 1998, but the fact that he was living quietly in Galway city for a number of months before that incident has not been lost on detectives investigating a number of very serious crimes, including one involving extreme and random violence.

Over seven years before he murdered Nancy Nolan, Murray was given his first temporary release from prison. In mid-1992, when he was 28 years old, he started getting accompanied visits home to Ballygar. In December of that year he was allowed home for seven days over Christmas. This was in spite of the fact that just a few months previously he tried to intimidate a female teacher at Loughan House Prison in Co. Cavan into giving him a kiss. He had hidden in the toilets of the education block of the prison until everyone else was gone, and he had then approached the woman's office. He told the teacher he had done a lot of cleaning around the school and wanted something in return. The woman used her professional experience to calm the situation. When Murray later apologised, no further action was taken. So in December 1992, less than 12 years after he stabbed Willie Mannion over a dozen times in the face and neck, Murray was allowed home to Ballygar to spend Christmas with his family.

Over the following years Murray was given occasional release from prison, first to attend a workshop in Ballinasloe, and later to live at home in Ballygar. Every time he was released the Gardaí voiced their objections, but eventually terrified locals were forced to accept that they were liable to meet Murray in Ballygar at any time. There were reports that he was making lewd gestures towards young girls in the locality, behaviour which would indeed tally with his later conviction for indecent exposure, but he was never charged with such offences. However, in 1996 he was put back in prison after he became the prime suspect for an arson attack on hay belonging to a garda. But, despite the deep suspicion that he was the guilty party, there was not enough evidence to bring a prosecution, and by mid-1997 the authorities had sourced a job for him in Galway city. He was given full temporary release until indecently exposing himself in July 1998. After serving his six-month sentence for this offence, he almost immediately started seeking further release from his life sentence. By October 1999 he was being released once a week for a 12-hour visit to his home in Ballygar. Despite his previous bad behaviour while out on temporary release, he was now being allowed out of prison unaccompanied every Monday, including 14 February 2000.

The murder of Nancy Nolan was a random, motiveless crime. Murray has never given any reason for attacking the 80-year-old woman with a lump hammer. There simply is no reason, no motive; it was a senseless act of gratuitous violence.

After murdering Nancy, Murray picked up her spectacles and took them with him. The glasses were the only item he stole from

Nancy's house. As with his attack on Willie Mannion in 1981, robbery was not a motive for Murray's attack on Nancy Nolan; nor was there any other obvious motive. Having pulled the front door shut behind him, no one saw the random killer walk out through Nancy's garden to his car and drive away, turning off the Roscommon – Galway road towards his own home, up a dirt track.

Before reaching his father's farmhouse, Murray stopped at a quiet location on the narrow laneway and threw Nancy's glasses into bushes. Further up the laneway he threw the lump hammer into bog water. He then drove on home and spent the late afternoon and evening helping his father with more chores around the farm. Just before 9 p.m. he returned to Castlerea Prison.

The following afternoon, Tuesday, 15 February, a neighbour of Nancy's phoned Roscommon Garda Station saying he was very concerned for his neighbour. Nancy's family had contacted the neighbour because Nancy wasn't answering her phone. He said he hadn't seen Nancy all the previous day and her car was still parked outside her house on the Galway road. The car had been parked there since the day before. She would always put her car in the garage overnight.

Just before 1 p.m. Sergeant Damien Lawlor and Gardaí Owen Crehan and Colm Corcoran arrived at Nancy's house. Using a key provided by a neighbour, the Gardaí opened the front door and found Nancy's body lying in the hall.

Within a short time of Nancy's body being found, the Gardaí knew they had a prime suspect. They had long feared something like this would happen, but despite garda warnings against giving Thomas Murray unaccompanied release from prison the authorities had let him out every Monday for the last four months. The Gardaí soon established that Murray had been given a 12-hour release from Castlerea Prison on the day of Nancy's murder.

As they sealed off Nancy's house, pending a forensic examination of the scene, many detectives simply shook their heads in disbelief that their long-held fears had been realised.

A shadow of terror descended over Ballygar in the immediate aftermath of Nancy Nolan's murder. Local people knew that Murray had been in the village on the day of the murder, and some feared he was still at large. Although he only appeared around Ballygar every Monday, returning to prison for the rest of the week, did that mean he might be back in the village the following Monday?

On Wednesday, 16 February, less than 24 hours after Nancy's body was discovered, Inspector William Gallagher received warrants from Judge John Neilan in Roscommon to carry out two searches. A team of Gardaí was dispatched to search the land owned by the Murray family at Cloonlyon, near Ballygar, while Gallagher and Detectives Alec Dempsey and Joe Conboy travelled to search Murray's property at Castlerea Prison. The Gardaí went straight to House No. 2 at Unit A, otherwise known as the Grove, a medium security section of the prison where inmates share houses rather than cells. After speaking with Murray and searching his room in the prison-house, the detectives seized a black knitted jumper and a beige-coloured jacket.

As the Gardaí began a protracted investigation to find Nancy Nolan's killer, prison authorities moved to cancel Murray's temporary releases. Within hours of Nancy's body being found, and detectives seizing some of Murray's clothing at Castlerea Prison, the enormity of what had happened was beginning to dawn on everyone. Even though it would take months to gather all the evidence in the murder investigation, the authorities now acted to ensure that the last temporary release Murray received was the day Nancy was murdered.

Although he was identified immediately as the prime suspect for the murder, it would be over two months before Murray would admit the killing. In the meantime, detectives tried to piece together his movements on the day of the killing, and searched for the murder weapon. The Gardaí had quickly established that Nancy's glasses were missing from her house and had most likely been taken by her killer. But there was so much open bogland in the area around Murray's home, it was like searching for a needle in a haystack. The older detectives remembered that when they arrested Murray in 1981 for the murder of Willie Mannion, it was only after Murray gave a detailed confession and outlined where he had hidden the knife that the Gardaí had found the weapon. It looked like that might be the case once again. The only way the murder might be solved was with Murray's assistance.

On 20 March 2000, the Gardaí went to Castlerea Prison and arrested Murray on suspicion of murdering Nancy Nolan. This was the first time he had been asked direct questions about the murder. He denied any knowledge of the killing and said the last time he had seen Mrs Nolan was two weeks before her murder, when he had spotted her in Ballygar village. He was released back into the custody of prison officials without charge.

Although the Gardaí still had no murder weapon, they were making progress. Two prisoners at Castlerea had come forward to say that on the night of 14 February 2000 Murray returned to Castlerea with a deep cut or scratch on his nose. The Gardaí wondered if he had received the mark walking through briars or bushes while hiding the murder weapon and Nancy's glasses.

The Gardaí meanwhile had sent Murray's black jumper and beige jacket to be examined by Dr Fiona Thornton at the State Forensic Science Laboratory in Dublin. Detectives had run the CCTV footage of Murray leaving Castlerea Prison on Monday, 14

February, and returning that night, so they knew what he had been wearing. A short time after Murray's clothing was seized at the prison, Dr Thornton told the Gardaí that there was indeed a primary and secondary transfer of fibres between Murray's clothing and the clothing Nancy had been wearing when she was attacked. Slowly but surely the net was beginning to tighten around Murray.

Shortly after he murdered Willie Mannion in 1981, Murray spent a number of months in the Central Mental Hospital. He was later transferred to Mountjoy Jail and later spent time in Dublin's Arbour Hill Prison and Loughan House in Cavan before being transferred to Castlerea Prison. Although he could never offer a motive for stabbing Willie Mannion to death, psychiatrists formed the view that he was not mentally ill but was instead someone of low intellect whose personality bordered on the psychotic. This description would also match the frenzied nature of Nancy Nolan's murder; it was a motiveless crime carried out by someone fuelled with a desire to kill innocent people. The murders of both Willie Mannion and Nancy Nolan were carried out by someone with no feeling, no humanity, no morals. But somewhere within Murray there was a need to admit his crimes. Perhaps it was a semblance of conscience or guilt that was eating away at him, or perhaps it was simply a desire to please people in authority. He had initially denied murdering Willie Mannion, only to come clean within days and lead detectives to the murder weapon he had carefully hidden. Now, 19 years later, as he thought about how he had attacked Nancy in the hallway of her home, something was happening within him. He didn't want to keep his crime hidden any more. He wanted to tell his father, and he wanted to tell the Gardaí.

On 24 April 2000, Murray told a chief prison officer at Castlerea that he wanted to speak with the detectives once again. He asked specifically for Detective Garda Basil Johnson, who travelled to Castlerea along with Detective Sergeant Tom Fitzmaurice. The detectives cautioned Murray that anything he said might be used against him. They immediately sensed that he had changed. He was more talkative; he indicated he had something important to say. Very soon he was no longer rubbishing their suspicions, but said he wanted to tell all. He told Johnson that he had sent for him specifically because the garda had always 'treated him fairly'. He then told the detectives, 'I want to give the whole thing up.' Over the following minutes he admitted he had murdered Nancy and he said he was sorry. These words were of cold comfort to her family and friends who will always be traumatised by her horrific death at the hands of one of the most dangerous men ever to live in this country. As the detectives listened in sombre silence, he continued his confession saying, 'It's an awful thing I did, to kill a woman like Mrs Nolan.' He then said he would show them where he had disposed of the hammer he had used to murder Nancy.

Murray's confession in Castlerea Prison was an extraordinary moment. While he failed to offer any reason for committing such a terrible crime, it was the only time he would outline in any way the sequence of events that led to him committing a second random murder. One detective believes Murray still has a lot more to say.

I think when Murray got Detectives Johnson and Fitzmaurice to visit him in prison, he had somehow changed for just a short time. The killer within him was replaced or overshadowed by a man isolated and alone and trying to 'do the right thing' for once in his life. By the time he made his jailhouse confession, other prisoners were looking at him and openly wondering if he could be the person who had murdered Nancy. While he was protected in a sense from the public gaze by being back in

Castlerea, he was under a lot of scrutiny from fellow prisoners and the prison officers. His father was visiting him in prison throughout February and March and into April, and Murray must have realised that his Mondays home in Ballygar were over for ever. I would describe Murray as being of a low intellect, but he could be cute sometimes. In a sense, when he told the Gardaí he wanted to 'give the whole thing up', he had come to realise that the game really was up, and that while it might take months or years, eventually detectives would find the murder weapon he had hidden close to his home. I think Murray felt it was in his own interest to admit what he had done, say he was sorry — for what little that was worth — and get on with prison life. But I think there is a lot more he could tell, especially about a particular unsolved attack near Galway city in 1997, and I think in time he will indeed tell all he knows, because the game is up now for Tommy Murray, and coming clean would help everyone, including himself.

The unsolved attack for which Murray is the prime suspect occurred north-east of Galway city in November 1997. At the time of this extremely violent and random offence, he was on temporary release from prison and was lodging with a couple near Ballybane in the east of the city. A person answering Murray's description was spotted close to the scene of this most disturbing incident. When he was later given a life sentence for the murder of Nancy Nolan, someone came forward with information putting Murray close to the scene of the other crime over two years before. The degree of violence used in the particular attack in 1997 is similar to the violence used against Nancy. As detectives continue to investigate the 1997 incident, they believe there are people who have crucial information about this crime and whose consciences are troubled every single day. Enquiries by the Gardaí into this particular attack have led them to now suspect that while Murray was on parole in 1997 and 1998, he was plotting random attacks similar to the murders of Willie Mannion and Nancy Nolan.

Shortly before 2 p.m. on 25 April 2000, Garda Kieran Doyle got a reading from a metal detector while searching a bog hole at Cloonlyon Bog close to Murray's old family home. Garda David Finn went to investigate and three feet down in bog water he found a lump hammer. He brought it to the surface and it was placed in an evidence bag. Murray had taken the lump hammer from the family farm and hidden it in late 1999, around the time he started going home on temporary release from Castlerea Prison every Monday.

As the lump hammer was being recovered, a search was under way in dense undergrowth a few hundred yards away for Nancy's spectacles. Murray had described to the detectives how he had stolen the glasses before making his escape from Mrs Nolan's house, but could give no explanation as to why he stole them. However, he could remember the general location where he had thrown the spectacles. The Gardaí who found the glasses treated them with great care. They were not only evidence in a murder investigation, but they were also the personal property of a highly respected woman who was a pillar of the local community.

It will take a long time for the community of Ballygar to recover from the crimes of Thomas Murray. The Co. Galway village was stunned by the horrific murder of Willie Mannion in July 1981, but there was at least some relief in the sense that the killer had been caught and convicted. That the same killer could be allowed to strike again in the same community in February 2000 is almost incomprehensible. Ballygar is a busy village less than ten miles from Roscommon town on the main road to Galway. It is a village with a strong community spirit, but it is also filled with memories of two elderly citizens whose lives were taken in the most horrendous way. One local woman who knew both tells me of the awful effect Murray's crimes have had.

Willie Mannion was a lovely man, very gentle and the sort that would stop to chat to anyone. I can well imagine him putting on the kettle and inviting Murray in for a chat and a cup of tea. Willie was a man without an ounce of badness in him, and those of us who remember him miss him dearly. But there are many people living in Ballygar now who weren't around in 1981, or who were too young to remember the murder. I remember I almost fainted when I heard how my own son had given Thomas Murray a lift to Galway city a few years before Murray murdered Nancy Nolan. My son had heard of Murray and the murder of Willie Mannion, but he wouldn't have known Murray to see, so he gave a lift to this man hitching outside the village. He only realised who it was some time later. For all we know Murray could have had a hammer or another weapon with him when my son gave him a lift. Those of us who remembered how he attacked Willie Mannion knew Murray was always going to be a danger. I mean, how could you ever trust him after something like that? But there was also a feeling that maybe the authorities knew what they were doing. Surely they wouldn't let him out of prison if he wasn't well. That's what we thought anyway. Nancy Nolan was in the wrong place at the wrong time and it is so sad. It could have been me or any other elderly person around here, or maybe he would have attacked children. It's just awful what happened to Willie and Nancy, and none of us will be the same again after it.

The murder of Willie Mannion in July 1981 horrified the community of Ballygar. The terrible injuries Willie had suffered to his face and neck left local detectives speechless. The Gardaí had quickly discovered that robbery was not the motive, as Willie still had around £200 in his pocket and a search of his prefabricated home revealed more cash in a secret hiding place. One detective remembers how Willie's murder made it clear to him and fellow Gardaí that Murray should never have been allowed out of prison alone.

We quickly decided that the person who killed Willie had done so purely to take a life. The person responsible had some rage within him. Willie Mannion had never harmed anyone in his life. He never did anyone a bad turn; he had no enemies. Later when we learned that Tommy Murray was the killer, we were surprised at the level of violence within him, but then again he was a very unpredictable teenager. Murray could be so quiet and docile, but to commit a knife attack such as the attack on Willie Mannion requires someone with absolutely no feeling. The murder of Nancy Nolan is clearly a crime where Murray shows he has no humanity within him. He is without a soul. But thinking back to Willie Mannion's murder and what he did to that poor man, the random killer within Murray was already evident.

The fear that came over the community of Ballygar following the murder of Nancy Nolan in February 2000 cannot be overstated. Decent law-abiding people found it difficult to understand how a random and brutal murderer could be allowed out of prison to claim the life of a second elderly person. There were simply no words to adequately describe the sense of loss, hurt, anger, despair and shock that engulfed the area in February 2000, and which still exists for Nancy's family and friends.

In December 2000 Murray stood in Court No. 2 at the Central Criminal Court and pleaded guilty to the murder of Nancy Nolan. In 1982, while Murray was still a teenager, he had stood in the same building to be given a life sentence for murdering Willie Mannion. Now he stood once again to receive a similar sentence for beating an 80-year-old woman to death with a lump hammer. If he had decided to fight the murder charge, there would have been 167 witnesses — from prisoners at Castlerea, to the locals in Ballygar who saw either Nancy or Murray in the village on 14 February of that year. There would also have been the evidence of fibres left by Murray's clothing in the hallway of Nancy's home. The fact that Nancy's glasses had been recovered and the lump hammer found only after specific information was given by Murray removed any doubt about his guilt. From the moment he made his confession in Castlerea Prison in April 2000, there was only one way he could approach the murder charge, and that was to plead guilty.

In a packed courtroom Murray stood meekly and faced the court registrar. As Nancy Nolan's five daughters, her son and all her family sat at the back of the court, Murray pleaded guilty for the second time in his life to murdering an elderly person in Ballygar, Co. Galway. After hearing a brief outline of the prosecution evidence, Mr Justice Paul Carney told Murray there was only one sentence that could be imposed in Irish law for the crime of murder — mandatory imprisonment for life. There were no cheers and no smiles from anyone in the courtroom. Murray sat back down beside a number of prison officers and looked at the ground, lost in his own private guilty thoughts. Nancy Nolan's family hugged and cried, and after thanking the Gardaí they left the court.

As the Gardaí watched Murray being taken away to begin his second life sentence, they too thought of Nancy Nolan. And they also thought of Willie Mannion, a man whose random and savage murder in the same village two decades before was not deemed serious enough by the State to keep his killer behind bars for ever.

Having admitted a second murder, Murray was sent to the high security Arbour Hill Prison in Dublin. He found the tight security in the Dublin prison very difficult to adapt to and missed his more comfortable surroundings in Castlerea. His experience of his first life sentence for the murder of Willie Mannion means that, despite admitting beating an 80-year-old woman to death, he still believes to this day that he will get parole again in the future. One garda says Murray has a totally skewed understanding of the destruction he has caused to so many lives.

Tommy Murray is the type of fella who blames other people for his problems and for what he has done. I know that he actually blames the authorities for 'allowing' him out of prison to murder Nancy Nolan. He actually feels it's their fault for letting him out when he 'wasn't well'. And he still hasn't come to terms with the fact that he will never get out of prison ever again. He thinks he'll get temporary release again in ten or twelve years. I don't think the authorities will ever be so stupid as to let him out of prison ever again, so if he stays in good health Murray could be inside for well over 50 years to come. But Murray just doesn't comprehend that his second life sentence will mean what it says. And it mightn't be the nicest thing to say but who could blame him for thinking like that when the State didn't believe back in 1981 that stabbing a 73-year-old man to death warranted a full and proper life sentence. Tommy Murray blames others for what he has done, and as long as 'life' doesn't really mean a full life sentence for the majority of murderers, there will be others like Murray who will kill again and blame the stupid system.

One Friday morning in 2004, Murray tried to attack two senior prison officials at Arbour Hill. He was working in the Fabric Shop where bedding is made for all the country's prisons, when he suddenly tried to hit the men with an iron bar he had removed from a piece of furniture. The iron bar caught in something and he couldn't strike either of the men. Within seconds a team of prison officers had dived on Murray to subdue him and he was placed in a padded cell. It later emerged that some weeks before this he had allegedly told a fellow prisoner that he wanted to get a hammer and attack a member of the staff. Within days of trying to attack the prison officials in Arbour Hill, he was moved to the Midlands Prison in Portlaoise. He is considered a high-security prisoner who should be constantly monitored, and will be kept in isolation in the future if that is necessary. While society can breathe a sigh of relief that he is finally off the streets, he has to be constantly watched so that he doesn't kill anyone in prison.

While Murray remains in prison, the Gardaí continue to investigate his movements during the time he was on temporary release and living in Galway city in 1997 and 1998. Detectives are convinced that there are people who have information that could help rule Murray in or out of particular crimes. One garda says the sense of fear that still exists is easing as time goes on.

I believe there are people who spoke to Tommy Murray during the time he was 'at large' around Co. Galway. We know he used to hitch lifts between Ballygar and Galway, sometimes standing in the centre of the road to force a car to stop for him. I believe there are people who gave Murray a lift who have not come forward to us yet. I can understand that people are nervous and afraid. It is the result of seeing Murray walking the streets only 15 or 16 years after murdering Willie Mannion. But Murray is put away for ever now. He'll never get out after murdering Nancy Nolan. I would urge people to come to us with whatever information they have. It might be something Murray said, or people might remember items he had in his possession. There are times that Murray was supposedly in bed asleep in Galway and honouring his curfew, but we suspect he wasn't always where he should have been. But we need help from the public.

The fear of Thomas Murray that still grips people is a legacy of the failure to properly monitor the life sentence prisoner when he was allowed out on temporary release. His crimes have devastated a community in Co. Galway and have shattered the confidence of ordinary decent citizens who cannot comprehend how such a random killer could have been allowed to operate under the noses of the authorities.

In Ballygar people try and get on with their lives. They have been let down by a system of justice where a life sentence has no real meaning. They have seen the life of an 80-year-old woman cruelly taken by a killer who should never have been let out of prison. It is as simple and as sad as that. Driving through Ballygar towards Galway, Nancy Nolan's former home lies on the right-hand side, close to Ballaghlea National School where she and her husband educated generations of local children. Travelling on towards Galway and up a laneway lies the spot where Willie Mannion lived all his life. Murray will never return to this village, but his crimes will forever remain in the minds of those who live here. It is here in 1981 that a 17-year-old future recidivist killer spoke the haunting words: 'I killed Willie Mannion. ... I had it planned, but I hadn't it planned too long. ... I wouldn't do it again in a million years.'

6

Murder at Tibnin Bridge

Corporal Gary Morrow, Private Peter Burke and Private Thomas Murphy knew they faced danger when they travelled to the Lebanon on peace-keeping duties. However, the three young men never thought that such danger would come from within. They never thought a fellow Irish soldier would turn on them and fire indiscriminately before moving in closer and firing again to ensure all three soldiers were dead. As the three sat on chairs at checkpoint 6.23A at Tibnin Bridge in south Lebanon on an October evening in 1982, they only had a split second's warning before the shooting started. Standing a short distance in front of his victims, 21-year-old Private Michael McAleavey first pointed his weapon at 20-year-old Gary Morrow and began firing. Keeping his finger on the trigger, McAleavey fired from right to left, hitting 19-year-old Thomas Murphy and then 20-year-old Peter Burke. Within seconds, McAleavey had fired 33 shots, 18 of which hit the soldiers, and he had taken the lives of three brave men. As reinforcements arrived at the bridge, McAleavey claimed he and his fellow soldiers had been fired on from the hills. It would take three months before McAleavey would finally confess he had killed his comrades, a confession that would ultimately leave him serving three life sentences, becoming the longest-serving prisoner in Mountjoy Jail.

Corporal John O'Connor was working in the UN Communications Centre near the Irish Battalion Headquarters in Tibnin in south Lebanon, when he heard the garbled message. It was 8.40 p.m. on Wednesday, 27 October 1982. O'Connor tried to make out what the caller was saying. All he could hear was heavy breathing, high static and incoherent speech. The corporal knew immediately that something was wrong and he tried to pinpoint which of the outposts was urgently seeking help. He quickly contacted checkpoints 6.22 and 6.23, but both reported all was calm. He then radioed checkpoint 6.23A at Tibnin Bridge. The telephone was answered by a male voice with an Irish accent. At the other end of the phone was Michael McAleavey, holding the phone tight, his heart racing and his mind concocting a plan to cover himself for three murders he had just committed. As O'Connor asked the caller to identify himself and report the outpost's status, he heard the voice again but this time more clearly: 'We've been hit. ... There's blood all over the place. ... They are still out there.'

McAleavey was only a week in the Lebanon when he murdered his three colleagues. When he left Dublin Airport with the 52nd Battalion in the early hours of 20 October 1982, he was a last-minute replacement for another soldier who had to pull out of the six-month tour of duty. From the Falls Road in Belfast, McAleavey joined the Irish Army in Dundalk on 7 August 1980 when he was 19 years old. He was later stationed in Cathal Brugha Barracks in Rathmines in Dublin, and soon applied to go to the Lebanon for United Nations peace-keeping duties. McAleavey had no previous convictions and had a good disciplinary record in the Defence Forces prior to going to the Lebanon. But on 27 October 1982, he committed a triple murder that ensures his name is forever linked with one of the darkest days in Irish military and criminal history.

Within minutes of O'Connor receiving the emergency message over the army radio, over a dozen soldiers were *en route* to Tibnin Bridge. It was only a three-minute drive north of the Irish UN Headquarters at Tibnin, and eight soldiers led by Lieutenant Brian Sweeney sped from there to the scene in an armoured personnel carrier. Meanwhile, five soldiers had grabbed rifles and were racing to the scene in a Land Rover from As Sultaniyah, just a few minutes west of the checkpoint. The soldiers knew a four-man team had been stationed at the outpost as normal. The radio message hadn't been specific but had sounded ominous — the men at the checkpoint were under attack, perhaps from the hills or under the bridge near the checkpoint. The soldiers about to arrive at the scene as back-up didn't know that three of the four soldiers at Tibnin Bridge were already dead.

Gary Morrow, Thomas Murphy and Peter Burke were all on their first tour of duty in the Lebanon. Like their killer, Gary and Thomas were both part of the 52nd Battalion that had arrived from Ireland the week before. Peter Burke, however, was due to go home from the Lebanon within days. The 20-year old was part of the 51st Battalion that had just completed its six-month stint keeping peace in south Lebanon. Peter couldn't wait to wear his uniform home to Dublin and see his family and his girlfriend. But towards the end of the 51st Battalion's six-month tour of duty, the troops were told that a few of them had to stay behind to show the 52nd Battalion the ropes. Peter Burke drew the short straw, and so on 27 October 1982, when most of his battalion were travelling home to their families in Ireland, he was doing one last checkpoint duty at Tibnin Bridge.

Nineteen-year-old Thomas Murphy from Dublin was the youngest of the soldiers to die that day. He joined the Defence Forces in June 1980, two months after his 17th birthday. With over two years' experience as a soldier, Thomas was a popular and highly regarded member of the 52nd Battalion.

Gary Morrow was 20 years old and married seven months to the day when McAleavey shot him dead. Like McAleavey, Gary was from the North; he was born in Lurgan in Co. Armagh. His dream of being a soldier in the Irish Army brought him to Cathal Brugha Barracks in Dublin, and while stationed there he met Collette, his wife to be. They married in Dublin on 27 March 1982. Collette was pregnant by the time Gary left for the Lebanon, but she didn't know it at the time. She tells me how, if she had had her way, Gary would have been to the Lebanon and back before the end of October 1982.

When we got married in March '82 I actually wanted Gary to go and do his tour of duty the following month, and not to wait until October. I didn't want to get used to him being around, only for him to go away after being married six months. But the Defence Forces wouldn't allow him to go in April because we were only married. I remember when he was preparing to go out in October the army told us to talk about the possibility that Gary might be killed while on peace-keeping duties. I remember Gary just came home one day and said we had to talk about it just in case. We made it a light conversation. It's the only way to do it. I asked him where he wanted to be buried and he said he didn't mind. But from then on I somehow realised he wasn't coming back.

Collette clearly remembers being at the airport when the 52nd Battalion flew to the Lebanon.

> Out at the airport the soldiers were advised to just wave to their relatives when they were going to the plane and not to stop. Being a corporal, Gary had to tell his men not to stop, but then he stopped. And I just got this feeling. A coldness came over me. Gary seemed to have changed. I said to him, 'There's something different. I don't want you going out', and he said, 'Why not?' I said, 'Gary, you're not going to come back if you go out. Please don't go out', and he said, 'I'll write to you', and he followed the others to the plane. A few weeks after Gary was murdered, I received a letter he had written shortly after arriving in the Lebanon. Although it had arrived in Rathmines, they didn't have the heart to give it to me until some weeks after the murders.

On the night of 26 October 1982, a young army private rostered for checkpoint duty at Tibnin Bridge asked Michael McAleavey if he wouldn't mind swopping a shift with him. McAleavey was due to start a shift at 22.00 hours that night, but the other young soldier said he preferred working nights and he asked McAleavey if he would take another shift at Tibnin Bridge the following day. It was fairly short notice, but McAleavey said he had no problem and they checked with their superior who said it was OK. McAleavey was now rostered to work between 14.00 and 22.00 hours at Tibnin Bridge on 27 October alongside Gary Morrow, Thomas Murphy and Peter Burke.

A few weeks before McAleavey killed his three colleagues, he had by chance sat opposite Gary and Collette Morrow on a train. McAleavey was travelling from Belfast to Dublin and was sitting alone when Gary and Collette got on the train at Portadown. The couple had been up visiting Gary's parents in Lurgan, and when Gary saw McAleavey in the carriage he said hello and they sat down opposite him. Collette remembers McAleavey as a very strange character.

When we got on the train and Gary saw this other soldier, I said that I didn't want to sit beside anyone else because we were into the last few days before Gary was due to go away. But Gary said there was nothing he could do and so we sat in the seats opposite McAleavey. I remember I said hello to him and sat down, and his face just went scarlet and his neck went peuce. His eyes just stared right through me. I thought maybe he was a bit embarrassed meeting his corporal and his wife on the train. I asked him if he was looking forward to going to the Lebanon, and he just stared at me and looked out the window. Gary went to the toilet and I didn't want to talk to McAleavey because I found him strange, so I started to read a book. I could feel him looking at me, and when Gary came back he took the newspaper McAleavey had and he turned it around to me and said, 'Look what McAleavey drew.' He had drawn a picture of me. I think he was raging he was caught, and he just went red. I felt strained sitting opposite him. I was very uncomfortable but I never said anything more to Gary about McAleavey. A friend of McAleavey's got on at Dundalk and they chatted away, and Gary and I chatted to ourselves. We got off the train at Connolly Station and Gary and I headed home. I know hindsight is a great thing, but Gary was killed less than two weeks later.

The early evening dusk had quickly turned to darkness, but the soldiers who rushed to checkpoint 6.23A saw bright lights as they arrived at Tibnin Bridge. Lieutenant Brian Sweeney and his fellow soldiers saw the headlights of a BMW car stopped at the checkpoint. As the back-up soldiers arrived at the scene, they saw a number of very disturbing things all at once.

Three men stood in front of the car. Two who looked like Lebanese civilians had their hands above their heads and appeared to be terrified. The third man, wearing an Irish Army uniform, stood two feet in front of the civilians pointing a rifle directly at them. His eyes were wide and he was turning his head from left to right as if looking for more people coming out of the darkness. The soldiers recognised the man as their fellow soldier, Michael McAleavey, and he appeared to be in deep shock. The soldiers also saw a large amount of blood on the ground. Behind McAleavey and in front of a bunker lay two bodies, both wearing Irish Army uniforms.

Peter Burke lay on his back with his head resting against the wall of the bunker. To Peter's left, Thomas Murphy lay on his front, with his right cheek resting against the bunker wall. It was obvious both men had been shot in the head. The legs of both soldiers were resting on the backs of upturned chairs, as if both had been sitting when they were shot. Sweeney immediately asked McAleavey what had happened. As McAleavey kept his rifle trained on the two Lebanese, all he said was, 'They came in, they came in.' Sweeney knelt beside the two soldiers and checked for signs of life. Peter Burke was dead; Thomas Murphy seemed to have a very faint pulse but wasn't breathing. With the bright lights of the BMW focusing on only a short section of ground, the body of Gary Morrow could not be seen lying in darkness at the side of the bunker. Sweeney radioed Battalion Headquarters, requesting urgent medical assistance and reporting one soldier dead, one dying, one missing and one survivor.

As Sweeney made the emergency radio call, the other soldiers were observing McAleavey's demeanour. He was still standing and pointing his rifle directly at the two Lebanese men. He was looking from left to right and his eyes were still wide as if he was in a daze. The soldiers noticed that his grip on the rifle was so tight his knuckles were white. A number of the soldiers brought the two Lebanese civilians towards the bunker and placed them on the ground to search them properly. The two men, Victor Nakhleh and Clouvies Hag, offered no resistance. Finding no weapons on the two men or in the BMW, the soldiers quite rightly assumed the two men had simply stumbled upon the scene. But someone had fired at the Irish soldiers, someone who might still be in the area preparing to fire again and who might use the bright car lights to pick their target.

One soldier asked McAleavey for his rifle and used the butt to smash the headlights of the BMW, bringing darkness to the murder scene. The soldier gave the rifle back to McAleavey and set about organising a search of the area. McAleavey was still in deep shock. Although not thinking at this stage that McAleavey might be responsible for the murders, one soldier wisely took back the rifle from McAleavey and brought him into the bunker to await the arrival of the army doctor. McAleavey offered no resistance. Moments later, as an ambulance arrived and parked close to the bunker, a number of soldiers spotted the body of Gary Morrow lying on his stomach at the side of the bunker. What nobody knew at that stage was that Gary Morrow had been sitting with Peter Burke and Thomas Murphy when McAleavey started firing, but had managed to crawl to the side of the bunker, only for McAleavey to come closer, stand over him and fire again.

When the Irish back-up soldiers arrived at Tibnin Bridge that night, they didn't know they were standing in the middle of a crime scene that would later be analysed at a murder trial in Ireland. They didn't have time to think about retaining forensic or ballistic evidence; they thought the next shot from the sniper was going to ring out at any second. They looked frantically around the checkpoint for any possible attack position. The T-junction at Tibnin Bridge links roads from the south, east and west. A corporal thought he heard a sound across the bridge to the south, and fired one round in that direction. Another soldier fired two rounds under the bridge, and fired a flare under the bridge too. Another soldier fired five rounds under the bridge from another side. They shone torches under the bridge and saw it was clear. Other soldiers ran towards a nearby water tank, thinking it might also provide a good vantage spot for a sniper. They fired at the tank as they approached it, but found there was no one there either. The Irish soldiers stopped firing and all was quiet.

As an ambulance prepared to remove the bodies of Gary Morrow, Thomas Murphy and Peter Burke, their fellow soldiers fought back tears as they lifted the bodies of their friends away from the scene. They picked up the blue United Nations berets that lay on the ground, and also the rifles that the three dead soldiers never had a chance to use to defend themselves before their sudden deaths. As well as being very shaken by the deaths of their comrades, many soldiers were puzzled as to who exactly had attacked the checkpoint and where they had gone.

Private Peter Burke was following a proud family tradition when he joined the Defence Forces. One of his grandfathers was in the army, and two of his uncles were soldiers too. When he decided he also wanted to be a soldier, he asked his father Noel to go down with him and help him join. The eldest of four children, Peter was a few months short of his 18th birthday when he signed up. Noel and Mary Burke remember how proud they were when they first saw their son in uniform. Mary tells me of the last time she saw her son.

When Peter was going off to the Lebanon, we were allowed out to the airport to say goodbye. And we were all there at the hangar, and he looked so brave heading off. He happened to be the last soldier going through the departure gate, and he turned around to blow a kiss, and when I saw him at that moment, I knew, I knew I was never going to see him again. And that feeling stayed with me the whole six months he was away. People told me not to be silly, but it became an obsession and I'd follow news reports of the happenings in the Lebanon, fearing the worst. But when it actually happened, when Peter was killed, he was due home and he should have been home.

Mary remembers hearing of the shooting at Tibnin Bridge.

My brother, who was serving in the same battalion as Peter, was coming home on 27 October. Peter had to stay behind for a few days to help the new battalion, so we went to Ballyfermot to visit my brother who had brought home letters from Peter for ourselves and his girlfriend. We called in to Inchicore to give his girlfriend her letter, and while we were there the news came on. It was a newsflash saying three soldiers had been shot dead in an ambush in the Lebanon.

Noel says they didn't think their son could be among those shot.

We first thought Peter wouldn't be there. Sure he was due to come home. We didn't think he could be out at a checkpoint. We thought he'd be back in the barracks.

But Mary had a bad feeling, the same feeling she'd had ever since her son had left for the Lebanon six months before. It was a feeling similar to the one Collette Morrow had when she said goodbye to her husband at the airport only the previous week. Within hours the Burkes, the Morrows and the family of Thomas Murphy would receive the heart-breaking news.

After hearing the news on the radio about the ambush, the Burkes went home to Kilmainham. Like dozens of other worried families that day, they rang the army to ask for information, but were told that the army didn't have the names of those killed and couldn't give out such information on the phone anyway. And so Peter Burke's family waited, and by half past ten that night when they had still heard nothing, they thought Peter mustn't have been involved and they went to bed. At around 11 p.m. they heard vehicles pulling up outside the house. They opened their front door to a priest and two officers.

Back in Tibnin, a number of army officers were quickly becoming very suspicious of McAleavey. When a soldier had taken his rifle from him, it was because he seemed edgy and unpredictable. Some soldiers thought it might naturally be from witnessing three of his comrades being murdered around him. But questions were beginning to be raised, such as how it was that he had not suffered any injuries. He mumbled something about being in the toilet at the time of the shootings and diving to the ground. An initial examination of the bodies of the three soldiers showed each had suffered a gunshot to the head at close range, so how did he not see the attacker or attackers? And then there was his very strange demeanour in the aftermath of the killings.

After handing over his rifle, McAleavey had gone into the bunker with a soldier who was instructed to 'mind' him. A doctor soon arrived and said McAleavey was suffering from shock and should be brought to hospital. As he was walking out of the bunker with the doctor, he suddenly ran towards the two Lebanese men who were still lying on the ground. He jumped on top of them and started hitting them and shouting, 'Bastards! They shot them.' Two soldiers managed to drag him away from the now very traumatised Lebanese men, but he kept kicking at them. He tried to grab a gun from one of the soldiers, but couldn't get at it. He calmed down eventually and willingly climbed into the ambulance to be taken away and sedated. Having witnessed this scene, many of the soldiers were now very thankful McAleavey's rifle had been taken away from him. Nobody dared say what many were now privately fearing, but something was definitely not right.

Collette Morrow was out with her friend Jennifer in Rathmines. They had been to the Leinster House pub and were going to the 24-hour shop close to Cathal Brugha Barracks to buy sugar when a car pulled up. An army captain got out and came over to them. He asked Jennifer if she was Collette Morrow, and Jennifer pointed to Collette. As she looked at Jennifer talking to the officer, Collette was smiling and in great form. But all of a sudden Jennifer wasn't laughing. The officer turned to Collette and said, 'Mrs Morrow, I have to speak to you.'

The day after her husband was laid to rest, Collette found out she was pregnant. She had been in Lurgan, having a cup of tea with her mother-in-law Mary, when she first began to feel sick. She went back to Dublin and her own mother Kathleen advised her to go to the doctor, and the news was soon confirmed. Collette had lost over two stone in the aftermath of Gary's death, and so hadn't realised she was pregnant. She would later give birth to a baby girl in the Coombe Hospital, just days before her husband's killer went on trial at the Curragh Military Court in the summer of 1983.

Two days after the three murders at Tibnin Bridge, McAleavey made a statement to the Irish Military Police in Tibnin. He had been sedated shortly after being taken to hospital, but apart from shock he had not suffered any physical injuries. A doctor who treated him noted that he did not make any reference to his three dead colleagues, but only seemed concerned with getting back to his unit. Indeed, apart from muttering the words, 'bastards killing them', while being brought to hospital, he had not spoken very much in the days after the shootings. When he came to make a detailed statement to the Military Police, it was the first opportunity to hear his recollection of events. Although he maintained that his colleagues had been shot while he was in the toilet, he did recount an incident that hinted at his own darker side.

McAleavey told the Military Police that at around 8 p.m. on the night of the attack, a jeep carrying two Israeli officers had approached the checkpoint from the western As Sultaniyah road. Gary Morrow had stopped the vehicle and asked for identification. McAleavey said the passenger in the jeep had pointed to gold bars on his shoulder and said something like, 'This is our identification.' McAleavey said he then intervened saying, 'The corporal asked you for identification, Jew boy.' The Israeli officer had grabbed at McAleavey's rifle and said, 'Talk with your mouth, not with your hands.' By his own admission, McAleavey continued to hurl racist abuse at the officers. Morrow intervened and allowed the jeep to drive on over Tibnin Bridge.

Army officers, on analysing this statement, described it as a potentially dangerous confrontation between Irish peace-keepers and Israeli officers. McAleavey was admitting to conduct that had inflamed a routine situation, but the danger had been averted by the calm manner of Gary Morrow and the Israeli officers. By admitting that he made a verbal attack on the Israeli soldiers,

McAleavy was displaying an unpredictability that the army had not seen in his character before he came to the Lebanon. However, while owning up to such behaviour unbecoming of a peace-keeper, he still maintained he knew nothing about the murders of his colleagues. He said he had hit the ground when the firing started and stayed there until it finished, and he hadn't seen a thing. He had then run down the slope from the toilet and found the bodies of Peter Burke and Thomas Murphy, and started screaming. He said he couldn't find Gary Morrow, but he heard something over by a water tank and fired a number of rounds in that direction. He said he had then radioed for help, and just then a car approached with two civilians, whom he ordered out of their car and held at gunpoint until reinforcements arrived.

The part of McAleavey's story about stopping the car was true, but the rest of his account about the shootings just didn't sound credible to the army officers. However, because of the geographical nature of Tibnin Bridge and the simple fact that it was a war zone, there was very little to be gained from a ballistic examination of the scene. Far too many bullets had been fired in this area in the weeks and months before. An examination of McAleavey's rifle showed it had fired 33 shots that night. He was now claiming to have fired a number of rounds at nothing in particular while in fear of his own life. Between them the three murder victims had suffered 18 gunshot wounds, including one each at very close range. It just didn't add up that McAleavey wouldn't have seen the killer or killers if they had walked right up to the bunker to ensure that the three soldiers were dead. But proving precisely which weapon had fired the fatal shots might be next to impossible. And the crime scene itself had been cleaned up soon after the killings, something which was entirely understandable in a situation where young soldiers had to take over checkpoint duty at Tibnin Bridge almost immediately after their colleagues were murdered. Army personnel suspected McAleavey was holding back on the truth, but what exactly was the best course of action? Never before had an Irish soldier been suspected of murdering three of his colleagues, and never had there been such a serious criminal investigation in an Irish-controlled peace-keeping area. Senior members of the Defence Forces consulted with the Minister for Defence and debated what to do. By early January 1983, it was decided that members of the Garda Murder Squad should travel to the Lebanon and directly question Michael McAleavey.

From late on the night of 27 October 1982 until 22 January 1983, McAleavey's movements were restricted. It wasn't that he was under arrest; it was simply that he had nowhere to go. After being released from hospital in late October 1982, and having made a statement admitting the use of provocative and racist language towards Israeli officers, McAleavey was confined to quarters at Gallows Green near Camp Shamrock, the Irish UN Headquarters in Tibnin. He was assigned clerical duties and he was escorted whenever he went out for exercise or to the shop. He was not given possession of a firearm and was closely monitored to ensure that he did not gain access to a weapon. And for three months McAleavey stuck to his story that he knew nothing more about the attack on his colleagues.

At 9.20 a.m. on Saturday, 22 January 1983, an army sergeant went to a bedroom of the Military Police Headquarters and told McAleavey he was required downstairs. McAleavey dressed himself and left his room where he met Captain Hugo Bonar on the landing. Bonar asked McAleavey to follow him downstairs and showed him into a room, where two men sat at a table. Bonar simply said to the men. 'This is Private Michael McAleavey', and he then left the room.

Chief Superintendent Dan Murphy introduced himself to McAleavey and introduced the other man as Detective Inspector Pat Culhane, also of the Investigation Section of the Garda Technical Bureau, otherwise known as the Murder Squad. Superintendent Murphy asked McAleavey to sit at the table beside them and advised him that anything he said might be given in evidence against him. McAleavey stared at both Gardaí for a long time as he struggled to come to terms with the fact that two detectives had travelled all the way to the Lebanon. In the three months since he made his initial statement, he hadn't been asked direct questions about the murders at Tibnin Bridge. He was getting very frustrated being confined to clerical duties at Gallows Green. He didn't talk to anyone about the murders, but he got the sense that while some soldiers believed his story, others looked 'knowingly' at him. In three months' time he'd be back in Ireland away from the heat, the insects and the suspicious eyes. But now, out of nowhere the Gardaí were at Camp Shamrock and it looked as if they had done their homework.

As Murphy introduced himself and his colleague, McAleavey continued to fix his stare at the officers. He was very taken aback at seeing the Gardaí and had the look of a caged animal. He tried to display a sense of bravado and said, 'I don't give a f*** who you are. You are no different than the f***ing MPs [Military Police].' Murphy calmly told McAleavey that they wanted to ask him some questions about his statement of 30 October 1982 relating to the murders at Tibnin Bridge. McAleavey replied angrily, 'I have made a statement and the next f***ing statement I will make will be to the f***ing papers.' The Gardaí gently persisted with their questions and McAleavey began to display even more bizarre behaviour saying, 'Did you not know I am a f***ing werewolf. I shoot everybody. I go around and shoot up the f***ing world.'

Before the Gardaí went into the interview room, they knew that perhaps the only way to solve the triple murder would be from McAleavey's own words. Taking into account the insurmountable difficulties with analysing ballistic information in a war zone, the primary evidence of what really happened would have to come from McAleavey himself. Murphy and Culhane had travelled to the Lebanon with two colleagues, Detective Sergeants Tom Connolly and Gerry O'Carroll. The Gardaí knew that proving that 33 shots had been fired from McAleavey's rifle would not be enough evidence. The bullets that hit the three soldiers could not be matched with any rifle, and there had been no witnesses. McAleavey claimed he had fired into the distance as he tried to protect himself and his fellow soldiers from further attack from the mysterious killer. With the crime scene long cleaned up and the 52nd Battalion trying to get on with the important job they were sent to do, there was very little further investigation that could be done, apart that is from talking once again to the suspected triple murderer himself. The key to solving the case, and perhaps the only way to solve it, lay with McAleavey and his conscience.

As McAleavey pretended to howl like a werewolf, Murphy and Culhane remained calm and let him continue to howl. It didn't take long for both officers to realise that McAleavey was a person with an unpredictable character and a bizarre streak. But somewhere within the suspected triple killer was the young man who had signed up to be an Irish soldier. The Gardaí simply waited until McAleavey realised that his werewolf act wasn't going to get him out of the room, never mind out of the Lebanon. Eventually, McAleavey settled down and he talked to the detectives about his background and how he always wanted to be a soldier. Murphy again asked him to discuss the events at Tibnin Bridge, and this time McAleavey didn't answer but looked down at the floor for around five minutes. Then he asked, 'What do you want me to say?' The Gardaí replied that they wanted the truth. McAleavey was silent for a few more minutes and then began to cry. Culhane offered him a cigarette and lit it for him. McAleavey looked at the Gardaí and began to cry again, saying, 'I shot them. I shot them.' He then said, 'I want to tell the truth of what happened that night. I am sorry I did not tell it before now.' Culhane asked him if he would like a cup of tea before making his statement, and McAleavey said yes. Less than ten minutes later Culhane came back into the room with tea and some biscuits, and when they had finished their tea McAleavey made his statement.

There was no trick, no coercion, just what one garda called the 'psychology of civility'. In the middle of a war zone, in intense heat, in a charged atmosphere, and having just admitted he had shot his comrades, the now self-confessed murderer Michael McAleavey shared a pot of tea. In the course of less than an hour McAleavey had reverted from being a violent aggressive character to the civilised young man who had once convinced army management that he was soldier material. And then he told all.

It took over two hours for McAleavey to outline the sequence of events that led to the killings. He described how he had originally applied to join the army before he had finished school in Belfast three years before. He recounted doing a medical examination and being accepted into the Defence Forces in Dundalk on 7 August 1980, and had applied to go to the Lebanon around April 1982. He told of arriving in the Lebanon on 20 October 1982 as part of the 52nd Battalion of Irish peace-keepers. And he told of how he agreed to swap his checkpoint duties with another soldier leading to him starting a shift alongside Corporal

Morrow and Privates Murphy and Burke on Wednesday, 27 October, at 2 p.m.

McAleavey told the Gardaí there were no incidents to report for the first six hours of the checkpoint duty, but then a jeep had approached the checkpoint from the western As Sultaniyah road. There were two Israeli officers in the jeep, and he described to the Gardaí how he had verbally abused them, only to be admonished by his corporal.

> Corporal Morrow stopped the jeep with the aid of a torch. … I got up [off a chair] to cover him off. … I heard Corporal Morrow ask the two men for ID and the passenger pulled down his jacket from his shoulders and pointed to his insignia and said that was the only identification needed. … I went over and pointed the rifle at the passenger and told him the corporal had asked him for his identification and to produce it … the passenger grabbed the rifle … I pulled back the rifle and told him that if he touched it I would knock his head off with it. … He started to talk in his own language … that is when I started calling him Jew boy and things like that. … Corporal Morrow said to me, 'Break it up', and he let the jeep through. … He then said to me, 'That was a stupid thing to do', and I said he was stupid to let them through.

According to McAleavey's statement, he and Gary Morrow then had a lengthy row that ended with Corporal Morrow saying he would ensure McAleavey would be put on the next plane home. Based on McAleavey's admitted conduct with the Israeli soldiers which was potentially so dangerous, putting him on a plane home would have been a good idea. It should be remembered that the only account of what happened that night is from the killer himself. But McAleavey's account shows he clearly had no respect for authority.

> After the jeep had passed I told him [Corporal Morrow] that he was an idiot. ... The corporal told me I should be quiet as I was only a sub coming out to the Lebanon. ... He told me to go out to the sand bag position at the bridge. I told him to wise up and he shouted, 'That is an order', and to go out to the bridge or he would report me. I said, 'F*** you', and went out and stood on the bridge. I must have been standing there half an hour, and I could hear them laughing, that is Corporal Morrow, Private Murphy and Private Burke. I came off the bridge and told Corporal Morrow to put a man in the mag [magazine] position or I wasn't going to f***ing stand out there on my own.

It is quite likely that Gary Morrow, Thomas Murphy and Peter Burke would have felt extremely uncomfortable in this whole situation and it is doubtful that they were laughing at anything at all. By McAleavey's own admission, in the space of a few moments he had threatened Israeli officers and had then cursed at his own corporal. Gary Morrow and Thomas Murphy would have known McAleavey as they were all part of the 52nd Battalion, but they had never before seen this dark and unpredictable side to his character. Peter Burke had only met the three men the previous week, and as McAleavey launched his verbal attack on the Israelis and then on his own corporal, it is likely that Peter was wishing he was back in Ireland. His colleagues from the 51st Battalion were already home, and his extra days in the Lebanon to assist the new battalion were now beginning to seem like an eternity. As he sat with Thomas and Gary outside the bunker at Tibnin Bridge and watched McAleavey approach them with an angry and wild look in his eyes, it is probable that Peter's thoughts were with his family in Dublin.

As McAleavey continued his confession, he outlined how he had turned away from his three colleagues before cocking his weapon, turning and firing at all three men. His confession tallies with the ballistic evidence, which indicated that each man was shot by someone standing a short distance in front of them as the three sat on chairs side by side. His confession also matches the evidence that all three were subsequently shot in the head by someone who moved in closer and fired at point blank range. However, anything McAleavey claims his fellow soldiers said or did before he fired must be treated with caution, as the men themselves cannot give the real story. He told how he walked directly up to the three men as they sat on chairs and confronted Corporal Morrow about the orders he was giving.

[After telling Corporal Morrow to put a man in the magazine position] I told him that he didn't even know his own orders and that he did not bother to read them. Corporal Morrow turned to Murphy and Burke and said to them that he did read the orders and he then said to me, 'The lads heard me.' ... I started on at him that he had forgotten his gun and had to borrow one, and I again told him he was a f***ing idiot. He then said to me that Chalk Three [a plane] had not come in yet and that there would be a vacant seat for me on it on the way back to Ireland. I started to walk away, and as I did I cocked the weapon, turned and opened up. I started spraying and just held my finger on the trigger. I remember the rifle jamming or I may have been changing mags, but I just cocked it and opened up again. I then remember running in beside them and mopping up. The last thing I remember was shooting Corporal Morrow,

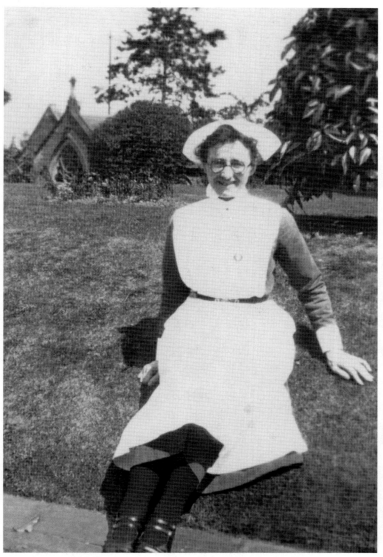

Nurse Katie Cooper, who was murdered on a Limerick roadside in 1953. Her killer became the last man hanged in Ireland.

Katie (third from left) with nursing colleagues in London in the late 1930s.

Phyllis Murphy, whose murder in 1979 led to a remarkable 23-year
investigation to catch her killer.

Phyllis

Mary Kitt. In 1980 Mary was murdered in her Galway home by an intruder.

Willie Mannion, who was stabbed to death in 1981. The 73-year old was
the first victim of random killer Thomas Murray.

Corporal Gary Morrow (on left) and Private Peter Burke, pictured just hours before they and Private Thomas Murphy were murdered by a fellow Irish soldier in the Lebanon in 1982.

Denise Cox, who was murdered in a random attack on a roadside in Ennis in 1983.

Marilyn Rynn (on right) with her mother Christina. Marilyn was murdered in a random attack in Dublin in 1995.

Marilyn

Mother of four Catherine Doyle. Catherine and her husband Carl were
murdered in their dream home in County Roscommon in 1997.

Farmer Paud Skehan who was murdered by a cowardly gang of thieves in 1998.

Paud in younger years.

Brian Mulvaney, who was beaten to death by a gang of thugs in a random attack in south Dublin in 2000.

Brian, his mother Annie and sister Aoife smile as dad Larry records the family celebrating Annie's birthday.

Friends Sinéad O'Leary and Nichola Sweeney. Nichola was stabbed to death in a random attack in Cork in 2000. Sinéad suffered stab wounds to her arms and stomach in the same attack.

Nichola

It took over two decades before advances in DNA technology caught John Crerar for the murder of Phyllis Murphy. (Courtpix)

Former Army Private Michael McAleavey (centre) on trial in 1983. He has spent over 20 years in prison for the murders of three brave soldiers. (Maxwell Photo Agency)

Thomas Murray was on day release from his first life sentence for murdering Willie Mannion when he committed a second random murder in County Galway. (Courtpix)

Double-killer Mark Nash is serving two life sentences for murdering a young couple at their 'dream home' in County Roscommon. (Courtpix)

The distinctive runners William Campion wore on the night he robbed and murdered farmer Paud Skehan have left him serving a life sentence. (Courtpix)

Brian Willoughby was awaiting sentence for random assaults when he murdered teenager Brian Mulvaney. (Courtpix)

Peter Whelan is currently serving a 15-year sentence for attempting to murder Sinéad O'Leary. He will then begin a life sentence for murdering Nichola Sweeney. (Courtpix)

who had gone around the side of the bunker. I then realised what I had done and started to run. I ran into barbed wire and cut my legs and tore my uniform. I then got on the radio and called [for help]. I told them there was a shooting, but I cannot remember exactly what I said.

A pathologist report would later show that as McAleavey pointed his weapon at the three soldiers and began firing, he shot Gary Morrow three times, Thomas Murphy seven times and Peter Burke five times. He then moved in closer and shot each man once in the head, ensuring that the three soldiers were dead.

Peter Burke's father Noel remembers that it wasn't until January 1983 that his family found out that Peter had been murdered by a fellow Irish soldier.

I remember leaving work and I got off the bus in Kilmainham and bought a paper and saw the headline, 'Soldier to be charged with murder of three comrades.' What made me feel sick was that we had been told we would be informed of everything. I came staggering up the road, and I had to tell Mary. We were totally shocked to think that a soldier could kill his own. To think that a UN soldier turned on his own comrades and killed them, for nothing. It wasn't accidental; it was cold-blooded murder.

Shortly after confessing to the murders of his three fellow soldiers, McAleavey met with Detectives Connolly and O'Carroll and drew a sketch, outlining where he had been standing when he opened fire, and where he moved in and opened fire again to ensure the three were dead. He drew the chairs where the three soldiers had been sitting and he wrote the names of his victims to indicate their position. Gary Morrow was to the right, Thomas Murphy in the middle, and Peter Burke on the left. The map was another crucial piece of evidence that came directly from McAleavey's own hand. It is an eerie document. He is a good artist and the detail on the sketch includes two disturbing pieces of text accompanied by arrows. The words read: 'General area where I fired at the soldiers — First shots' and 'Position where I fired last shots at Cpl. Morrow.'

On 24 January 1983, two days after he confessed to murdering his three colleagues, McAleavey was escorted from the Lebanon to Dublin where he was kept in military custody. His murder trial began in July 1983 at a Court Martial Hearing at the Curragh Military Camp in Co. Kildare. There had never been a murder trial like it — seven senior soldiers sitting in judgment on a young soldier accused of murdering three colleagues. McAleavey wore his army uniform for every day of the trial and walked purposefully into the room when the court began each day. Twice the Court Martial tried to go to the Lebanon to hear witnesses there, but it wasn't possible because of the tensions in the area. The court heard evidence from over 60 witnesses in a trial lasting 36 days, before taking less than five hours to reach a verdict on all three counts of murder. The families of Gary Morrow, Peter Burke and Thomas Murphy all broke down as the verdict was announced — Private Michael McAleavey was guilty of three counts of murder. He was jailed for life and was immediately discharged from the army 'with ignominy'. His army uniform was taken from him a short time later.

Collette Morrow attended every day of the trial. She had given birth to a baby girl only two days before the trial started, but she insisted on moving down to Kildare for the duration of the court case. McAleavey looked at her once during the trial, and Collette just kept staring back at him. She had already seen photographs of him and recognised him as the strange soldier she and Gary had met on the train from Belfast the previous October. At the trial when she stared back at McAleavey, he looked away.

Collette married again in 1990; her husband is a widower who lost his first wife close to the time Collette lost Gary. Her daughter is now a young woman. Collette gave birth to a son in 1992, and she and her family live in west Dublin.

Peter Burke's family moved to Spain before the murder trial started. They just had to get away from all the publicity and all the talk about the case. Mary and Noel Burke wanted to protect their three other children, and decided they had to get away for their sake. They never sold their house in Kilmainham; they just closed the door and went off. They returned for the trial and eventually moved back to their family home. Noel Burke remembers staring at his son's killer. 'I'd stare at McAleavey during the trial and he looked at me once. I was staring at him with one question in my eyes — why? I never got an answer.'

As the families of the three murdered soldiers tried to piece their lives together, McAleavey was beginning his life sentence in Mountjoy Jail. He was regarded as a cocky individual and a prisoner without fear of others. In October 1985 he received a fractured skull and a fractured arm when he was attacked by another prisoner after a verbal confrontation. He was in the prison library and was selecting books to read, when another prisoner waiting his turn told him to hurry up. McAleavey said he'd be another 20 minutes if he wanted to be. A short time later as McAleavey was leaving the library, a prisoner attacked him out of the blue and beat him repeatedly with a brush handle. By the time other prisoners intervened, he had suffered serious head injuries and had to be rushed to the nearby Mater Hospital, where an armed garda stood guard at his bed. Despite the injuries he suffered he would not make a complaint against the other prisoner. He was later moved to Portlaoise Prison before returning to Mountjoy. However, less than 15 years after murdering three brave Irish soldiers, McAleavey was given temporary release from prison.

It is deeply saddening to consider that when a decision was taken to grant McAleavey day release from the Mountjoy Training Unit in 1996, no one in authority thought to pick up the phone and inform the three victims' families. It was left to journalists to break the news that the triple killer was being allowed out of prison unaccompanied, having served the equivalent of less than five years for each of the three lives he took. Photographs revealed how the thin killer of the early 1980s had been replaced by a bulky life sentence prisoner who was freed from prison each day to attend a work course. McAleavey's day releases were later stopped, and he is now the longest serving prisoner in Mountjoy Jail.

The families of the three murdered soldiers are understandably still outraged that McAleavey was freed from prison less than 15 years after being given three life sentences. They rightly point out what a mockery such releases make of the so-called mandatory life sentence for murder. Although the families are relieved he is back behind bars, Collette Morrow describes her frustration with those in authority:

I remember we met with one prison official to express our objections to McAleavey's temporary release and we did not like the approach of this official one bit. He referred to McAleavey by his first name, saying things like 'Michael is a changed man, we are rehabilitating him, and the panel believes Michael is ready for the outside.' But this official was so sure that McAleavey was a changed man, yet he was brought back to prison a few weeks later for some reason. It's quite simple, Michael McAleavey will always be a danger to the public. And anyone who says, 'Oh he's served over 20 years. Do you not think he should be released?' I'd say no, he took away three lives. He took away my husband, a father, a brother, a son, a grandson. He didn't just murder three men; he injured so many families as well.

McAleavey has now been in custody for well over 20 years. The Belfast man has declined to seek a transfer to a prison in the North, and instead chooses to serve his life sentences in Mountjoy Jail. He is already actively seeking further parole, and based on the way 'life' rarely means a full life sentence, it is quite possible he will someday be considered for some form of release. The Parole Board will be conscious of the fact that McAleavey made a full confession to the murders of his colleagues, and that without this confession there might not have been a successful conviction. However, if ever the triple killer is given further temporary release from prison, he must be monitored for every single moment he is on the streets.

Collette Morrow tells me she will never allow the memory of her first husband to fade.

For over 20 years I'm watching McAleavey, that he doesn't get out. And even though I started a new life, I always swore and promised that I would keep fighting for Gary and the other men. I believe McAleavey would have been released a long time ago, only for there was pressure put on the government by the families, and it's really up to the families to keep fighting. In a way you're doing yourself justice.

Mary and Noel Burke travelled to the Lebanon in 1998 and visited the spot where their eldest son was shot dead 16 years before. As they approached Tibnin Bridge they got a sense that they were close to where their son was murdered. The army chaplain brought the Burkes down to the scene, and they then went to Camp Shamrock and met the Irish peace-keepers. Some soldiers played the guitar during an open air Mass. Mary and Noel thought of their murdered son, and they felt a wonderful pride in the work of the Irish soldiers. Mary says her son's killer must never be released from prison.

At the trial we learned the extent of the injuries that Peter and the other two men suffered. There were three dolls at the trial that were used to show the injuries. There were pins in the dolls to show where each bullet wound had been. What McAleavey did was barbaric, opening fire from a distance and then going to each man and executing them. He shot Peter under his chin, and he shot Gary Morrow in the back of the head. How can anyone ever think this man could be worthy of release from prison?

Collette Morrow has also been to the scene of the murders. She had decided she'd wait until her daughter was 18 and then ask her if she'd like to visit the spot where her father had travelled on peace-keeping duties before she was born. Collette got a call to say the Irish troops were pulling out of the Lebanon and that there was a chance to go out before the soldiers left. So she and her daughter and Gary Morrow's mother and brother travelled to the Lebanon and visited Tibnin Bridge. As Collette visited the scene of her first husband's murder, she was overcome by emotion and started to shake uncontrollably.

There is no plaque to mark the spot where three brave Irishmen were slain by a fellow soldier. Tibnin Bridge is now a busy roundabout, and southern Lebanon is now a much more peaceful part of a beautiful country blighted by years of conflict. While life has thankfully moved on at Tibnin Bridge, the terrible events of 27 October 1982 will forever be etched on the minds of all Irish soldiers, and in the hearts of three proud families.

Forty-seven Irish soldiers died while serving as United Nations peace-keepers in southern Lebanon. The last battalion left Camp Shamrock in 2001.

7

Time Bomb

Repeat random attacker Frank Daly was about to take an innocent life for no reason. It was just after eleven o'clock on the night of 29 August 1983, and 20-year-old Denise Cox sat on a low timber fence outside a pub near Ennis. The shy, attractive woman had no idea that the stranger walking towards her was an incredibly violent character with murder on his mind. She had no idea this man had previously attacked a number of children in the 1970s, and more recently had stabbed a man during a row. She wouldn't have seen the knife that Daly had clipped to his trousers. When Daly approached Denise, his girlfriend Nora was only a short distance up the road, unaware she was about to witness the random murder of a young woman. As Daly walked by Denise he said hello to her, but as she didn't know the scruffy character she didn't reply. He walked on a short distance towards where his girlfriend was waiting for him, but he suddenly stopped and stood in a gateway. He looked back down at Denise still sitting on the wall. She looked like she was waiting for someone. Inside the pub people were still drinking, but the roadside was quiet with no cars or pedestrians approaching. Daly climbed through a gap in the bushes and sneaked back towards Denise, silently approaching her from behind. Denise only had time to scream before Daly began to stab her.

The murder of Denise Cox was a crime of shocking violence. Daly stabbed her 20 times, in her chest, stomach, neck and back. Some of the wounds struck her heart and her lungs, and she died quickly. Having committed his random attack, he dragged Denise's body to a quieter part of the grounds of the pub and left her lying face down on the grass with her hands tucked under her. His girlfriend walked down, saw what he had done and fainted. It would be the next day before Nora told the Gardaí what she had witnessed. In the meantime, she and Daly walked away from the murder scene. He washed his bloody hands in a nearby river and then the couple hitched a lift home.

By the time Daly murdered Denise Cox, he had spent over ten years in either prison or psychiatric care. His case serves as another prime example of the need to either tag violent recidivist criminals or keep them off the streets permanently. By the time Daly murdered the young woman in a random and motiveless assault he was already known to the Gardaí as one of the most dangerous threats to people in Ennis and beyond.

It was almost 20 years before he murdered Denise Cox that Daly first emerged as a very violent character. In April 1964 he was just 15 years old when he was given a two-year sentence to be served at an industrial school in Daingean, Co. Offaly, for assaulting a woman. This was to be the first of many such violent offences he would carry out in both Ireland and England. After leaving Daingean he spent his late teens travelling between Ennis and London, supposedly trying to get work as a labourer. He tried to fit in with people and not show his true colours, but he had a short fuse and no respect for authority. He tried to join the Irish Army in December 1969, but he lasted just over two weeks of probation before he was told he wasn't wanted. He headed back to England and within four months had assaulted two young girls.

The 7 and 8-year-old victims were playing on a recreation ground at a village just south of London when Daly approached them, exposed himself and physically assaulted the girls. Incredibly, he was not sent to prison, but instead was given a three-month suspended sentence and fined £100. Within six months he would commit another violent assault.

In October 1970, at a court in Essex, Daly was sentenced to a total of eight years for attacking a young woman. His *modus operandi* was to try and blend in with the many Irish labourers lodging in villages around London, where he would look for quiet locations to attack young girls. However, by the middle of 1970 the British police were watching out for him. They were aware that he had recently been given a suspended sentence for attacking two girls in a village in Surrey, and so shortly after the assault on a woman in Essex he emerged as the prime suspect, was caught and convicted. He was sent to a secure prison in Gloucestershire, where he soon emerged as a troublesome prisoner. He carried out three brutal assaults on prison staff and five other inmates and was placed in solitary confinement. Released from prison in July 1976, having served less than six years of his eight-year sentence, Daly left England for good and returned to his native Co. Clare.

Denise Cox was only beginning to socialise around Ennis. She was a quiet woman, happy with the company of close friends and family. She had plans to become a beautician and was very much a home bird. On the night of her murder in August 1983, she said goodbye to her family at around eight o'clock and headed out the door of her home at Marian Avenue in Ennis. She walked the short distance over the River Fergus to the Queen's Hotel in the town centre, and at around half past nine she walked out to the Greengrove pub at Roslevan, about a mile outside the town centre. She was alone for the entire evening, but it appears she may have been expecting to meet someone who never showed up. She had earlier told a cousin that she was meeting friends that night. No one has ever come forward to say they were due to meet Denise, but between ten and half past ten she had looked around the Greengrove for someone and apparently didn't see them. She then went out and sat on the three-foot high white wooden fence at the front of the popular pub.

Patrick and Maureen Cox will never come to terms with the murder of their only daughter. As well as being parents to their three remaining children they are now proud grandparents, but a part of them was lost when Denise was murdered. Patrick tells me how they think of Denise all the time.

We are never going to get over this. You go to bed with it, and you get up with it in the morning. Denise had everything ahead of her. She wanted to be a beautician and she was looking for a good job. It's affecting us still. They say time is a healer, but not in this case. Any parent who loses a child knows that. We try not to think of how Denise died. We try to think of the many happy times, the family holidays, and the young woman who was so full of life.

Seven years before he murdered Denise Cox, Daly attacked a 13-year-old girl. He was only back in Ireland a few months after serving six years in an English prison for a similar offence, when in December 1976 he attacked the teenager on open ground near Ennis town centre. He pushed the girl to the ground, knocking her unconscious, but he was spotted by passers-by and fled the scene.

The Gardaí were already aware of his assault convictions in England and he was quickly arrested. He was kept in custody and at Ennis Circuit Criminal Court in March 1977 he pleaded guilty to attacking the young girl.

One garda who knew Daly during this time says he should never have been allowed out on the streets after the attack in 1976.

It is so frustrating to think of how obvious it was that Frank Daly was an extremely dangerous man. Here he was after serving time in England for a serious assault on a young woman. He'd previously attacked children in England at a play area, and now he was admitting attacking a young girl in Ennis. And although he could often look scruffy, he sometimes cleaned himself up and could almost pass for a normal person. But to those who really knew him, Daly was bad news, a dangerous and vicious man who if left unchecked would continue to be a 'time bomb'. I think the English authorities were only too happy to be rid of him when he was released from prison in 1976, but here he was only back in Ennis a short time and he was attacking a child here. But the real frustration for me is that after pleading guilty to this particular attack he never even saw the inside of a prison cell at all.

By the time Daly came to be sentenced for attacking the 13-year-old girl in Ennis, he had carried out at least five separate assaults over the previous 12 years, and many naturally thought he was facing a lengthy spell in prison. But as he stood to be sentenced at Ennis Circuit Court in March 1977, a return to prison was not about to be prescribed for serial attacker Frank Daly.

In a decision that shocked many people in Ennis and beyond, Daly was not given a prison sentence for attacking the 13-year-old girl, but instead was released on probation on the understanding that he enter Our Lady's Psychiatric Hospital in Ennis for treatment. The judge hearing the case took the decision after hearing a submission that Daly had a very strong sexual drive that he couldn't control when he took alcohol. And so Daly paid a £50 recognisance to the court and signed himself in under the care of a doctor at the psychiatric hospital. He was given drugs to reduce his sex drive and underwent psychological tests and therapy sessions. But doctors soon became aware that Daly was sneaking out of the grounds to go drinking and then sneaking back to his ward at night. He lasted just over four years as a patient before walking out the door on 27 August 1981. Because he was a voluntary patient, the hospital staff were powerless to stop him. He left Ennis and headed for Co. Kildare, where he got work as a stable-hand close to the Curragh. Shortly he would return to Ennis and within two years he would murder Denise Cox.

Daly looked at the knife. It had a brown handle and the blade was about six inches long. It was early on the evening of Monday, 29 August 1983, and he and his girlfriend Nora were sitting in a pub in Ennis. Nora had bought the knife earlier that day from a store in the town, paying £4.45 for it. She had also bought a pink maternity dress that afternoon. The 26-year old was now three months pregnant and she and Frank were looking forward to the birth of their child. She was a traveller who had lived in Counties Galway, Offaly and Clare. She and Frank had been going out for about six months. He had met her in a pub the previous year, but their budding romance was halted when he was given a six-month prison sentence in December 1982 for stabbing a man with a knife. When he was released after four months Nora was waiting for him, and they first lived in a tent near Kilkishen, a quiet village 12 miles east of Ennis. Frank, or Rockie as he was known to his friends, was apparently making a go of it with Nora. He was signing on the dole and trying to get some work. They eventually found a house to rent in Kilkishen for £7 a week, and now he was going to be a father. Nora knew about her boyfriend's conviction for stabbing a man, but she wasn't aware of his much darker past.

As the couple sat in the pub that evening Nora drank glasses of Harp and Daly had about five pints of Smithwicks. He asked if he could see the knife she had bought and she took it out of a plastic bag and handed it to him. He turned it over in his hands and then clipped it to his hip. He had what Nora later described as a 'strange look' in his eyes. A number of people saw him holding the knife, including a psychiatric nurse who knew him from his time as a voluntary patient. A young woman serving behind the bar also saw Daly with the knife dangling from his hip. Both she and the nurse knew Daly was a volatile character, and both were concerned to see him carrying a knife so openly. But Daly hadn't committed any crime and so neither the nurse nor the bar worker phoned the Gardaí. At around 11 p.m. Daly and Nora left the pub and walked out the Tulla Road towards their home in Kilkishen, a journey that would bring them past the Greengrove pub.

Denise Cox was wearing one of her favourite outfits, a white jumper, white top, blue jeans, maroon pop socks and matching shoes. She had entered the Greengrove pub at around ten o'clock and looked around as if expecting to see someone, but they weren't there. She ordered a Coke and sat alone. The Marian Athletic Club was holding a meeting in the pub and Denise sat quietly sipping her drink near by. She looked at her watch and saw it was now almost eleven. She left the pub and went to the front of the car park and sat on the wooden fence.

Frank and Nora had a plan they often used to hitch lifts. They knew they looked like a fairly dishevelled couple, so Daly used to walk ahead of Nora and let her try and hitch a lift by herself. Once in the car, she would ask the driver if he wouldn't mind picking up her 'husband' a short distance ahead. It was a plan that often worked for them. It was a 12-mile walk from Ennis to Kilkishen but local motorists, unaware that the male hitchhiker was a violent criminal, were often only too happy to give a lift to the couple.

Daly approached the Greengrove pub with the knife in his pocket. His girlfriend was some distance behind him trying to hitch a lift. He looked back and couldn't see her on the road. He saw a car approach from that direction with Nora in the passenger seat. He expected the car to slow down and let him in. That was the way she normally got a lift for the two of them. But the car approaching this time didn't slow down. It continued on past the Greengrove and towards Kilkishen.

As Nora stepped into the car she had asked the driver if he wouldn't mind collecting her 'husband' walking on further up the road. The driver pulled off but then told Nora he wouldn't stop for her husband. He drove past Daly, on past the Greengrove pub and past Denise Cox who was sitting close to a street light on the fence outside the pub. Nora asked the driver to stop and she got out of the car some distance up the road. She started to walk back towards Daly and she saw him walking towards her. They would have to try again to hitch another lift. Suddenly Daly stopped and stood in off the road. He looked away from Nora, back towards the Greengrove, and stepped in through some bushes and out of view.

As Denise sat enjoying the calm August night, perhaps waiting for someone to show up as arranged, the car carrying Nora had driven past, heading for Tulla. It was quiet out on the roadside, there were still many people drinking in the pub, but there was little traffic outside. Denise may not have noticed that the car had stopped a good distance away and a woman had got out. Denise may also not have taken much notice of the man walking up the road to the other side of her from the Ennis direction.

Daly said hello to Denise. She didn't know him; he looked like a rough character and had drink taken. Daly walked on in the direction of Nora, who was walking back towards him. Denise took no more notice of the man until suddenly he was behind her. She only had time to scream before he began to stab her.

Nora heard the screams, but by the time she got down to see what was happening, her boyfriend had murdered Denise. Nora could not believe her eyes and she fainted. When she came to a few minutes later, she got up off the ground and walked over to Daly, who by this time had dragged Denise a short distance along the inside of the grounds of the Greengrove, out of sight of the entrance to the pub car park. Nora couldn't speak. Daly came out of the car park with the knife still in his hand, and blood on both hands and on his upper clothing. He put the knife in the plastic bag Nora was carrying and took the bag from her. He said he felt as if he was going to be sick. Nora stumbled in a daze and followed her boyfriend away from the Greengrove and away from Denise's body. The couple walked on towards Tulla and Kilkishen, and at a small river Daly knelt down and washed the blood from his hands and dried them on Nora's black dress. They walked on towards Spancil Hill, saw a car coming behind them and put out their thumbs. When the car stopped, Nora got into the front passenger seat and Daly got into the back of the car. The young man driving the car suddenly recognised Daly, but it was too late to stop him getting into the car, and the man nervously drove the couple all the way to Kilkishen. As he dropped Nora and Daly off in the village, he would remember that Daly gave the roof of the car a few light taps in appreciation of the lift. The motorist knew he had just given a lift to a very dangerous man who had previously attacked both children and adults, but he had no idea Daly had just committed murder.

Just before Daly and Nora got the lift home that night, an off-duty garda had driven past them as they were hitching. The garda immediately recognised Daly and didn't stop to offer the couple a lift. The garda was one of a number of officers frustrated at the fact that Daly was free to walk the streets without any monitoring, despite the fact that he was a proven danger to both children and adults. Just moments earlier the officer had driven past the Greengrove pub. By this time Denise Cox's body lay close to a tree trunk out of sight of the main road.

It would later emerge that one man actually saw Daly, Nora and Denise shortly after the murder. A motorist had driven into the Greengrove car park to do a U-turn, and as he was coming back out towards the main road he saw a man and two women to his left. The motorist said the man had his arm around the waist of one of the women as if to keep her standing. The witness thought the woman might have been ill, and he drove on thinking nothing more of it. What this man had actually seen was Daly dragging Denise's body further away from the roadside fence.

James Corry, a director of the Greengrove pub, pulled up to the premises just before 9.30 the following morning. He lived about 300 yards away and had driven up to feed the guard dogs. As he stepped out of his car he looked back towards the road and saw what looked like a bundle of white clothes about 70 yards away lying inside the perimeter wall. There was something odd about the clothes, but there had been a local athletics club meeting in the pub the night before and James thought perhaps one of the athletes had left clothes behind by accident. He walked into the pub's kitchen to feed the dogs, but something still wasn't right. A thought struck him — what if the bundle of clothes was a person? He left the dogs and walked up towards the front entrance towards the 'bundle'. As he got closer he could see long fair hair and a white top and blue jeans, and he knew it was a woman. He knelt down and felt the woman's arm. It was cold.

Detective Garda Joe O'Neill was at home that morning. He lived close to James Corry, just a few hundred yards from the Greengrove pub. He heard a knock at the door and saw it was his neighbour, James Corry, who was very distressed. James told him he had just found the body of a woman in the grounds of his pub. O'Neill asked his wife to phone Ennis Garda Station, and he raced to the scene. He saw the body of a woman lying face down on the grass, with her hands under her body and bloodstains visible on her back and underneath her. He noticed trampled grass and bloodstains near by. There were also drag marks near where the body now lay. He immediately stood guard to preserve the scene.

At Marian Avenue, Denise's parents were getting very worried. Their daughter had not returned home and it just wasn't like her to stay out like that. She would always come home. Patrick phoned other relatives to check if she had stayed over anywhere, but no one had seen her.

Over in the village of Kilkishen, despite having committed such a heinous crime, Daly was not making any plans to flee. He and Nora had arrived back at their rented house less than nine hours before, at around 1 a.m., and their housemate, Tony, would remember how Daly went straight to the bedroom and Nora to the kitchen. A short time later when Tony was going upstairs to bed, he saw Daly sitting at the end of his bed, wearing just his vest and underpants, and with a basin of soapy water near by. Tony thought nothing of it and went into his room.

Before going into the house, Daly had hidden the knife out the back on a high wall close to a soccer field. He had told Nora to wash his bloodstained clothes. He was deluding himself in thinking Nora would stay with him and protect him. She was still in total shock, and was perhaps wondering if she might also be blamed for the murder. She felt bad that she hadn't tried to call for help, and that she had now washed the killer's clothes for him. Daly thought her silence meant she was going to protect him, when in fact she was simply traumatised by witnessing such awful violence. Daly instructed Nora to 'play it cool', should the Gardaí come knocking at the door.

When Daly entered the psychiatric hospital in March 1977, he knew the alternative to undergoing the treatment was another lengthy prison sentence. Shortly before he left the hospital for good in 1981, he told the staff he preferred prison because at least in jail you had 'a definite sentence to finish'. By 30 August 1983 events were unfolding at a pace that would ensure that Daly would become one of the longest serving lifers in Ireland, serving an indefinite life sentence.

Within hours of the discovery of Denise's body, the Garda Murder Squad was *en route* from Dublin. Based on his numerous past crimes, the local Gardaí had already earmarked Daly as a suspect. Then a man came forward to say he had given Daly and Nora a lift at around 12.30 a.m. that morning from just past the Greengrove out to Kilkishen. The man said it was only during the journey that he recognised Daly and realised he was giving a lift to a man who had seriously assaulted a teenage girl in the 1970s and, more recently, had stabbed a man during a row. The detectives knew it was time to talk to Frank Daly.

In Ennis, Denise's distraught parents and her three brothers had been told the awful news of her murder and were being comforted by family and friends. As details emerged of the injuries their precious daughter had received, Patrick and Maureen had to be sedated. Denise was their second eldest child. She had a brother two years older and two younger brothers, only 16 and 11 at the time she was murdered. In time, each would battle to come to terms with the almost unspeakable pain visited upon their family. Patrick told me how he left his job within a year of his daughter's murder and could never work again.

I was only struggling to keep my job after Denise's murder. I had been 24 years in a factory making spectacle frames. I had to retire in 1984. My message is that the person responsible ruined all our lives. It is still affecting us today. I haven't held down a job and often we feel we're just living away. Maureen and myself have beautiful grandchildren, and Denise would have loved them. She would have been a wonderful aunt. She would have been a wonderful mother, but she never had that chance. We go up to Denise's grave, and we put her anniversary in the *Clare Champion*. It's with us every day.

When four Gardaí arrived at the house in Kilkishen, Daly was courteous. Nora was there too and offered the detectives a cup of tea. Detectives Gerry Kelly and Andrew Curtin took Daly into one room and asked him about his movements on the night of Denise's murder. While Daly was busy lying to the two officers, claiming he knew nothing about the 'terrible' murder, Detectives James Breen and Patrick Cahill were talking to Nora in another room.

Within minutes of Nora speaking to the detectives, she went upstairs with them. Breen picked up a plastic bag from a dressing table in their bedroom. The bag contained a pair of ladies' shoes, but what caught their attention were the clearly visible blood marks on the bag.

When the detectives first arrested him, Daly continued to deny any knowledge of the murder. He said he'd heard about it on the news but knew nothing about it. He agreed he and Nora had walked out of Ennis towards the Greengrove pub, but said they had got a lift with a stranger all the way home and had not seen anything suspicious. However, he would shortly crack once he realised Nora was already telling detectives the real story.

Nora had remained in a trance from the time she saw Denise's body and her boyfriend's blood-soaked hands. It was only late the following day, when the Gardaí separated Nora from Daly and after the detectives found the bloodstained bag, that she told the real story. In a tearful statement at Tulla Garda Station, she outlined how she and Daly had gone into Ennis early that Monday afternoon and she had bought a knife in a shop. She described how he took the knife and then later on the way home they had separated and she got a lift, but the driver wouldn't stop for Daly. She told how she got out of the car and walked back towards him, but he looked different and then disappeared into bushes near the Greengrove, and that's when she heard the woman scream. She told the detectives how she had seen Denise's body and had frozen with fear. She cried as she told how she couldn't tell the Gardaí the truth until she was alone with them.

After making her statement identifying Daly as the murderer of Denise Cox, Nora asked to be brought to see her boyfriend. Despite having witnessed Daly committing murder, she still wanted to see the father of her unborn child. In a room at Tulla Garda Station, they embraced and both began to cry. In his second statement to local Detective Gerry Kelly and Superintendent John

Courtney of the Murder Squad, Daly admitted attacking Denise Cox by sneaking up behind her. But the one thing he couldn't say was why he carried out the attack.

I saw a girl sitting on the fence and I said hello to her. She did not make any reply. I walked on a bit and noticed there was a divide in the bushes on the top of the wall. I climbed through and walked towards where the girl was sitting on the fence. She heard me coming and she acted in a very startled way. She kept sitting on the fence. ... She said something, but I am not sure what she said. I do not really know what I did next. I was carrying a sheath knife in my back pocket and I remember taking it out. ... She was still sitting on the fence when I stabbed her. I stabbed her mainly in the front. ... I remember her shouting at me to stop. ... I stabbed her a lot of times and I could not stop myself from stabbing her. I remember picking her up and I brought her in further away from the fence. That is when Nora was standing below on the road and she asked me what I was doing. ... I jumped off the wall on to the road. I still had the knife in my hand. Nora asked me for the knife. I gave it to her.

After Daly drew a sketch of where he had later hidden the knife, a search was carried out near a soccer field at the back of the house in which Daly and Nora lodged. The sheath for holding the knife had already been found lying on the roadside some distance away from the Greengrove pub. Late on the night of 31 August 1983, two days after Denise Cox sat on the wooden fence, Garda Maurice Greehy found the knife. Greehy was searching an eight-foot wall at the back of Daly's house when he saw the knife stuck in ivy. If Daly had decided to contest the murder charge, the Gardaí now had the murder weapon.

Back at Tulla Garda Station Daly knew he was caught and there would be no more second chances. The enormity of the situation was clear: he was going to prison for a long, long time. In the presence of two Gardaí he made a comment that accurately summed up both his criminal career and his deeply disturbed mind. And considering that the State's failure to tag recidivist criminals allowed him to walk the streets of Ennis unchallenged in August 1983, his comment is chilling.

Well I have really done it at last. ... I stabbed them. ... I attacked them again. ... And now I have reached the f***ing top. ... I have really killed.

When Daly pleaded guilty in November of the following year to the murder of Denise Cox, there was no evidence heard about the crime. The whole process at the Central Criminal Court in Dublin lasted less than two minutes, during which Daly was given a mandatory life sentence. Patrick Cox remembers feeling relieved that his daughter's murderer was caught, but was unhappy with the court process.

I remember the court case only lasted a couple of minutes. I only saw Denise's killer on that day. I hadn't seen him before. A full court case would have been upsetting for us, but we never got any explanation at all, no information about the murder. I felt cheated. And because he pleaded guilty there was little media interest, and no one really spoke about his previous convictions and the fact that he was a proven violent person. People should know that. And we've never been kept informed about his progress through the justice system. I know he's serving a life sentence, but he fooled people before when he went into the psychiatric hospital.

Except for repeat offender Jimmy Ennis from Co. Kildare and the English serial killers John Shaw and Geoffrey Evans, Frank Daly has spent more time behind bars than any other prisoner in Ireland. He has spent over 30 years of his life in prisons in England and Ireland, including over 20 years of a life sentence for the murder of Denise Cox. In recent years he has been placed in the Training Unit of Mountjoy and has been granted temporary release a number of times. The prison is a semi-open, low-security facility, where prisoners take part in extensive workshops to learn skills in woodwork and metalwork. Daly has not exhibited any anti-social behaviour similar to his attacks on prison staff and inmates in Gloucestershire in 1970. Life sentence prisoners who are placed in the training unit are normally nearing the end of their prison sentence. This is where fellow random murderer Malcolm McArthur was housed prior to being moved to the even lower-security Shelton Abbey Prison in Co. Wicklow in 2003. Like Daly, McArthur took the life of a young woman in a random attack. He used a lump hammer to beat 26-year-old nurse Bridie Gargan to death while stealing her car in the Phoenix Park in July 1982. However, there are a number of distinctions between these two prisoners who have both been in prison since the early 1980s. While the Parole Board has already recommended that McArthur be granted parole, it is not clear what the State's plans are for Daly. Unlike McArthur, Daly has a number of previous convictions for random assaults. Recently, Daly has taken part in a work release programme, whereby he occasionally leaves prison to attend a work course in Dublin and then returns to prison at night. So far he has not been detected reoffending.

In August 1983, as Frank Daly sat in a small room at Tulla Garda Station making a confession that would lead him to become one of the longest serving lifers, he told detectives he was sorry for murdering Denise. He also made a plea to the State that should be heeded until the day he dies. His exact words at the end of his confession were: 'I am sorry for doing it. Don't anybody ever let me do anything like that again.'

Frank Daly was the third eldest of a family of 19 children. He attended the local Christian Brothers School but was a poor student. He dropped out of school in his early teens and worked as a messenger boy. It is now known that during his early years he either witnessed or was aware of a particular man abusing a number of women. He knew this man for many years, and during his childhood he spent a lot of time in his company.

Psychologists and criminologists spend years trying to understand the minds and actions of murderers like Daly. What drove him to take the life of a young woman who was sitting on a fence minding her own business? For how long had he harboured such murderous intent? What more could society have done to reduce or eliminate the danger this repeat offender posed to everyone, especially children and young women? Despite his convictions from the 1970s, what happened to Daly that he was able to form a relationship with Nora, albeit for less than a year? What has now changed within him so that more than two decades later he is occasionally trusted to walk the streets of Dublin alone?

Soon after her boyfriend was charged with the murder of Denise Cox in 1983, 26-year-old Nora, who was three months pregnant and alone once again, left Co. Clare and moved to another part of Ireland.

Ennis has changed a lot in the more than two decades since Denise Cox was murdered. The population has grown rapidly and the town has expanded greatly. The Greengrove pub and restaurant is gone, replaced by a new shopping centre to cater for the north-east of Ennis. The white timber fence where Denise sat is also gone, replaced by a stone wall. When the wall was put in place some years back, a special stone was set to mark the spot where a young Ennis woman's life was so brutally cut short in August 1983.

Patrick and Maureen Cox still live at Marian Avenue, from where Denise set off that Monday night. Denise was a shy young woman who didn't like her photo being taken, but the Cox family have one photo of her taken shortly before her murder that sits proudly in their living room. The Cox family have suffered more than any family should ever have to suffer. With the support of neighbours and friends they have battled on, supporting each other in trying to come to terms with one of the most violent murders this country has witnessed. The peaceful roadside of Marian Avenue is one of the oldest parts of Ennis town. Patrick tells me he and his wife have lived there for over 40 years. And there they will remain.

We thought of selling up and moving away somewhere else after Denise was murdered. But where do you go? No matter where you go it's still in your mind. We realised we did nothing wrong; we shouldn't have to move. Besides, Denise is laid to rest here. We couldn't bear to be far from her.

8

Murder at Christmas

Marilyn Rynn was almost home when her killer grabbed her from behind and dragged her to her death. It was just after 3.30 a.m. on Friday, 22 December 1995, and David Lawler was about to commit one of the most shocking crimes this country has witnessed. Forty-one-year-old Marilyn, a single woman, adored by her family and much loved by her work colleagues in the civil service, was just moments from the front door of her home in Blanchardstown in west Dublin. She had enjoyed a long night at her office Christmas party across town and now only had to go through the unlit shortcut known as 'the Tunnels' and she would be home at Brookhaven Drive. She knew the area and had walked this way many times. It was a wet, miserable night and she kept her head low with her chin into her coat as she walked briskly through the shortcut. She didn't notice the stranger with long hair and a bushy beard walking behind her. Lawler was also just minutes from home, but as he saw the woman walking alone ahead of him he made a conscious decision to attack her. A young man had run past both of them in the opposite direction, but he was now gone and there was no one else around.

Lawler was now intent on committing a sexual assault. He increased his pace and grabbed Marilyn from behind, pinning her arms to her waist. She screamed for help, but Lawler put his hand over her mouth and began to drag her in off the road towards bushes in the adjoining park. In a split second Marilyn wriggled free, but she slipped down an embankment in the park. As Lawler pursued his victim he also slipped down the deep ravine. She tried to run from her attacker, but in the darkness she couldn't find her way out of the mucky terrain. Within seconds Lawler was attacking her. Marilyn was subjected to an appalling assault before being murdered. Lawler strangled Marilyn to death and then left his victim lying in the undergrowth. In a further callous act, he took Marilyn's belongings from her handbag and scattered them around the park. Then the married father of one walked to his house, put his filthy clothes in the washing machine, and got into bed with his wife. But he had left crucial evidence at the scene, his own DNA. Freezing temperatures would conspire to preserve this evidence, and seven months later the Gardaí would come for him.

For 16 days Marilyn lay in Tolka Valley Park. For 16 days her parents, brother and sister, nieces and nephew hoped against hope. They knew Marilyn would never choose to go missing. She would never miss staying over with her parents in Ballyfermot on Christmas Eve and Christmas Day. It was a tradition she looked forward to every Christmas and there was no way she'd just go away somewhere leaving everyone so worried. And there was no way she'd be out of contact for more than a day from either her family or one of her friends from the civil service. Something was terribly wrong, but for 16 days, in the absence of a body, there was still a glimmer of hope.

The murder of Marilyn Rynn has devastated her close-knit family. At the time of her murder she lived alone at Brookhaven

Drive in Blanchardstown, but she was hardly ever alone. Her brother Stephen and his family lived just around the corner, and his three children were forever visiting their Auntie Marilyn and staying over with her. Her elderly parents lived just a few miles away at the old family home in Ballyfermot, and her younger sister Rosaleen kept in regular touch too. Marilyn led an active and happy life, and the pain her random murder has caused is all too evident when I meet the Rynns. Her mother Christina says that in the fortnight the search for her eldest daughter was under way, she knew they were going to get terrible news.

Marilyn was a beautiful person, kind and gentle and loving. She was the life and soul of the party. In some of the photos we have of her, she is smiling so much you'd think she was about to reach out of the photo and talk to you. Once we heard Marilyn was missing, we knew something awful had happened. We knew Marilyn didn't choose to go missing. I used to dream about her when she was missing, and I thought of her lying somewhere all alone. Marilyn's murder has caused havoc in our family. We never recovered from it. How anybody does this to a family, I don't know. I still think of what happened to her. And I think what kind of a brute was he?

By Christmas Day 1995 the Rynn family knew something was wrong. Amid the rush in the run-up to Christmas no one had seen or heard from Marilyn since the previous Thursday. Her family knew she was going out to her work party over in Raheny that Thursday evening. When no one heard from her on the Friday or Saturday, they thought she might have stayed over with friends after a night out. By Sunday, Christmas Eve, her absence was being noted. She would normally stay over with her elderly parents in

Ballyfermot on Christmas Eve. The three of them usually went to the carols and then Mass would start at nine o'clock. But Marilyn never arrived. Her brother Stephen remembers how the search really began on Christmas Day.

Myself and Catherine and the kids went over to my parents on Christmas Day and I was very alarmed to find Marilyn wasn't there. She was supposed to have been with them since the previous evening. Something was wrong. I didn't want to worry my parents, so myself and my wife Catherine suggested Marilyn might have stayed with friends somewhere. But we left Ballyfermot that little bit earlier than we normally would and we went home to Blanchardstown. I went around to Marilyn's house and immediately became even more concerned when I found Christmas cards lying on the floor in the hallway. It was obvious Marilyn hadn't been home in a few days. We spent that Christmas night phoning around to friends, trying to find out if they had seen Marilyn. And we made contact with a friend in the ambulance service to check if there were any cases of unidentified women being brought to hospital after traffic accidents or the like, but that drew a blank. Early on St Stephen's morning we went to Blanchardstown Garda Station.

It was a dog called Ben that found Marilyn. The search of Tolka Valley Park began at first light at 7 a.m. on Sunday, 7 January 1996, 11 days after Stephen Rynn first reported his sister as missing. During the last few days of December 1995 and the first week of January '96, the Gardaí were concentrating much of their efforts on suggestions that Marilyn might have last been seen in Dublin city centre, but now the indications were that she might well have disappeared closer to home. After reviewing all the information they had collated, the detectives decided an inch-by-inch search of the local park should be conducted immediately. Garda Eddie O'Connor and his Alsatian Ben were part of the search team which began its work that Sunday morning. Eddie let Ben off the leash so the dog could get down a slope to an area of dense undergrowth in the valley. Within minutes Eddie heard Ben making agitated sounds, and soon found him standing over the body of a woman.

The scene where Marilyn lay for over two weeks left many detectives aghast. She was provisionally identified by a necklace she was wearing and a mark on her neck from a thyroid operation. She would later be formally identified through dental records. Detective Inspector Derek Byrne immediately got into his car and drove towards Stephen Rynn's house to tell him of the probable discovery of his sister's body. The garda wanted to get to Stephen before the discovery made it on to radio news bulletins, and he just made it.

The subsequent image of Marilyn's covered body being brought up the slope on a stretcher accompanied by visibly shaken detectives was captured by television cameras, and will remain with many people. And while the general public feel anger and sadness at such a terrible random crime, the impact of Marilyn's murder on her family can never be adequately described. She was a loving daughter, sister and aunt. She was the only one of the three Rynn siblings not to marry, though all who knew her say she was 'brilliant with kids'. Her brother Stephen and his wife Catherine have three children whom Marilyn adored. Her sister Rosaleen and husband Derek have children born following Marilyn's murder, children who will never get a chance to meet an aunt who would have doted on them.

Marilyn lived alone, yet she played a central role in so many lives. She had a wide group of friends in the National Roads Authority and other government departments where she worked. The solitude of her death is in total contrast to the active life she led. Stephen Rynn remembers how he had to break the news of his sister's murder to his parents.

Detective Derek Byrne called to me that Sunday morning. He'd been keeping us up to date on the search, and he told me they had found a body and thought it was Marilyn. They were about 99 per cent sure it was Marilyn. I immediately drove to tell my parents. I knew my Ma was at Mass, and I went immediately to the church in Ballyfermot. She had gone to the half eleven Mass and I met her there. I didn't tell her immediately, I wanted to tell herself and my Dad at the same time. But she knew there was something strange when I picked her up from Mass. I told my Ma as we drove home in the car, and told my Dad when we got home.

On the Monday night before her murder, Marilyn had celebrated her 41st birthday with her brother Stephen and his wife Catherine and their three children, who all dropped around to Marilyn to wish her a happy birthday. The actual day of her birthday was the next day, but some of 'the girls' in the civil service had arranged to take her for a meal and a night out to celebrate. This was the happy pattern to her life. She had family close to her in Blanchardstown and she had great friends where she worked in the National Roads Authority and in other parts of the civil service. Having gone out 'on the town' on the Tuesday night, she took it easy on Wednesday night. Her sister-in-law Catherine dropped around to her, and the two of them wrapped Christmas presents. The two women were good friends. Catherine's husband

Stephen was in the Defence Forces. During the time he had spent three six-month tours of duty overseas, Marilyn had been a great support. As the two women sat wrapping gifts, they had a pre-Christmas drink and were looking forward to the holiday. Marilyn told Catherine she was going to her office Christmas party the following night at the Old Sheiling Hotel in Raheny, and she was also looking forward to heading to her parents in Ballyfermot that Sunday.

As Marilyn sat wrapping presents, less than a quarter of a mile away David Lawler was sinking lower and lower. The 32-year-old father of one was now addicted to phone sex lines, and was accessing pornography on his home computer. He was spending more and more time in the bedroom where he kept his computer, and he was taking less and less interest is his role as a husband and father. It was left to his wife to assist their young son in almost every way. When his wife tackled him over the large phone bills they were getting, he admitted he was ringing sex lines. He worked as a technician with Telecom Éireann and his work rate was very good. However, by December 1995, outside of work Lawler was spending four or five nights a week drinking and much of the rest of the time ringing sex lines or accessing internet pornography.

One garda who was involved in the investigation into the murder of Marilyn Rynn says there are similarities between Lawler and some of the other men who randomly targeted women.

I think it is interesting to consider that David Lawler is not the only seemingly happily married man to target a woman in such a callous way as he did. There are many examples of men who appear to be good 'family men' who are now in prison for some of the most disturbing crimes in recent times. You only have to think of John Crerar, Larry Murphy and Richard O'Hara.

Crerar was married with children when, as a jury found, he abducted and murdered Phyllis Murphy in 1979. Richard O'Hara was married with three children when he murdered Deborah Robinson in 1980 and then hid her body in a ditch. And it is chilling to consider how Larry Murphy, a father of two, abducted, raped and tried to murder a woman in 2000 before going home and getting into bed with his wife. There are many more cases where seemingly upstanding citizens have finally let their mask slip to show what they really are. It would make you wonder about some of the missing and murdered women such as Jo Jo Dullard and Annie McCarrick. Perhaps their killers are men who are married and are rearing or have reared a family. If so, their wives or children must suspect them at some stage. You can't keep a mask up for ever. In David Lawler's case, I've often wondered since if we could have stopped him. But he had no serious previous convictions, and although he was scruffy and considered odd, he was still for all intents and purposes a happily married man. His mask only slipped when he attacked Marilyn, and by then it was too late to stop him.

Both Marilyn Rynn and David Lawler attended Christmas parties in the hours before their paths crossed close to the Tunnels. Although they lived in adjoining estates in Blanchardstown, they didn't know each other. Marilyn was a familiar sight on the bus going to and from the city, while Lawler worked away from the city in Lucan. Marilyn was involved in community activities, while Lawler's only social activity was drinking in one pub in the village. While she was making her way to Raheny to attend the National Roads Authority Christmas party, he was already enjoying his work Christmas party in the city centre.

Lawler had boarded a bus from Blanchardstown at around lunchtime, got off at a stop along the Liffey and walked over Capel Street Bridge to the Central Hotel. He met over half a dozen work colleagues and they had a few drinks before going upstairs in the hotel for their meal. He drank two or three pints of beer before they sat down to eat. After their meal the group continued drinking, first going to a nearby pub, then going over to a pub in Temple Bar. The others decided they were going on to a disco, but Lawler said goodnight to them and walked towards a takeaway at the bottom of Grafton Street. With his long greasy hair and bushy beard, he might have had difficulty getting into a nightclub anyway. Having bought a cheeseburger, chips and coffee in the takeaway, he ate his meal and started to look for a taxi.

Marilyn stayed at the Old Sheiling Hotel until around 1.50 a.m. She was in great form, laughing and joking with her colleagues. The group of women she worked with in the civil service were by now much more than work colleagues, they were good friends. These were the same women she had been out with two nights before, celebrating her 41st birthday. But it had been a long week and while others were still dancing away, Marilyn decided to call it a night. She had a long journey across the city still ahead of her. As she left the hotel she met a man she worked with. He was also looking for a taxi. He managed to hail one, and let Marilyn take it, wishing her a merry Christmas.

Having failed to get a taxi, Lawler walked towards Westmoreland Street to get a Nitelink, but he missed one and so began walking home in the rain. He turned down Aston Quay, hoping to find a taxi, but none was available so he continued walking past the Phoenix Park through Castleknock, finally arriving in Blanchardstown village at around 3.30 a.m.

Meanwhile, Marilyn's taxi took her from Raheny to Abbey Street in the city centre. She went over to Eddie Rocket's diner on O'Connell Street, bumped into a friend and spoke to him for a short time. At around 2.50 a.m. she said goodnight and headed up Westmoreland Street. She got the 3 a.m. Nitelink bus heading for Blanchardstown and arrived in the village at around 3.30 a.m.

Lawler was watching Marilyn. He saw her walking by a vegetable shop in the centre of the village and he began to follow her across the road as she took the same direction he would normally take home himself. Lawler's house at Edgewood Lawns was only a few hundred feet away, while across a wide grass margin lay Marilyn's home in the Brookhaven estate. As he lurked some distance behind her, Lawler saw a young man half running and half walking towards both of them. The man walked quickly past Marilyn and then past Lawler and hurried on towards Blanchardstown village. This man would later prove to be a crucial witness. At the time he had no idea he had just passed by a woman who was minutes from being murdered, and the man who would commit the crime.

Lawler later told the Gardaí he attacked Marilyn on impulse. In one statement to detectives he said:

> I had no intention of going near her. I don't know what came into my head. … I grabbed the woman from the rear. The idea only came into my head seconds earlier … murder was not the intention.

There are some people who can partly appreciate the terror Marilyn felt that terrible night. There are men and women who have survived random sexual assaults, people who have been terrorised and violated. There are those who are alive today because their attackers either chose not to commit murder, or because they were disturbed before they could kill their victims. But down in the deep ravine of Tolka Valley Park in December 1995 there was no one who could come to Marilyn Rynn's aid. Lawler would later say he murdered Marilyn because after he had sexually assaulted her, she said she recognised him. Again, he was trying to explain his behaviour as a sudden or spontaneous act. He told the Gardaí, 'All this was just panic when she said she knew me.' It's an obvious point but important to state — Marilyn cannot tell us the real story.

At least four people heard Marilyn scream for help as Lawler attacked her. None of the four raised the alarm at the time. Each thought it was the sound of someone messing or joking, or they thought they might be imagining things. One young girl heard someone screaming, 'Help, help!' while a woman also living near Tolka Valley Park thought she heard a woman shouting, 'I am telling you.' Another woman living near by heard screams, while a woman passing by the park on a minibus thought she heard a woman's loud voice. Each of the four people listened carefully for a number of minutes after hearing the sounds, but there was total silence, so no one phoned the Gardaí.

After strangling Marilyn to death, Lawler pulled her by the legs further into the undergrowth to conceal her from view. He then took her handbag and threw away cards from her purse into undergrowth in various sections of the park. These items would not be found until almost eight months after her murder.

Having discarded Marilyn's possessions at a number of almost inaccessible parts of the park, Lawler began walking home. His house was only a short distance away, but he took a circuitous route home, hiding behind trees. For someone who later claimed he did not intend to murder Marilyn when he attacked her, he was already displaying a high degree of cunning. He arrived home shortly after 4.30 a.m. His clothes were filthy, so he took them off and put them in the washing machine and he wiped his runners with a J-cloth. As his blue zip-up jacket, wine coloured sweatshirt and denim jeans were being cleaned of evidence, his wife heard the sound of the washing machine and came down to the kitchen at around 5 a.m. He told her he had been splashed by a taxi and got drenched and had put his clothes in the washing machine. It was the next morning when his mother-in-law, who was visiting, took the clothes out of the washing machine and hung them on the line. She noticed that a pair of black runners on the floor of the sitting room were sopping wet also.

Over the following days Lawler thought of how well he had covered his tracks. His clothes were washed and he hadn't heard anything on the news about a woman's body being found. As he thought of what he had done, he didn't feel very well and didn't go into work the day after murdering Marilyn. As Christmas approached he tried to turn his attention towards his family and forget about his crime. Soon he was back drinking in his local and laughing heartily as fellow customers joked that his long hair and beard gave him a biblical appearance. And all the while Marilyn Rynn's body lay hidden in the nearby park, as her parents and brother and sister and their families wondered where she was and if she was all right.

Garda Ciarán Noone was on duty on St Stephen's Day when Stephen Rynn approached the front desk of Blanchardstown Garda Station. Within moments of listening to Stephen outline how his sister was missing, Noone knew the Rynn family had genuine cause for concern. Over the coming days an extensive Garda investigation would be under way to find Marilyn. But despite hundreds of house-to-house enquiries and large media coverage of the 41-year old's disappearance, no one came forward with any sighting of her or, indeed, any information, and no one had said at this stage that they had heard the screams in the park. The Gardaí also had to contend with three separate 'sightings' of Marilyn in the days after she had been murdered

One person insisted they had seen her in Penney's shop in Dublin on Christmas Eve, while a young neighbour of Marilyn's said he had seen her on a bus going into town. Another of Marilyn's friends insisted she had spoken to her on the telephone early on 22 December to arrange meeting in Dublin for a drink. By the time this supposed conversation took place Marilyn was already dead, but the woman was so sure in her recollection that the detectives had to consider that Marilyn might have arrived home safely from her Christmas party, only to disappear the next day in Dublin city. Because of the holiday period, it wasn't until early January that the detectives could get access to Marilyn's phone records. On Friday, 5 January, the Gardaí discovered that the telephone conversation as described by Marilyn's friend did not take place on Friday, 22 December, and the investigation was now focused on Blanchardstown, to where Marilyn had travelled home from her Christmas party. At first light the following day Marilyn's body was found.

One detective involved in the search says it's very regrettable they didn't search Tolka Valley Park sooner.

In hindsight, we should have gone right over that park from very soon after Marilyn's disappearance. I think we've learned a lot for future missing persons cases, but it's sad to think of Marilyn lying there all that time when we were knocking on doors just a few hundred yards away. The initial problem was that we had a number of people who could put Marilyn in town the night of her Christmas party, but we had no one to say she ever travelled home. We had to approach the case as if Marilyn could be anywhere. She might still be in Dublin city centre, or she could have gone any direction. When we searched her house we even got up into the attic and went over every inch of her home with a fine toothcomb. Looking back, we should have done the same at every piece of open ground near by. What I'd like to say is that while it's terrible that Marilyn lay there for over two weeks, it was David Lawler through his despicable crime who caused that to happen. Yes, we should have found her sooner, but thankfully, and I know it means something, when we found Marilyn, the semen her killer had left at the scene of the murder was still preserved. If it had been a few more days before we found her, that evidence might have been gone, and so the way I look back on it is, that while we should have found her sooner, we still found Marilyn in time to get justice for her.

In the days immediately after the murder of Marilyn Rynn a particularly cold spell hit Ireland. From the end of December '95 right through to the start of January '96, there was a sharp to severe ground frost most nights with air temperatures falling below zero. It was the coldest period in 14 years and in the undergrowth at Tolka Valley Park the cold temperatures preserved the semen Lawler had left at the location. When Ben, the Alsatian dog, found Marilyn on 6 January 1996, her body had been exposed to the elements for 16 days and nights. But just like the abduction and murder of Phyllis Murphy in 1979, whose body lay hidden for 28 days in woodland, something remarkable had occurred at the spot where Marilyn lay — the killer's DNA was preserved.

Lawler was in his spare bedroom, searching the internet for

information on DNA. It was a month after Marilyn's body had been discovered and the Gardaí were now asking him for a blood sample. He knew they were asking many men in the area for a blood sample, and he was very concerned. He wanted to know how long semen remained identifiable in the open air. As he surfed the net he read that by the time Marilyn's body had been found, over two weeks after he killed her, his DNA should have diminished so as to make such evidence unidentifiable. He breathed a sigh of relief, and on 27 February 1996 he walked into Finglas Garda Station by appointment and gave a sample of blood.

Lawler didn't know it, but detectives had already earmarked him as a suspect, along with a number of men who were known to be capable of extreme random violence. Just days after Marilyn's body was found, Gardaí Gary Tobin and Malachy Dunne had called to Lawler's home and completed a standard questionnaire about his movements on the night of her murder. By the time the Gardaí came knocking, he had concocted a tale that was a mixture of truth and fiction. It was to be his undoing.

Lawler told the Gardaí how he had gone to his Christmas party in town and had then walked all the way home to Blanchardstown. He described walking through the unlit shortcut close to his house and seeing a woman walking in the same direction. He also mentioned the man who ran past him in the opposite direction. He described this man as being about 6 foot 4 inches, with short brown hair. He said all this happened shortly before he arrived home at 4.50 a.m. The Gardaí examining his statement wondered if the woman he described might be Marilyn. But if Lawler had seen her around 4.30 a.m., where had she been since 3 a.m. when she got the Nitelink home? Or what if he was lying about the time he walked through the laneway? What if he had murdered Marilyn and then arrived home at 4.50 a.m. just like he said? The Gardaí knew he had no previous violent convictions, that he might be telling the truth, and that the woman he described might not have been Marilyn at all. There were many convicted rapists out on the streets who would fit the profile of her killer. But one detective wrote down on Lawler's completed questionnaire, 'This is a real suspect — blood him.'

In all, 354 men emerged as potential suspects for the murder of Marilyn Rynn, 336 of whom volunteered a blood sample, including Lawler. Fifteen other men declined to give a blood sample but offered to provide hair samples to eliminate themselves from the investigation. Three men refused to co-operate and give any sample, so they were treated as prime suspects and arrested for questioning; they soon decided to give a sample. The investigation was eventually solved by DNA technology, but it is important to remember that Lawler was only caught because he volunteered a blood sample, and he only did that because he believed his DNA would not be detected by the time Marilyn's body was discovered. For years the Gardaí have expressed their frustrations that the inability to forcibly take DNA samples has allowed a number of murder suspects to remain free to walk the streets. Lawler might have been among their number if he had declined to give a blood sample, but one detective says they were on to him before the results came back.

It's true that the DNA match solved the murder investigation for us, but by the time the positive result came back we were already watching out for his name. We had tracked down the mysterious man whom Lawler described running in the laneway, and what he told us meant that we would be watching Lawler for ever. Without the DNA match it wouldn't have been enough to build up a circumstantial case. We now believed David Lawler had indeed arrived home at 4.50 a.m. that morning, but we also believed he had spent the previous hour murdering Marilyn and trying to cover his tracks.

What made the Gardaí so suspicious of David Lawler was when a young man named Keith finally came forward to say he was the person who had run through the laneway in the early hours of that Friday morning. Keith told of how he had been out with two friends in Blanchardstown and was going towards the village to get a taxi, when he decided to take a shortcut through the unlit laneway known as the Tunnels. But he said he suddenly got nervous and started to run through the laneway, only slowing down when he saw a woman coming towards him. He now knew that this was Marilyn Rynn, and the man he saw walking behind her must have been her killer. What really nailed Lawler was when Keith said he had seen the woman and the man in the laneway at around 3.30 a.m. Lawler had previously stated to the detectives that he walked through the laneway shortly after 4.30 a.m., so there was a discrepancy of 60 minutes. Keith had to be the young man Lawler described seeing that night — he was 6 foot 4 with brown hair, just like Lawler said. Through his mixture of fact and fiction Lawler had ended up accurately describing to the Gardaí seeing this man in the laneway, but lied about the time he saw him. The detectives knew that either Keith or Lawler was telling lies. They already suspected it was Lawler, but they needed the DNA results to prove it beyond any doubt.

A team of Gardaí gathered early at Cabra Garda Station on the morning of 6 August 1996. It was eight months to the day since Marilyn's body had been found in Blanchardstown, and now it was time to bring in her killer. The Gardaí travelled to Edgewood Lawns where the killer lived, but they decided not to arrest Lawler then and there when they saw him come out of the house with his son. Lawler and the young boy got into the family car and began driving towards Blanchardstown village. The detectives rightly assumed Lawler was dropping his son off to school, and they followed at a discreet distance.

The news that Lawler's DNA matched the semen recovered from Marilyn's body had been relayed to the Gardaí from the Northern Ireland Forensic Science Agency in Carrickfergus. A decision to send most of the samples to Northern Ireland had been taken because of the constraints the State's own Forensic Science Laboratory in the Phoenix Park was being forced to work under. By mid-March 1996, Dr Maureen Smyth and Dr Geraldine O'Donnell working in Dublin had cleared 10 negative samples and were awaiting results on a further 13. This still left over 300 samples to be analysed, including Lawler's. The Gardaí obtained financial approval to send the remaining samples to forensic scientist Brian Irwin in the North and soon received very interesting news. The blood sample provided by Lawler matched the semen recovered from Tolka Valley Park by a figure of 1 in 2,634. Within weeks, following further tests, the final calculation would show a 1 in 4 million match between Lawler's blood and the semen.

Shortly before 8.45 a.m. on 6 August 1996, the Gardaí stopped Lawler's car at Church Avenue in Blanchardstown village. Just moments earlier he had left his son to school, and now the time was right to bring him in. One garda reached in through the window and turned off Lawler's ignition. Detective Inspector Derek Byrne asked Lawler to step out of his car and he then arrested him for the murder of Marilyn Rynn on a date between 22 December 1995 and 6 January 1996. At 8.54 a.m. Lawler was put into a garda car. Within a few hours he would be confessing to one of the most disturbing murders in recent Irish criminal history.

Before news of Lawler's arrest was released to the media, the detectives had gone to see the Rynn family. They told them that someone was being arrested for Marilyn's murder and that there would be further developments later that day. Meanwhile, as Lawler was being brought to Cabra Garda Station for questioning, a female garda went to break the news to his wife that would change her life for ever.

The Gardaí already had the DNA evidence they believed gave them a strong case to put before a jury, but they wanted to hear Lawler's account of how he had become a killer. Soon after his arrest his wife arrived at the garda station in a shocked state. She wanted to see her husband, and he said he wanted to see her too, so the Gardaí gave them some time together in a secure room.

Lawler had met his wife to be at a niteclub in Dublin in the mid-1980s. They got engaged soon afterwards, but then they split up for a time before getting back together again. They were married in the Dublin Registry Office in September 1989, and for a while they were happy, delighted when their son was born, and content with their life in Blanchardstown. But slowly they had drifted apart as Lawler spent more and more time drinking and accessing pornography and sex chat lines. They were now distant people living in the same house. Just hours earlier they had sat down to breakfast with their son, and now Lawler found himself confessing to his wife that he had murdered a woman. Just as he had previously admitted ringing sex lines, when confronted by his wife about Marilyn Rynn's murder Lawler simply couldn't lie to her any more. Nobody listened in to what Lawler and his wife spoke about, but once their meeting was over Lawler said he wanted to make a full confession.

Over the following few hours Lawler outlined to the detectives how he followed Marilyn in the laneway close to his home and attacked her from behind.

I was walking slightly faster than her. ... I had no intention of going near her. I don't know what came into my head. ... As she was near the end of the laneway there's a gap in the railings beside the big stone. I grabbed the woman from the rear. The idea only came into my head seconds earlier. Murder was not the intention. ... She started to shout, so I put my hand over her mouth and started to drag her towards the bushes. She fell and started to roll towards the bushes down in the valley. I fell at the same time and was rolling after her. ... I started to pull her clothes off. ... She [later] said she knew me and I just panicked completely and I went to try and strangle her. ... All this was just panic when she said she knew me. ... I dragged her body by her legs into the bushes. ... I could not go into work [the following day]. I sat in the house and thought about it all day.

Up to the time of her brutal murder, Marilyn Rynn was very active in the local community. She had helped out as an organiser with the local Girl Guides and the Brownies. She played badminton in the local college and during the winter months she took up a pottery course. She loved it when her nieces Karen and Clare and nephew David called around to see her. Clare was only 11, while David was 16 and Karen was two years older. They simply loved their auntie Marilyn and she loved them. She was keen to hear how they were getting on in school and what plans they had for their future careers. Whenever they called around she would have snacks for them, and they would sometimes rent out videos.

On the afternoon that Lawler confessed to murdering Marilyn, he travelled with the detectives — Derek Byrne, John Dennedy and James Clinton — and pointed out various locations where he had thrown items belonging to Marilyn on the night of the murder. A fresh Garda search got under way using rakes and shovels and four days later, on 10 August 1996, Garda Michael Walsh found Marilyn's Chartbusters video card, her Superquinn Club card, her Xtravision card and Coolmine Sports Complex card. On 13 August Garda David Cullen found Marilyn's personal address book. Other Gardaí soon found her VHI card and blood group card, and in nearby dense undergrowth Sergeant John Carr found Marilyn's black mascara brush. Each item was placed in an evidence bag in silence. As much as any photograph of Marilyn smiling with her friends and family, the discovery of her personal property depicted a woman full of life but whose life had been tragically cut short.

On the night of 6 August 1996, David Lawler was charged with the murder of Marilyn Rynn. Her family held each other tightly when they heard her killer had been caught. Over the following months they would have to face the ludicrous situation whereby Lawler was granted bail, despite the fact that he had made a full confession to the murder. When he eventually pleaded guilty to the murder, the Rynn family sat and listened as Marilyn's killer was given a mandatory sentence of life imprisonment. Her parents, Christina and Stephen Snr, both attended the court. Stephen Snr was deeply upset by the murder of his eldest daughter, but he was happy to at least see her killer jailed before he passed away some years later.

On the night that Lawler was charged with the murder, two detectives went to visit his wife. They found her sitting alone in her house. Her son was up in bed and she was sitting in the dark feeling totally numb. Over the course of that day her life had been turned upside down. Her husband had just confessed to her that he had murdered a woman. Another detective who worked on the case says he can fully understand what brought the detectives to the woman's house.

David Lawler's wife was a pleasant woman, and she had done no wrong. When Lawler was charged at Dublin District Court that night, we were all happy to get him as far as being charged, but we weren't jumping up and down. We had seen his wife come in to see him earlier that day, and that really brought home to us that kind of human dimension. Of course Marilyn's family are the most important people to consider in all of this. They have lost their loved one in the most cruel way. But also we had to think of how Lawler's wife told us everything she could to help us. It can't have been easy to tell us about how her husband phoned sex lines, but she did it. That woman's whole life changed in 24 hours. She was now faced with being a one-parent family immediately, and it just seemed right that the Gardaí should sit with her and answer the questions she had about courts and that kind of thing.

A psychological assessment of Lawler carried out after his arrest found he was a very intelligent man. He had worked with Telecom Éireann since leaving secondary school in the early 1980s. He had attended school in his native Baltinglass in Co. Wicklow and passed his Inter and Leaving Certs with little or no study. He had been drinking heavily since the age of 15, and had no other outdoor pursuits. The eldest of four children, he was regarded as a loner but knew many people to say hello to. He is still regarded as a bookworm, interested in astronomy and economics, and enjoys doing cryptic crosswords in newspapers.

Lawler is currently housed on the West 2 landing of Arbour Hill Prison, where he is allowed to associate freely with other prisoners. He is considered to be arrogant but doesn't cause any trouble for prison staff. He spends his days working in the Braille Shop, where he helps to print books and other reading material for blind children. Based on the way this State treats life sentence prisoners, Lawler stands a chance of getting parole at some stage many years from now. When the Parole Board comes to seriously consider his case, they will be mindful that he pleaded guilty to the murder charge and that his only previous conviction was for petty theft in the 1980s. On the other hand, the Gardaí who investigated the murder of Marilyn Rynn will understandably object in the strongest terms to any suggestion that this random murderer should ever be allowed back on the streets. As one garda put it:

During our investigations into David Lawler's habits and interests, we found that he is very interested in the future, and one of the books he read was entitled *The World in 2020*, which dealt with political and economic forecasts for the future. Consider for a moment that in the year 2020 David Lawler will only be 57 years old. Will he still be in prison? I hope so, but will he? If ever he is to be released in any shape or form he must be watched for every single moment, because look at what he has done. He is a danger to every woman.

Marilyn's mother Christina believes her daughter's killer should remain in prison for the rest of his life, even if that means 60 or 70 years. She believes prison life is too easy for people such as Lawler, where prisoners have their own television and video and computer games. She is visibly upset when she talks about the circumstances of her daughter's murder, but she also glows with pride when she talks about Marilyn's life.

I'm sure Marilyn could still have had a family if she had wanted. She was still young and could have got married. Whatever she put her mind to, she did it to perfection. She was one of only four to do her Leaving Cert in her year in Ballyfermot. She was a great daughter. We used to have long chats on the phone. She was really great with Stephen's kids. She was murdered before Roisín's children were born, but she would have loved them. They are the cutest kids you'd ever come across, and I'm sure she does love them. Marilyn is laid to rest beside her father in Palmerstown Cemetery. I miss them both terribly.

Marilyn's brother Stephen says he understands that most Irish people will always recognise Marilyn's name for a sad reason, but he also paints a totally different picture of the little sister he has lost.

The average Joe Soap will always think of Marilyn as the woman who was murdered, and it's very difficult to get that image out of your head. But we also remember Marilyn for all the great times. I remember even back when we were kids, our Dad worked for CIÉ and in the '60s we had subsidised travel and we went to Belgium and France, and I remember sitting down with Marilyn in Belgium eating waffles and it was a real treat. And my own kids have great memories of Marilyn. They used to treat her house as a second home. When we think of Marilyn we think of good times.

Christina Rynn dreamt about Marilyn for the 16 days she was missing. She still dreams about her daughter.

Recently I've been dreaming constantly about Marilyn, and it's all normal as if I'm talking to her here in this room, and it's as if she's coming for a visit. We have big conversations and when I wake up in the morning I remember I was talking to Marilyn during the night, but then I think, sure I couldn't have been. But it seems so real to me at the time, it takes me about ten minutes to realise that she's not here any more.

9

Double Killer

There were six little children in the house the night Mark Nash stabbed Carl and Catherine Doyle to death. Mercifully, none of the children was physically harmed during the frenzied attack that also saw Nash savagely beat his own girlfriend with an iron bar, leaving her for dead. Two babies, including Nash's own daughter, lay on a couch just a few feet away from where he stabbed Carl Doyle four times in the chest. Upstairs, two girls and two boys, the eldest only 7 years old, lay sleeping as Nash crept up the stairs to attack their mother Catherine and her sister Sarah Jane, his girlfriend of five months. The knife had broken when he attacked Carl, so he picked up a different weapon, an iron bar used to open the kitchen stove. The two women were getting a bed ready for the babies when Nash silently entered the room. In the following agonising moments it dawned on Sarah Jane that her boyfriend was a different person. She saw a mad, wild look in his eyes and she saw the 'hammer' in his hand. Without a word he began beating her on the head with the iron bar, causing her to collapse to the floor. Stunned, Sarah Jane put her hand to her head, saw blood all over her hand and she looked up at Nash and screamed. As he brought the bar down again on to Sarah Jane's skull, he said in a cold and distinct voice, 'You have to die, Sarah.' Catherine, as shocked as she was, tried to intervene and screamed at Nash to stop, but next he turned on her. Catherine stumbled towards the stairs, screaming for Carl to come and help, not knowing her husband was already dead. Catherine managed to make it downstairs, but Nash followed her. He caught her by the neck and began to strangle her. He saw another knife in the kitchen and picked it up. He stabbed Catherine Doyle 16 times. The 26-year-old mother of four died on the kitchen floor of her home, the dream home she and her husband had yearned for when they moved from Dublin many years before. In a matter of minutes the tranquillity of life near Ballintober, Co. Roscommon, was shattered by a man who had only been there a few hours. Nash had finally let his mask slip; the cocky charmer was actually one of the most dangerous killers to ever set foot in Ireland, someone fuelled by an unexplained murderous rage, who killed without motive, without reason. Leaving a married couple dead and thinking he'd also killed his own girlfriend, Nash ran from the house.

At the bottom of the stairs Sarah Jane Doyle pretended to be dead. She had suffered extensive injuries to her head when Nash attacked her in the bedroom, and she had passed out for a time. When she came to, there was no one in the bedroom, but then she saw Nash coming back up the stairs. He came back into the bedroom and hit her again on the skull with the iron bar. She tried to curl herself up on the ground to protect her head, blood pouring down her face and her head swimming. Nash seemed to be laughing at her, telling her to get up, but she couldn't stand. She was only half-conscious. Nash began to push his girlfriend towards the stairs, kicking her and hitting her with the iron bar, and he then pushed her down the stairs. What Sarah Jane did next was instinctive, requiring incredible strength of character, and it ultimately saved the teenager's life. As she fell to the bottom of the stairs she closed her eyes, lay very still and pretended to be dead. There was nothing more she could do. She was dazed, traumatised and losing blood, but she somehow knew that pretending to be dead might be her only chance. Nash came down the stairs and stepped over her. She waited for the next blow to her head, waited for what seemed like an eternity, but no more blows came. After a few minutes, and not knowing if her boyfriend turned killer was still standing over her, she found the strength to open her eyes and look around. Nash was gone.

Sarah Jane dragged herself towards the kitchen. She was losing a lot of blood and in danger of passing out, but her mind raced with the thought of her baby boy on the couch, and the other children, and her sister Catherine and brother-in-law Carl. She knew she had to get help. She tried to stand but her left leg wouldn't move, so she dragged herself on her hands and knees out the back door towards a shed. She finally reached the long grass and crawled for 200 yards to the closest neighbours. With her heart pounding and her breathing heavy, she tried desperately to be quiet, not knowing if her attacker was still around. After what seemed like an eternity she reached the house. It was around half one in the morning when the Hester family opened their door. Sarah Jane was bleeding profusely, she was crying, dazed and distraught, but she was alive.

Less than five months before this awful night, Sarah Jane Doyle met Mark Nash for the first time. It was April 1997 and she was at the Vatican Niteclub in Dublin with her sister Jenny. Only 18 years old, Sarah Jane had recently given birth to a baby boy, but she was no longer seeing the father and tonight was one of her first real nights out in a while. She was walking towards the bar when she met Nash. With his long curly hair set in a ponytail and his dark features, he stood out in the crowd. The two of them got talking.

In his broad Yorkshire accent Nash told Sarah Jane he was 23, worked in telesales and had only arrived in Ireland a few months ago. She told him she had a baby boy, and Nash said he had a five-month-old girl, and they both revealed they were now single. As the music continued the pair made arrangements to meet up the next day outside Burger King on O'Connell Street.

The following afternoon at 1 p.m. Sarah Jane and her son met Nash and his daughter. They headed towards Stephen's Green, wheeling the two buggies and chatting away. Within a few weeks Sarah Jane and her son had moved in with Nash, first living in a flat at Manor Street in the north inner city, and then moving two miles to share a house with two women at Clonliffe Road. However, beneath the friendly 'family man' exterior Nash was hiding a much darker side.

Unbeknownst to Sarah Jane, it was shortly after being charged with drugs offences in Britain that Nash had arrived in Ireland in late October 1996. He had been arrested in Yorkshire for possessing ecstasy with intent to supply, but was released on bail. He decided to leave England once and for all, and moved to Dublin with his 22-year-old girlfriend Lucy, who was in the late stages of pregnancy. The couple had been living together in Leeds for nine months, where Nash was working in telesales. Their daughter was born in Dublin on 9 November and five days later Nash managed to get a job working in telesales in Dublin city centre. He was a smooth talker; some thought he was 'over friendly' or even smarmy, while many others fell for his cocky and self-assured manner. From November 1996 until he murdered Carl and Catherine Doyle in August 1997, Nash worked for three different telesales companies in Dublin. But none of his employers and none of his new Irish friends was aware of his criminal convictions in Britain dating back to 1990.

Nash was 17 years old when he first appeared at Huddersfield Juvenile Court in 1990, charged with assaulting a woman. He was sentenced to 18 weeks in a young offenders' institution. By this time he was already smoking cannabis on a regular basis, and he knew many dealers in Yorkshire. Over the following years he appeared in court six times for motoring offences, including driving with no insurance and dangerous driving. In March 1994 he appeared at Bradford Crown Court, charged with theft and handling stolen goods, but didn't serve a prison sentence. He was a loner, dabbling in petty crime and smoking dope while concealing from most people his violent character.

Lucy, his girlfriend before Sarah Jane Doyle, told the Gardaí that he had once beaten and threatened her during an argument. She said that during the confrontation he caught her and banged her head on the sofa, grabbing her by the throat and threatening her with an iron. He was never charged in relation to this allegation. One young Irish woman who had a relationship with him for less than a week in early 1997 later told the Gardaí that he hadn't been violent towards her, but she broke it off because she got bad vibes and considered him 'too intense, too possessive, coming on too heavy'.

Nash liked to carry a knife. He told one girlfriend that he carried a knife around Dublin 'for protection'. She saw it at the end of the bed one day and he told her he carried it at night when he walked alone. It was a big flick-knife with a large blade and a black handle. This fits with the profile of a predatory killer who later used two knives to murder two people in a horrific random crime.

Carl and Catherine Doyle were childhood sweethearts who doted on each other. Catherine's maiden name was Doyle too. The couple shared the same goals in life: they wanted a nice home, many happy and healthy children, and the peace and quiet of the countryside. Both were from Dublin, and the lure of life outside the capital would eventually bring them to Carane, near Ballintober in Co. Roscommon. They were married at the Registry Office in Dublin in October 1990, when Catherine was 21 and Carl a year older. They moved to Roscommon under the Rural Resettlement Scheme when they were around two years married. At the time of their death less than five years later, they were the proud parents of two boys and two girls. Carl had got a job with Avonmore Meats in Ballyhaunis, and they had bought their 'dream house' near Ballintober with the assistance of Roscommon County Council. Their detached house was set on half an acre just eight miles from the town of Castlerea. There were flowers and trees and nature all around. Catherine loved little figurines and statues of fairies, and they named the house Cnoc na Sióga. It was to this idyllic setting that Nash travelled with Catherine's sister Sarah Jane on the evening of Friday, 15 August 1997.

No words can adequately describe the emotional pain endured by Catherine Doyle's family. Her parents Patrick and Catherine Snr have lost their eldest daughter and their son-in-law Carl in the most horrific way. And they have witnessed another daughter Sarah Jane lying in hospital suffering extensive head injuries, not knowing if she would live or die. But the Doyle family were already in mourning when Catherine and Carl were murdered. Just two months before, in June 1997, Catherine's 20-year-old brother Richard died tragically. Catherine and Carl had travelled back from Roscommon and helped Patrick and Catherine Snr organise Richard's funeral. Amid their own tears the couple had consoled

Catherine's five other siblings, Patrick, Jenny, Sarah Jane and the young teenage twins James and Claire. The Doyles are a close-knit family who have battled through more than any family should have to endure. The two Catherines were as much like sisters as mother and daughter. Catherine Snr tells me how she got the news that her eldest child had been murdered.

I remember on that Saturday morning the Guards were banging on my door, and I wouldn't let them in. I just knew they had terrible news, the way they arrived at the door. I eventually let them in and they walked into the sitting room and just turned around to me and said Catherine and Carl had been murdered. I remember I just couldn't take it in. I was thinking it was a car crash. I just couldn't get it into my head. And they told me Sarah was in transit to Beaumont Hospital with very bad head injuries. Paddy was in town that morning and they got Paddy home to me. We were just in a complete state of numbness, not so much shock as total, total numbness. Your brain just seems to shut down.

Catherine Snr never liked Nash. She met him soon after her daughter Sarah Jane began going out with him, but Catherine felt something about him wasn't right. She wanted to learn more about him.

I wanted to learn about his background, about his job or his family. But he wouldn't talk about himself and I was getting more and more suspicious. Here was this person coming from England, and we knew nothing about him. It was a closed shop, and that's what made me worry. I'd ask about his family in England and if he was in touch, or where they lived, and he'd just change the subject.

Mark Nash finished work at around 4 p.m. on Friday, 15 August 1997. He took a taxi home to Clonliffe Road and got the car to wait while Sarah Jane got the two babies ready for the journey all the way to Co. Roscommon. She was really looking forward to seeing her big sister and her family. She hadn't seen Catherine since Richard's funeral. They had spoken a good bit on the phone, but Sarah Jane was looking forward to having a long chat over the weekend. She thought a change of scenery might help herself and her boyfriend too. She had had her first really serious row with Nash that Wednesday and needed to talk about it.

During the row Nash had shouted at her, smashed a television and hit a wall, and insulted one of their housemates. She had never seen that side of him before. The row had been over her desire to move from Clonliffe Road back closer to her parents in Hartstown in west Dublin. Naturally, she was still very upset over Richard's sudden death and she missed the closeness of her family. Nash didn't want to move that far from town and began to raise his voice. As their discussion became heated a housemate intervened. It was then that Nash showed his nasty side, screaming at this other young woman and passing comments about her weight and general physical features. Nash's mask was beginning to slip. This young woman left the house and didn't return. She had sensed the particularly hateful venom in his hurtful comments. Meanwhile, he had followed Sarah Jane upstairs and as the argument continued he kicked and broke a television and then kicked some chairs. He punched a wall but he didn't physically harm Sarah Jane. The two of them later made up and Nash told her he was really looking forward to going to Roscommon for the weekend. They had been going out for four and a half months and this had been their first big row. Sarah Jane hoped the relaxed atmosphere in Co. Roscommon might make things better.

Nash and Sarah Jane and the two babies arrived at Heuston Station at around 5.30 p.m. and Sarah Jane bought two return tickets to Castlerea. They sat in the smoking carriage and Sarah Jane settled down both her own son and Nash's daughter for the journey. It didn't seem like a big deal at the time, but Nash was on edge. He walked up and down the carriage a number of times and couldn't sit still for very long. He drank a brandy and a vodka, and by the time they arrived at Castlerea Station at 8.30 p.m. he seemed OK again.

Carl Doyle was there to greet the couple and their children. On their way from the station they stopped for some supplies including vodka, whiskey and soft drinks, arriving at Cnoc na Sióga, three miles outside Ballintober, just after 9 p.m. Catherine greeted the visitors at the door, telling them their own four kids were asleep upstairs. Everyone seemed in great form and looking forward to a happy weekend in the countryside. Within four hours Carl and Catherine Doyle would be dead.

Mark Francis Nash was born in April 1973 to 21-year-old Bernadette Nash. He never knew his father and he grew up with his mother and her parents at Fitzwilliam Street in Huddersfield. When he was 13 his grandparents moved to Co. Mayo, and he and his mother moved to the town of Bradley, where he left school three years later in 1989. By this time he was already smoking cannabis and hanging around with undesirables. Relations between Nash and his mother were strained, and in 1991 she put him out of the house. This was a year after his first conviction for assaulting a woman. He moved to Leeds and in early 1996 he met Lucy and moved in with her. When their baby was born in Dublin in 1996, Nash and Lucy were living on Prussia Street in the north inner city and they seemed happy. However, their relationship soon became strained and soon after one incident in early 1997 where he repeatedly screamed at her, they split up. Initially, they were forced to continue living in the same house and Nash had full access to his daughter, but around March and April 1997 he often found himself wandering the streets of Dublin alone. He socialised with workmates but spent a lot of time by himself. He was forever looking to fit in somewhere, and when he met Sarah Jane Doyle and then her family, he thought he had found his niche. But Catherine Snr knew something was wrong.

Nash was a very cocky individual. He didn't so much walk as strut. He was trying to fit in, just be accepted into the family. But I couldn't accept him. He was too secretive, and I didn't like the way he spoke to us. He was over-friendly, creepy.

Catherine Snr had no idea Nash was capable of the extreme violence he displayed against two of her daughters and son-in-law. But in hindsight she now believes that if Nash hadn't killed in Co. Roscommon, he would have killed in the Doyle family home in Hartstown.

He hated the closeness of our family, and he hated that I was a strong character. I think he has a problem with strong women. He used to say to me, 'You're too strong.' It was a weird thing to say. I just couldn't take to him, and he knew it. A few times he stayed over here with Sarah Jane and I heard him pacing around the house at night. It's only looking back you can see what that could have meant. There was one time when he made a threat, and only I really took notice of it. Cathy and Carl were here and the two of them were talking to Paddy and myself. Nash came into the room and his daughter was here, and she was crying. He was trying to get involved in our conversation, and he was in a dark mood, and he turned to us and half-pointed and said, 'I'll do you' to the others and then 'but I'll get you in the end' to me. The others didn't take it seriously, but I now believe he had thought about attacking my family. It was in his head; it was premeditated. If he hadn't done it in Roscommon, it would have been Hartstown.

Initially, everyone seemed in a happy, relaxed mood in Cnoc na Sióga. Carl and Catherine's four young children were asleep upstairs. Sarah Jane had carried her five-month-old son in from the car and Nash had carried his daughter, who was now nine months old. Sarah Jane gave the babies a bottle each and put them on a two-seater couch in the sitting room. The four adults spent the following four hours listening to music, drinking and chatting. There was a general party atmosphere and Catherine brought out some chips and bread from the kitchen. Nash took out his Nikon Compact camera and began taking snaps. Little did anyone know he was taking photos of those he would shortly attack. He was recording a future crime scene.

Sometime around 12.30 a.m. Nash went to the toilet and vomited. He also had diarrhoea and he spent around three-quarters of an hour in the bathroom. While he was in the bathroom, it appears that something happened within him to bring his murderous streak to the surface. One garda says it is still unclear just when Nash decided to kill the Doyles.

Nash gave us different stories. He claimed Carl Doyle was playing with a knife and jokingly told Nash to stab him, but we know that is totally untrue. Carl Doyle was fast asleep when Nash killed him. So this murder was premeditated. Nash picked up a knife or took a knife out of his pocket and stabbed Carl as he slept. It's just a matter of guessing when Nash first decided to kill, and we all have our theories. During questioning he spoke to us about this 'red mist' descending around him in the bathroom that night, as if he suddenly decided to be a murderer as he sat on the toilet, but we have a different theory, one which is very scary to consider and which is much more likely. But based on the belief that Nash used to carry a knife around Dublin city, and other information, it's more likely that he thought about committing murder long before he travelled that night to Co. Roscommon.

As Nash was in the toilet getting sick, the others continued chatting and laughing, but it was getting late. Catherine and Sarah Jane decided to go upstairs to get beds ready for the two babies. Catherine was going to bring a mattress from her room into a spare room and they left Carl asleep on the three-seater couch. Carl normally started work during the week at 5 a.m. with Avonmore Meats, so by the early hours of Saturday morning it was no surprise that he fell asleep on the couch. The two babies lay on the other settee. Nash came out of the toilet and headed for the sitting room.

When Nash later claimed that Carl Doyle had been holding a knife and playfully handed it to him, the detectives were able to disprove this claim very easily. Thanks to the photographs taken by Nash before he went to the bathroom, he left clear evidence that Carl never had a chance to defend himself. Of the 13 photographs that were successfully developed from Nash's camera, one photo showed Carl asleep on the couch with a red cigarette lighter resting on his lap. A photograph taken by a garda crime scene examiner after the murder showed Carl still half-sitting and half-lying in the same position, with the cigarette lighter still on his lap. The camera couldn't lie. Carl Doyle was murdered while he was asleep.

Nash stabbed Carl four times in the chest. One of the wounds pierced his heart and he died almost instantly. Carl was a 29-year-old man who had dedicated his life to his family, leaving home early each day to travel to Ballyhaunis where he worked at the Avonmore Meat factory so as to provide for his family. His £200 weekly wage was spent on the family he adored. He and Catherine had dreamt of a life outside Dublin, a detached house with open space to the front and back, room for their four young kids to play safely, a place for them all to live safely, where he could not only provide for his family but also protect them. As Carl's life was callously taken while he lay sleeping, so too was that dream.

Upstairs, Catherine and Sarah Jane were carrying the mattress into the spare room. They never heard a sound from downstairs; they never heard Nash stab Carl; and they never heard him pick up a stove handle and creep up the stairs. Both women were looking forward to a good night's sleep after a night's craic. They were trying to keep quiet so as not to waken the four children already sleeping upstairs. The two women had no idea of the imminent danger they faced.

Such was the force that Nash used to stab Carl that the knife broke, leaving fragments lying on Carl's shirt. With Nash's own baby daughter and Sarah Jane's baby son lying asleep on an adjoining settee, he had left Carl's body sitting half-slumped in the middle of the other settee. He walked to the kitchen looking for another weapon. It was quiet upstairs, and Nash may have thought Sarah Jane and Catherine were sleeping. The Gardaí would later wonder if this had been his original plan. Had he intended carrying out his killing spree when he thought his victims were in bed? He picked up an iron bar in the kitchen, a device Catherine used to open the big kitchen stove. He clutched it tightly and crept up the stairs.

The two Doyle sisters were to show remarkable courage over the following moments. Through admirable inner strength and restraint, Sarah Jane would manage to lie still and convince Nash that she was dead, after he beat her repeatedly on the head and then threw her down the stairs. And her elder sister Catherine was to fight Nash, grappling with this bully brandishing the iron bar, trying to stop the attack on her sister, while screaming out for Carl to come and help. And then somehow Catherine was downstairs, continuing to battle for her life. The extent of her injuries serves as evidence that she fought the coward with the iron bar, she fought to escape.

As well as stabbing Catherine Doyle 16 times, Nash tried to strangle her. He had chased her down the stairs towards the kitchen and grabbed her around her neck. As Catherine struggled furiously to escape, Nash saw another knife and he stabbed Catherine ten times in her front and three times in her back. Catherine, a 28-year-old mother of four, died on her kitchen floor from stab wounds to her lungs and heart.

Catherine Doyle was living her dream, she was a 'free spirit' who loved the open air and was devoted to her husband and children. She took to life in Co. Roscommon like a duck to water. She just loved being surrounded by nature. The Doyles never went on holiday — they couldn't afford it — but they were living the life they had dreamed of. Naturally, Catherine missed her parents and brothers and sisters, but they were only a train journey away and they were always at the end of the phone.

Paddy Doyle smiles as he thinks of one of his fondest memories of his eldest daughter. It is one of Catherine Snr's favourites too. Paddy tells me how they one day found themselves watching her from afar in Dublin city.

We went into town and we were due to meet her. Cathy was working in a restaurant and we saw her coming down the street. She'd long hair at the time, and she was wearing a straw hat. Catherine and myself were peeping out from a doorway at her. She was walking along and the breeze blew her hat off. And whatever way she put her hand up to catch her hat and with her hair blowing — it stays with us. She was actually having a look at herself in a reflection of the window of Brown Thomas. She was wearing dungarees and a straw hat, and with her long hair — we just stood back and watched her. That image will stay with Catherine and myself for ever.

Gardaí Thomas King and Muireadach Colleary were in the local patrol car when they got the call at 1.50 a.m. They arrived at the Hester home just after 2 a.m. They found Sarah Jane being comforted by members of the Hester family. She was covered in blood, with a large gash on the top of her head and blood running down her face. She was shaking uncontrollably. When she saw the Gardaí she gasped, 'Help me, please help me.' She told them she had been attacked by her boyfriend, that Carl and Catherine had been attacked and that there were six little children up in the house. An ambulance had just arrived, and when they saw her head wounds the crew said they had to get Sarah Jane to hospital immediately. The two Gardaí headed up the road towards the Doyle house. The lights were on downstairs, but there seemed to be no movement at all inside. Sergeant John O'Gara arrived at the house at the same time, and the three Gardaí went inside.

If any solace can be found in the terrible events in the Doyle house that night, it is that none of the children was physically harmed. The two babies who were on a couch close to Carl's body were much too young to remember that night. In time, Nash's daughter, then nine months old, would return to England with her mother Lucy to start a new life away from her father. But that night she was in the middle of a horrific murder scene. Beside her lay Sarah Jane's son, only five months old. The two babies had been 'brother and sister' for just five months. They would soon be separated for ever, but in the early hours of Saturday, 16 August 1997, they lay crying side by side on a settee. Unaware of the terrible events occurring around them, the babies were crying for their bottles.

Three of Carl and Catherine's children slept through the terrible attack. They had been asleep since early that night. But one of the boys woke up. When the Gardaí entered the house, they first found Catherine's body in the kitchen, and they then found Carl's body sitting slumped on a settee with the two babies crying on the other settee. Then they heard a sound. A little boy ran towards them very upset. His words were simple and heart-breaking — 'Mark killed Mammy and Daddy.'

Mark Nash ran through fields, keeping low to avoid being seen. His mind was racing, he knew he had finally let everyone see what he was capable of. He needed to make his escape, he needed to get away. Near Castlerea he approached a farmhouse; all was quiet and he ventured closer to the house. He saw a toolbox and he stole a hammer. At another farmhouse he broke into a shed and stole a bike and a cap and jacket. He began to cycle towards Galway, but he knew the Gardaí would come looking for him. He began to imagine that people passing him by were looking at him strangely, as if they knew. He thought he had killed Sarah Jane as well as Carl and Catherine, but as he cycled towards Galway city he somehow found out she was alive, most likely hearing a radio bulletin somewhere. He knew they would soon be after him. He was getting tired, and near Tuam he stopped cycling and sat by a river. And there he began to write two letters to the girlfriend he had tried to kill just hours earlier.

As detectives were breaking the news to Paddy and Catherine Doyle in Dublin that one of their daughters had been murdered and another was in a very serious condition in hospital, they were also delicately trying to ask for a photo of their prime suspect. The Gardaí in Roscommon had been able to locate the Doyles in Dublin quite quickly because of a Mass card for Richard that had been on the mantelpiece at Cnoc na Sióga. But now as the Gardaí from Blanchardstown were dispatched to bring the awful news of Carl and Catherine's murder, they simply had to get a description of Nash as soon as possible. An incredibly vicious killer was on the loose and had to be caught immediately. Sarah Jane had been able to give a general description before being rushed to hospital, but the Gardaí needed a photograph and the only way to get it was to ask the family to whom they were bringing the most dreadful news. Catherine's youngest sister Claire found a photograph of Nash for the Gardaí, taken less than two months before. The description was soon relayed to all garda stations around the country.

Nash sat by a stream known as the Sinking River. He was tired; he had been cycling all day, hiding whenever he thought traffic was approaching. Now he had somehow heard that Sarah Jane had been rushed to hospital in Dublin and was still alive, and he needed to talk to her. As he sat by the river bank he wrote two letters. The first was addressed to Dublin's Beaumont Hospital for the attention of 'Sarah Jane Doyle (patient, head injuries)'. In the letter he wrote: 'Sarah, there is a letter at home for you which you must read. There is also £140 in there. Goodbye, Mark.'

The second letter Nash wrote continues to be of great interest to both the Gardaí and the police in England. Part of its contents clearly suggests that he previously harboured murderous intentions. Just hours before he was arrested by the Gardaí in Galway, he wrote to Sarah Jane at her family home in Hartstown enclosing seven £20 notes, and saying he was glad she was alive. He also wrote:

> … I went mad. In the space of ten minutes I went from a sane person to a madman and then back again. I don't know what to say or how to say it. What have I done? This is the second time I've gone this way. I am insane. … I can't understand what I've done or why I've done it. Somebody please help me.

Late on the night of Saturday, 16 August 1997, a man answering Nash's description was spotted two miles outside Galway city on the Tuam Road near Castlegar. Gardaí Gerard Curtin, Caroline Sewell and Ray Wimms sped to the scene where they were joined by Garda Eoin Griffin. In the townland of Two-Mile-Ditch near Castlegar the Gardaí saw a man pushing a bike, with his head low. Sewell and Wimms got out of the patrol car and approached the man. Suddenly Nash looked in the direction of the officers and shouted: 'I'm Nash. Stay away or I'll kill you.' He let go of the bike, rummaged in his pocket and took out the hammer he had stolen earlier in Castlerea.

For some moments Nash was again out of control. He stood in the centre of the road and tried to stop cars approaching. Terrified motorists braked to a halt, but their doors were locked so they were safe. He saw a blue van approaching and threw himself in front of it, smashing the windscreen with the hammer. The driver of the van and her two children were shocked, but Nash couldn't get into the van so he ran towards a nearby house, pursued by the Gardaí.

Nash saw a woman trying to get in the front door of her house. She had seen the commotion and was trying to get inside to safety.

She was almost inside when he arrived at the front door and forced his way in. However, the woman's son managed to restrain him and keep him subdued, and seconds later the Gardaí were at the door.

During the hours that Nash was at large in Counties Roscommon and Galway, armed detectives were guarding Sarah Jane Doyle at Beaumont Hospital. It was a necessary precaution in case Nash made his way to Dublin where he might attack Sarah Jane again. Eventually the detectives would come to the conclusion that there was no motive for the killings, and that Carl and Catherine Doyle were the victims of a random killer who happened to be staying in their house that night.

Sarah Jane underwent extensive surgery to treat the multiple deep cuts to her head. She was left with two steel plates in her head, but just as she had battled to make her way to the Hester house to raise the alarm, she fought to recover from her injuries. In the first few hours at the hospital doctors feared for her life, but she found the strength to come through. When she came around from the anaesthetic after life-saving surgery, she was talking about Carl and Catherine as if they were still alive. Her mother had to tell her that they were dead.

By the time Nash's letter arrived for Sarah Jane at her family home in Hartstown, detectives were ready to seize it. Unbeknownst to the Doyle family, anything Nash now said or wrote had taken on a bigger significance after the double murder he had committed in Roscommon. Two detectives were waiting for the postman and when he arrived at the Doyles' front door with the letter, the Gardaí ran up to the Doyles saying, 'Don't touch the letter.' The Gardaí said they needed the letter as part of their investigations, and the Doyles signed a note permitting the detectives to take the letter away. The officers brought the letter to Beaumont Hospital and read its contents to Sarah Jane but told her they had to keep the letter. This is the letter where Nash suggests he previously had murderous thoughts. Indeed, within hours of being arrested in Galway he was making statements relating to another double murder carried out in Dublin only five months before.

On the night of 7 March 1997, two women were murdered as they lay sleeping in their beds at sheltered accommodation in Grangegorman in Dublin's north inner city. Sixty-one-year-old Mary Callinan and 59-year-old Sylvia Shiels were stabbed repeatedly in one of the most disturbing crimes ever investigated in this country. The State Pathologist, Dr John Harbison, would conclude that the attack on the women continued after they were already dead. Both women suffered horrific injuries to their throats, chests and lower bodies. Their killer broke in through a downstairs window and took knives from the kitchen before going upstairs and attacking the women as they slept. After committing the double murder, the killer went to a third bedroom and stood beside a third woman who also lay sleeping. But something happened within the killer that stopped him from committing a third murder, and he left the house and walked home. The woman whose life was spared by this evil man would later find the bodies of her housemates.

As Nash confessed to the double murder of Carl and Catherine Doyle, he said he also wanted to talk about another double murder. He wanted to talk about the murders at Grangegorman, which had occurred a short distance from where he had been living on Prussia Street in Dublin. Detectives in Galway wrote down what he had to say about the double murder in Dublin and when they read it back over to him, he agreed that that was what he had said. He first mentioned the Grangegorman murders shortly after his arrest on Saturday, 16 August 1997. He described the killings as having occurred 'about three months ago', when in fact the double murder had occurred over five months before, but everything else he had to say about the murders seemed to be accurate. On the following day Nash made a further statement where he again mentioned the double murder in Grangegorman. At this stage he had spoken to four detectives about these murders, and now he had also made a verbal comment to a senior garda. Another matter that was beginning to intrigue the Gardaí was the fact that when Nash was being transported to Mountjoy Jail after being charged with the murders of Carl and Catherine Doyle, he pointed out a particular location in the Grangegorman area. A garda immediately wrote down what exactly Nash had pointed to, and its significance. The Gardaí in Galway passed on all this information to their colleagues in Dublin, who found it of great interest. But there was one drawback — a man was already in custody charged with one of the Grangegorman murders.

Just over two weeks before Nash murdered Carl and Catherine Doyle, 24-year-old Dean Lyons from Tallaght was charged with the murder of 61-year-old Mary Callinan. At that time the Director of Public Prosecutions believed there was enough evidence to bring a charge against Lyons in relation to one of the murders, and it followed that a second murder charge might be forthcoming in the future. However, Lyons, a heroin addict, was innocent of the murders — it would later emerge he had been charged on the basis of a confession relating to a crime he did not commit. The murder charge against Lyons remained in place for nine months before it was suddenly dropped during a short hearing at Dublin District Court. In the meantime, from his prison cell Nash had withdrawn the original statement he made which implicated himself in the Grangegorman murders. Lyons later moved to England to try and rebuild his life and kick his drug habit, but he died in 2000. The investigation into the murders of Mary Callinan and Sylvia Shiels continues, and detectives believe advances in DNA technology may one day identify the killer by evidence he left at the scene of the double murder.

On Monday, 12 October 1998, Nash was found guilty of the murders of Carl and Catherine Doyle and was given two life sentences. The families of Carl and Catherine were happy and relieved that the killer was going to prison, hopefully for the rest of his life. Nash was also convicted of assault causing harm to Sarah Jane Doyle, and received an eight-year sentence to be served at the same time as the life sentences. During the five-day trial Sarah Jane had recounted how Nash had told her she 'must die' as he repeatedly beat her with an iron bar. Her mother Catherine believes as a matter of principle that Nash should have faced more serious charges for the attack on her third youngest child.

I was annoyed that he only got eight years for the attack on Sarah. I was very annoyed he wasn't charged with attempted murder, because that's what it was in my opinion. Because in all honesty he thought she was dead, and he had said to her as he attacked her, 'You must die, Sarah.' He had shown intent to murder.

Today Sarah Jane Doyle lives in west Dublin close to her parents and is trying to get on with her life.

The woman who came to Ireland with Nash also gave evidence against him at his murder trial. Lucy described how volatile Nash was and how his mood could change so quickly. Shortly after he committed the double murder in Roscommon, she took their baby daughter and moved back to England.

Nash is still every bit as cocky as the day he arrived in Ireland. When he was first put in Mountjoy Jail, he was placed in the Medical Unit, also known as F6. This is where prisoners are isolated for their own protection, or for the protection of other prisoners. While there, he allegedly made a threat to take a prison officer hostage. In recent years he has adapted to prison life in the high security Arbour Hill Prison, where he is allowed to mix with other prisoners who are also serving long prison sentences. He passes his day by working in the Braille Shop, but he is very keen to be transferred to a British prison to continue serving his life sentences. However, when he applied to be transferred to England, his request was denied and he was told by the Department of Justice that the refusal stemmed from the fact that he is still considered a suspect for the murders of Mary Callinan and Sylvia Shiels at Grangegorman in March 1997.

In October 2002, the Dublin City Coroner, Dr Brian Farrell, wrote to Nash asking him to attend the inquests into the deaths of the two women murdered in Grangegorman. The coroner made the request on the understanding that Nash might have information relevant to establishing the circumstances by which the women met their deaths. A section of roadway outside the Coroner's Court was reserved in the expectation that a prison van might arrive ferrying Nash from Arbour Hill Prison. However, Nash employed a solicitor to state that he would not be attending the inquests voluntarily. He said he believed himself to be in a 'particularly vulnerable' position because he was a prime suspect for the murders. The coroner deliberated until the following month before deciding that he would not seek to compel Nash to attend the inquests. Dr Farrell lamented the 'glaring anomalies' in the 40-year-old Coroners Act whereby Nash could refuse to attend the inquests.

The Gardaí and the British police have met a number of times to discuss the movements of Nash in the months and years before he murdered Carl and Catherine Doyle. The two forces have tried to discover if he really had killed before then. The degree of random and motiveless violence he used against the couple naturally makes him a suspect for any such killing in an area where he was living. While this clearly makes him a suspect for the murders of Mary Callinan and Sylvia Shiels in 1997, the British police have also examined whether he committed any unsolved crimes in England before moving to Ireland. Once he was convicted of murdering Carl and Catherine Doyle, police from Huddersfield travelled to Dublin to investigate him as a suspect in a random violent attack carried out in May 1996 while he was still in England. Another man was later convicted of the crime, only to have his conviction overturned, and this violent incident remains officially unsolved.

One garda who investigated the murders of Carl and Catherine Doyle says it is wrong that Nash can be allowed to spend his days in Arbour Hill without being questioned at length about his movements before he committed a double murder in Roscommon.

Nash is a perfect example of what I would call the need to 'debrief' any random murderer. Basically, we've successfully prosecuted him for two such killings and naturally he would be considered a suspect for any other such killings that occurred anywhere near where he was living or working. Consider that Nash was only in this country ten months when he murdered Carl and Catherine Doyle. Even today so little is known about him, so little about what drove him to commit such a terrible crime. I really think people convicted of such random murders should go through a detailed interview in prison, over months if need be, where they would be forced to co-operate and outline everything they can remember about their lives. If they choose not to co-operate, they should lose prison privileges. Such an idea would only operate if random killers were told in no uncertain terms that they were going to remain in prison for the rest of their lives, and that if they convinced us they had nothing more to hide, their life in prison might be that bit easier. It is so wrong to just let suspicion hang in the air, and I believe there are some convicted murderers who have an awful lot more to tell us, but there are others who do not. Sitting down with killers would allow some of them the opportunity to convince us they were not involved in other violent incidents, yet they choose to hide behind this right to silence, and so the suspicion remains. The only way to find out what our random killers know is to debrief each and every one, just like prisoners of war. It's not a crazy idea; it's something that could help solve the murders of many Irish citizens.

Nash is a restless prisoner. He wants to be sent back to England and continue serving his life sentences there. Catherine Doyle's parents are absolutely opposed to such a move. They keep a letter which was hand delivered by an official from the Department of Justice in April 2001, which states clearly that the then Minister for Justice, John O'Donoghue, refused Nash's application to transfer to a prison in England. Nash will continue to try every legal manoeuvre to be allowed home, and argues he is being unfairly treated because of a cloud of suspicion hanging over him which does not relate to the crimes of which he is convicted. One detective says Nash cannot have it both ways.

When Nash decided not to attend the inquests into the

murders at Grangegorman, he was clearly stating he wanted to maintain a silence. The Coroner had said he believed he could protect both Nash's constitutional rights and his fears for his personal safety, but Nash chose to remain in Arbour Hill. If that's the attitude he took when he was being given a clear opportunity to publicly state his case about the suspicion hanging over him, that's fine, and we have to live with that. But is it right that he can then turn around and say he wants to leave the country entirely, and if the Gardaí ever want to ask him questions they can come and visit him in prison in England? Quite simply, as things stand I don't see Mark Nash ever leaving Arbour Hill. And whose fault is that?

Nash receives few visitors at Arbour Hill Prison. Before he was identified as a random killer he had a number of casual relationships with young women. With his cocky self-assured manner, he promised them the sun, moon and stars while managing to disguise the violence within him. None of these women visits Nash now. However, one of the few people who does visit him is an official from the British Embassy, who routinely checks on British citizens incarcerated in Irish prisons. Two of the other men the official visits in the Dublin prison are English serial killers, John Shaw and Geoffrey Evans, who abducted and murdered two Irish women in separate attacks in 1976. Both men have been in prison for over a quarter of a century and both know they will most likely die in an Irish prison. Nash on the other hand has already gone to the High Court to argue, that just like republican prisoners who have been transferred from British to Irish prisons, he should be allowed back to Huddersfield.

The dream home that Carl and Catherine Doyle bought in the mid-1990s was sold after their murders. On a night in August 1997 the house was the scene of a terrible crime carried out by someone who had never been to Co. Roscommon before that night. A Dublin family's dream of leaving the hustle and bustle of city life for the peace and tranquillity of the countryside was shattered by a person fuelled by an unexplained rage. The settee on which Carl Doyle was sitting when he was murdered was removed and burned by his family. Carl and Catherine were brought home to Dublin and laid to rest at the cemetery in Mulhuddart. Hundreds of people had attended their removal in Co. Roscommon to pay their respects to a young couple who wanted only the best for their four young children. Their two boys were aged 7 and 5 when their parents were murdered and the two little girls were aged 3 and one. As the bodies of Carl and Catherine Doyle were slowly driven from Co. Roscommon to Dublin, each coffin bore a red rose.

For five months in 1997 Nash tried to infiltrate the family of Paddy and Catherine Doyle. The murder of their daughter and son-in-law, and the death of their son Richard two months before, has left a void in their lives. The Doyles still have five loving children, including Sarah Jane, and their collective strength has brought them through much heartache. They are a close-knit family, and what is so upsetting for them is that for five months in 1997, Nash, a stranger from England, tried to be part of that group. He stayed in their house, sat in their sitting room and stood in their kitchen.

Catherine Snr shudders when she thinks of how Nash was privately plotting to murder someone in her family.

Looking back now I know it was in his head, it was premeditated. I know that if Nash hadn't attacked Carl and Cathy in Roscommon, he would have tried to kill myself and Paddy and our twins James and Claire in this house. He wasn't being accepted, he was just too secretive and wasn't being accepted. I think he was envious or somehow jealous of the closeness of our family. I just know in my heart that he wanted to cause us pain.

As Paddy and Catherine Snr sit remembering their eldest daughter, they get very upset whenever they think of how she died. But they also smile when they think of the full life she was leading up until her murder. They have many good memories that keep them going through all the horror a stranger caused their family. Catherine Snr describes to me a special memory of her murdered child.

Catherine loved to pick wild flowers. Once in Roscommon she saw some flowers growing by the side of the road and she shouted, 'Stop the car, stop the car', and she got out and picked the flowers, and she brought them home to the fireplace. Herself and Carl just loved that house at Ballintober. They saved and saved until they got enough money together to make it theirs. I remember she rang in the springtime to tell me about all the daffodils that had grown in the garden, and there were plum trees out the back. She loved daffodils, and from the time she was a little girl she'd bring me a big bunch of daffodils at Easter, because I always did our house up in the spring, and I'd fill the house with daffodils.

10

One Killer Caught

It was the coldest Holy Thursday/Good Friday in living memory, the night Paud Skehan was left bound and gagged, lying on a concrete floor with his legs tied to the banisters of his home. For hours the 68-year-old bachelor farmer lay semiconscious, unable to free himself and suffering severe and ultimately fatal head injuries. Paud's killers had taken their time. They had been watching him and they knew he lived alone. And as Paud slept in his upstairs bedroom, the cowardly gang of criminals from Limerick city had silently entered the house. There were at least two attackers and possibly some look-outs on the laneway outside. The degree of violence used against Paud and the lack of respect for humanity continues to shock everyone in the quiet countryside of O'Briensbridge in Co. Clare. During the prolonged attack Paud's killers dragged him from his bed and beat him repeatedly about the head. He lost a lot of blood on the upstairs landing as his attackers punched him in the face and kicked him. They blindfolded him with a handkerchief, bound his hands and feet with a necktie and television cable, flung him downstairs and trussed him to the banisters. As they screamed at him to tell them where he kept his cash, his killers doused him with lighter fluid and threatened to set him alight. It is not known whether his killers found any money in the house that night, but they effectively tore his home apart pulling out floorboards, ripping his couch and throwing religious pictures from the walls. Finally, the killers left the house, leaving Paud lying on his sitting room floor with a blood-soaked blindfold on his face, his hands bound, and his feet tied to the stairs. He had suffered fatal brain damage, but his suffering was not over. For hours he lay shivering in sub-zero temperatures as his two dogs Shep and Puppy wandered distressed around the house trying to comfort him. He developed bronchial pneumonia and by the time he was found unconscious next morning, it would be too late to save him. As his killers made their escape, they didn't think of raising the alarm. They simply didn't care. But one of the killers had left unique evidence at the scene that, through dogged detective work, would eventually result in him serving life for the murder of Paud Skehan.

For 54 days Patrick 'Paud' Skehan fought for his life. When he died, it was quietly, in the care of staff at the Mid Western Regional Hospital in Limerick. For the almost eight weeks he was in a coma his family had kept a bedside vigil, but he never recovered. Paul's only recognition of sounds or voices was on the day he was rushed to hospital, when he turned his head as his nephew's wife called out his name, but that was it. Paud Skehan effectively died during the attack in his home, eight weeks before the life support machine was switched off.

It was Paud's friend and neighbour, Michael Browne, who found him lying bound and gagged in his house. It was early on Friday, 10 April 1998, and Michael knew something was wrong. He had seen Paud's jeep parked oddly over a mile away from his house, something Paud would never do. Michael had gone to

Paud's two-storey farmhouse to see if his friend was all right. Within moments of arriving at the house, he found the front door open and he walked in calling Paud's name. He had only turned left into the sitting room when he saw the house in disarray, and he saw Paud lying in a pool of blood.

Michael knelt beside his friend and felt how cold he was, so he ran upstairs to get a duvet which he brought back down and wrapped around him. As well as being practically frozen, it was obvious Paud was very badly injured from a beating. Michael Browne went to raise the alarm.

O'Briensbridge is a normally peaceful village in south-east Co. Clare. It is less than five miles south of the scenic town of Killaloe on the shores of Lough Derg. It is also less than ten miles north of the outskirts of Limerick city. The townland of Ardnatagle, Bridgetown, near O'Briensbridge, is where Paud Skehan lived his entire life, growing up as one of five children. He was the only one of the five not to marry, and he remained living at the old family home. His two brothers emigrated to England and one sister moved to America. However, Paud's other sister, Margaret Kennedy, remained in O'Briensbridge, living just up the laneway from her brother and the home she grew up in. One of Margaret's sons, Paddy, also still lives on the laneway with his family, so although Paud lived alone for much of his life, he always had family and friends close by. However, the thoughts of how he lay suffering for hours on the concrete floor of his house will forever cause great upset for his family. Paddy Kennedy tells me how his uncle Paud was dedicated to his work.

Paud had a small farm, about 65 acres, but he worked seven days a week. He'd take it easier on Sundays. He'd go to Mass, but he'd be back out then after changing into his wellies. Paud had a heart by-pass about ten years before he died, but he recovered and was back out working within a short time. He lived to work, and we'd see him every day because he had farmland up past our house here, so he'd drive by from his own house in the tractor. You'd always know Paud was coming because you'd hear the dogs first and then the sound of the tractor.

Paddy's wife, Antoinette, was one of the first people at the scene after Michael Browne raised the alarm. She will never forget seeing Paud injured and so distressed.

It was early on Good Friday morning when I heard this car coming into the yard and banging on the window. I saw it was Mike Browne and he said, 'Come quick. Paud's been attacked.' I got such a fright. I rang Paddy and left a message for him in work, and I went to Paud's house and saw him lying there and moaning. Mike had already untied Paud from the banisters and had put coats and blankets on him to try and warm him up. Paud never regained full consciousness, but when he was brought to hospital I remember I called out his name, and his head turned and he looked at me. But he didn't answer, he just looked at me. And that was it.

It was just before 9 a.m. that morning that Garda Gerry Brassil took the call at Killaloe Garda Station from Michael Browne. Three Gardaí immediately sped to the scene, Gardaí Ollie Nevin and Bernard Kennedy in one car and Pat Ryan in another. The Gardaí who arrived at the farmhouse could smell the paraffin from Paud's clothing, and they quickly saw how the house had been systematically ransacked. As Paud was put into an ambulance,

Ryan followed in his car, hoping Paud might regain consciousness and be able to give a description of his attackers. Nevin, meanwhile, took up a post outside the farmhouse to preserve the scene and await the arrival of the garda forensic team. Such a move is a standard procedure in any criminal investigation, but preserving the scene of the attack on Paud, in what would soon become a murder investigation, was to reap great rewards.

Four days after Paud Skehan was attacked, Garda Jarlath Fahy approached a suspicious looking man loitering in the forecourt of a garage just outside Ennis. It was shortly before 11 a.m. on Tuesday, 14 April 1998, and as Fahy looked at the man standing in wet and filthy clothes, he knew there was something definitely out of place about him. The Gardaí were already on the look-out for a man who had been involved in ramming a garda patrol car in Gort in Co. Galway the previous night, and this person was believed to have headed south towards Ennis. The patrol car had been chasing two cars when it was rammed by one of them. One man had already been arrested at around 6 a.m. at an industrial estate on the Gort road, but his accomplice was still at large. The man standing at the garage in his filthy clothes certainly fitted the bill of someone up to no good. But what really gave the game away was the balaclava Willie Campion had rolled up on his head like a little hat.

Garda Fahy approached Campion and asked him his name. In a distinct Limerick accent Campion said he was James Ryan from Limerick. The garda searched him and found he was carrying a small black-handled knife in a scabbard. He also found the keys to a Toyota car which would later be identified as belonging to a car Campion had tried to steal near Gort. Despite being caught with the knife and the stolen car keys, Campion was displaying a brazenness he would later maintain during his trial for the murder of Paud Skehan. As Fahy asked him what he was doing out on the Gort road, Campion replied that he was looking for horses. Asked what he was doing wearing a balaclava, he said he had it to 'keep me ears warm'. Fahy arrested Campion on suspicion of causing criminal damage to property in Gort earlier that day. He brought him to Ennis Garda Station and arranged for the Gardaí from Galway to travel and see if they could identify Campion from the earlier car chase. A sequence of events was quietly unfolding that no one could have foretold.

Within hours of the attack on Paud Skehan being discovered the previous Friday 20 miles east of Ennis, a specialist garda team had subjected the entire house to a thorough forensic examination. Detectives who examined the crime scene soon came to the conclusion that Paud had first been attacked as he slept in his bed. He had then been dragged or pushed out on to the landing where he was severely beaten. There was congealed blood on a large section of the wooden floorboards on the landing, and the Gardaí were left in no doubt that Paud had been the victim of an incredibly violent attack during which he was repeatedly punched in the face. The blood spatters on the walls downstairs revealed how he had been pushed down the stairs before being tied to the banisters and left with his head and shoulders lying on the concrete floor. The degree of violence used by the robbers left many experienced Gardaí stunned.

Detective Garda Eugene Gilligan looked at the floorboards on the landing upstairs. Amid all the blood that would later be identified as Paud's were a number of footprints. The detective could see two distinct sets of prints that were not Paud's, clearly indicating at least two other people were present. Gilligan looked closely at the footmarks, knowing each one might contain some unique aspect that could identify the footwear and the owner. It was apparent that both sets of prints had been left by people wearing runners. The garda could see there were drag marks in the blood, showing where Paud had been dragged along the ground after losing a lot of blood. One particular footprint caught the detective's eye. It was on the edge of the scene of the attack, towards the right-hand side as you came up the stairs. This one seemed to be a full-length footprint and it looked like it might hold some clues. Gilligan knew that the print would reveal more when treated with chemicals. Time was of the essence, so the Gardaí took Paud's own chainsaw and cut a section of the floorboards measuring around two square feet. Gilligan took this section of flooring back to Garda Headquarters in Dublin to examine it more thoroughly.

Willie Campion was a career criminal who was first arrested in Limerick before he was even a teenager. By the time he murdered Paud Skehan, he had racked up 15 convictions including robbery with violence. He was only 12 years old when he first appeared at Limerick District Court in July 1980 charged with malicious damage. He was given the Probation Act, and received a similar sentence when he was convicted of burglary the following December. In May 1982, when he was 14, he was sentenced to two years' detention for carrying out burglaries in Limerick. In January 1984 he received a further two years for burglary, larceny and malicious damage, and in September 1985 a 17-year-old Campion was given another 17 months for other robberies. One garda who dealt with him says he was a criminal without any conscience.

Willie Campion simply knew nothing only badness. He mixed with other young thugs in Limerick and when he was put away during his teens he was still mixing with them. The only time Campion could have been saved from a life of crime was when he was put in a detention centre. But it's like dealing with any vicious child. You need to isolate them while they're inside, keep them away from other children, re-programme them to be proper human beings. By the time Willie Campion was an adult he had already received sentences totalling over five years, and was fine-tuning his thieving ways. He was on a downward spiral, a bad egg who was only going to get worse.

Campion specialised in 'tie-up' jobs, where he and fellow cowards would break into people's homes and tie them up while ransacking their houses. Over eight years before he murdered Paud Skehan in this way, he and a close associate broke into the home of a former Limerick coroner and subjected him to a terrifying ordeal, during which they tied him up and robbed him. The coroner lived in a house close to the Moyross estate where Campion was living and terrorising his neighbours. In May 1990 Campion appeared at Limerick Circuit Criminal Court after being extradited back from England. He was convicted of the attack on the coroner and jailed for seven years. Some people on the Moyross estate lit bonfires to celebrate the fact that they and the rest of Limerick were rid of Campion, at least for a few years.

Eight years later, Campion sat in an interview room at Ennis Garda Station. He was cold and hungry, he had walked over ten miles through fields during the night to get away from the Gardaí in Gort, and now he was under arrest in Ennis. He didn't know how much the Gardaí knew about what he and his accomplice had been doing that night. He had stupidly held on to the car keys for the Toyota, so they would soon find out he had tried to steal that car near Gort. The alternator had gone within seconds, so he had abandoned the car after driving about a hundred yards. He had had a very bad night, and now he was wet and shivering in a garda station. He wasn't going to let the Gardaí know anything. They would have to prove what he had been up to that night. He knew they had him for the theft of the Toyota, and it looked like he was in trouble for carrying that little black knife as well. The detectives had now found out he had given them a false name, another stupid mistake. They would be gunning for him now. He was probably going to get a few months for all this.

Gardaí from Gort had travelled down to Ennis to look at Campion, but they couldn't identify him as being involved in the ramming of a patrol car in the early hours of the morning. But there was no doubt in the minds of the officers that he had been involved in something untoward. There had been an attempt to break into a shop in Labane, just north of Gort, which had started the car chase; and nobody believed Campion was wearing a balaclava simply to keep his ears warm. Garda Fahy told Campion he wanted to take his clothing as part of their investigation into the crime for which he had been arrested, and any other crimes. Campion readily gave his clothing over, as his sister had by this time arrived at the garda station with a set of fresh clothes for him. Among the items he gave to the Gardaí were his wet, muddy black FILA runners, footwear he had been wearing four days earlier when he and his accomplice attacked Paud Skehan.

At Garda Headquarters, Eugene Gilligan examined the section of flooring he had taken from Paud's house. There was already a fairly distinct visible pattern to the footprint one of the killers had left in Paud's blood. It was clearly a runner print. Now it was time to treat the footprint with the Amido Black test. This test is a three-part process whereby a special chemical binds itself to the protein in blood and helps to show up any blood mark that might be invisible to the naked eye. Gilligan first sprayed a fixative on to the section of floorboard; he then sprayed on the black Amido dye; and finally he sprayed a special wash that cleaned away any part of the floorboard not covered with blood. Immediately the garda had not only uncovered a clearly visible footprint but one that would eventually be matched perfectly with Campion's FILA runners.

While events were unfolding in April 1998 that would eventually lead to one of his killers being caught, Paud Skehan was still in a coma at the Mid Western Regional Hospital. Paud was a strong but gentle man who never did anyone a bad turn. His killers never gave him a chance, beginning their assault on him while he was still asleep, and then continuing to kick and punch the 68-year old while he was disoriented. But for almost eight weeks Paud's family hoped he might come around. Antoinette Kennedy remembers hoping Paud might wake up from his coma.

At the start we hoped Paud would regain consciousness and might recover. We were actually wondering if we should make plans to get him into a nursing home. We knew he could never go back to living alone, but we thought he might come out of the coma, that he might live. But sure we were just hoping. We were even talking about getting our own sitting room ready for him just in case he might get a little better. But Paud had gone to nothing, he had just faded away. It was so sad. Paud was a man who worked almost every day of his life, a strong man who had previously battled through a heart operation, but the effects of what his attackers did to him were awful, and eventually Paud just faded away.

On Wednesday, 3 June 1998, Paud lost the fight for his life.

During the 54 days he lay unconscious in hospital, he would sometimes move his head when a light was shone directly on his face, but it was just a reflex. When he died he had family near him. One relative ran to fetch a nurse when she realised something was wrong with Paud's breathing, but by the time the nurses came into the room, Paud was gone.

Detectives in Co. Clare, led by Chief Superintendent Liam Quinn and local Superintendent Seán Corcoran, were now dealing with a murder investigation. The Gardaí already had a list of over a dozen suspects — people who were all capable of the violence that Paud Skehan had been subjected to. The detectives knew from the forensic examination of the scene that there had been at least two people involved in attacking Paud. Shortly, one of the killers would be identified by his runners, but there was another intriguing aspect to the investigation, and it is a question that remains to this day — who drove Paud's jeep away from his house and left it on the road towards Limerick?

There may well be a simple answer in that it could have been Campion or his co-killer, but both murderers had stepped in Paud's blood and must have had blood stuck to the soles of their runners. However, a detailed examination of Paud's jeep did not reveal any blood traces on the floor. So was there a third person who was a look-out? One detective says the investigation considered every scenario.

What we know for definite is that there were two killers in Paud's house and one of them was Willie Campion. How they got to Paud's house was never established. It's a good ten miles from Limerick. Did they drive or were they dropped off by someone else? We've often thought about whether there was a third person who might have kept watch outside while the others attacked Paud. When we searched Paud's jeep it was as clean as a whistle, no evidence at all, and we never found the keys. You could speculate all day about whether there was a third or fourth person involved. What I would say is that Willie and his fellow killer must have been tipped off by somebody more local who knew that Paud lived alone and that he might have cash. There must be someone who spotted Paud at a mart or somewhere else, and they watched him and they passed on information to the killers. The way the killers spent so much time in Paud's house would indicate they were taking their time searching the house inch by inch, as if they knew what they were looking for. So whether there was a third person at the house that night or not, there was a third party involvement in the overall crime.

In the days after Paud died, local farmers got together and offered a £10,000 reward to anyone who came forward with information about the murder. Paud was a well-liked man who was a familiar sight around the locality, and feelings were running high. Antoinette Kennedy says Paud was a quiet man, but was very interested in his community.

Paud would know everything that was going on. He'd meet people at the shops or at the creamery or at Mass. He knew all the local scéal. He didn't drink but he met people out and about all the time. He was a quiet, reserved man, old fashioned. He was a familiar sight out in his jeep with the dogs. We all miss him terribly.

After the Gardaí took Campion's runners and other clothing, they examined them to see if there was any evidence on them linking him to the incident where the garda car was rammed in Gort. But there was no evidence linking him to the car chase or the attempted break-in at the premises in Labane. A day after his arrest in Ennis, the Gardaí established that the car keys Campion was carrying belonged to a Toyota that had been stolen from a farmhouse in Gort, only to be abandoned a short distance away. Campion appeared at Ennis District Court and was convicted of the theft of the Toyota and possession of the small knife he had been hiding the morning Jarlath Fahy arrested him. When he was jailed for three months for stealing the Toyota, Campion began his sentence thinking that all in all he had got away fairly lightly. But as he served his short spell behind bars, his FILA runners were about to ensure he would be spending a lot longer in jail.

Dr Tom Hannigan of the State Forensic Science Laboratory had received the section of floorboard from Eugene Gilligan. Both knew the floorboard contained a unique runner print. If they could find the runner and its owner, they had the equivalent of the killer's fingerprint. A FILA runner had been found in a ditch some distance from Paud Skehan's house, but Dr Hannigan ruled this runner out. The Gardaí gave him a few other pairs but none was a match. Then on 15 June 1998, almost two weeks after Paud's death, Dr Hannigan received a pair of runners from the Gardaí in Ennis. The black FILA runners had been taken from a criminal named Willie Campion four days after the attack on Paud Skehan, and perhaps they might prove a match. Dr Hannigan examined the soles of the runners, and very soon he knew he had the killer's print.

On the sole of the right runner Dr Hannigan found eight separate wear marks that matched perfectly the impressions left in blood at the scene of the murder. On the sole of the left runner he found six wear marks that also proved beyond any doubt that it too had left marks on the floorboards. Because the correct chain of evidence had been kept, it was easy to prove that the runners had come directly from Campion's feet four days after Paud Skehan was battered and tortured. In time Campion would claim he had got the runners from someone else, but the Gardaí knew they had identified one of the killers.

Campion left the gates of Cork Prison early on the morning of 30 August 1998. He had finally completed his sentence for stealing the Toyota in Gort the previous April, and he was now looking forward to getting back to Limerick and planning more robberies. He had been moved from Limerick Prison just a few weeks before, after the home of a prison officer was petrol bombed. Campion could not have been responsible for the attack, as he was behind bars, but it was felt he might have information about who was responsible. One of his close associates had been overheard making a specific threat to a prison officer, and another associate had been spotted near the prison officer's home shortly before it was attacked. But as he stepped outside of Cork Prison Campion felt all that was behind him and he was looking forward to getting home. However, he was only out the door when he saw the team of detectives, and he knew in his heart what it was about and that he wasn't going anywhere. One detective says he will never forget the look on Campion's face.

From the very moment we arrested Campion for the murder of Paud Skehan he maintained he knew nothing about the attack. And right throughout the trial he maintained his innocence, claiming he had borrowed the FILA runners from someone else and that he'd been at home with his wife on the night in question. But I will never forget the look on Campion's face when he came out of Cork Prison, only to see us. We had detectives at both ends of the street. He wasn't going anywhere.

Maybe he's guilty of more than we know, but at that very moment you could see that he knew he was caught for something very serious he had done.

Within hours of being arrested, Campion was charged with the murder of Paud Skehan. He was also charged with the theft of property belonging to Paud. It would never be known what items were taken from Paud's house on the night he was attacked. It was known that Paud dealt a lot in cash. He had a cheque book, but he would often be seen with a roll of cash at a mart. It was clear that his attackers had literally torn his home asunder, plundering every possible hiding place in a search for money. The torture and murder of Paud Skehan was motivated by greed, and it was only right that one of the alleged murderers should face a charge of burglary too.

Paud's nephew, Paddy Kennedy, says his uncle's view of life was from a different and safer era.

Paud could remember a time when people could leave their door unlocked. He trusted people, he saw the best in them. He was the type of man who would lock his door and then leave the key in the lock. He was just of a different time, a better time, when it came to trusting people.

Campion and his fellow murderer broke into Paud's home through the front door. As they approached the house they had circled around the back, thinking they could sneak in by the back door, but they found there was no back door. There was only one way into the house, so they tried the front door and with a bit of pressure the door gave way. The house was in darkness and one of the killers picked up a sleán, a wooden-handled implement for cutting turf. They crept up the stairs and entered Paud's bedroom and began to beat him. They pushed and kicked Paud out on to the landing as they screamed at him to tell them where his money was. Paud's family shake their heads in sorrow when they think of what he must have endured before his death. One relative says it is simply dreadful.

They gave Paud an awful time. Just to imagine the fright he would have felt, it's a wonder he didn't suffer another heart attack during the assault. The fear must have been terrible for him. And Paud was such a strong man and he would have been powerless when these cowards struck.

When the Garda crime scene examiners studied Paud's house, they could see the mentality of the attackers, men who were willing to go to any lengths to get money. Floorboards had been pulled away, drawers had been ripped out, and even part of the fireplace had been pulled from the wall. A Sacred Heart picture had been flung on to Paud's bed, a cardboard box containing some of his clothes had been upturned, as had his television, and copies of the *Farmers Journal* were strewn across the kitchen floor. The callous killers who left Paud blindfolded, with his hands tied and his legs bound to the staircase not only invaded his home, they desecrated it. For 68 years Paud Skehan lived in this house; it was where he and his two brothers and two sisters had grown up. His family home was set in off a quiet country lane that is so infrequently used that a line of grass still grows right down the centre of it. For 68 years Paud felt safe in his home, but when his killers struck they shattered this safety, leaving him a prisoner in his home, tied to the banisters as the temperatures dropped to between −6° and −8°C.

To this day Campion has never made any verbal admission that he was one of the people who tortured and murdered Paud Skehan. Soon after his arrest in August 1998, he made a number of comments to Detective Sergeant Jeremiah Healy that show his mentality. Although Campion had a conviction for possessing a small amount of drugs, he didn't have a serious drug habit. When he broke into Paud Skehan's home he wanted cash or any other valuables, and he was prepared to torture and kill to get whatever he could. Campion stole because that's what he did. He was a career criminal who knew no different. Having been in trouble since before he was a teenager, he was a hardened criminal, a callous and crafty killer who right to the very end simply couldn't believe a pair of runners would nail him for murder. When Healy asked Campion what he had to say about the fact that a footprint in Paud Skehan's blood matched the print of the runners Campion had given the Gardaí in Ennis, he replied that it was 'astonishing'. In a further act of bravado he told the Gardaí that even if they could prove the runners had been in Paud's house, it didn't mean he had been. Campion told the Gardaí: 'It is up to your scientists to prove I was there. ... I will take my chances this time, gentlemen. ... You will have to get your famous scientists to prove it.'

Campion was charged with the murder of Paud Skehan, but despite his large number of previous convictions and the seriousness of the charge he faced, he was later granted bail. From soon after he was charged in early September 1998 until the murder trial finally began in March 2000, he was living in Limerick city and detectives fear he may have been involved in a number of other serious incidents during this time. One garda says he was very surprised that Campion actually turned up for his murder trial.

Campion is not a dumb criminal; he was a clever enough criminal. When he and his fellow killer went into Paud's house they didn't leave any fingerprints, and no one saw them come or go from the house. He knew the general tricks of the criminal trade, and being caught by your shoes was practically unheard of to thieves like Campion. He was caught because he was ignorant and stupid enough to keep wearing the same runners after attacking Paud and stepping in his blood. He simply couldn't comprehend how a pair of runners could be identified from a footprint. He did understand that a particular make of runner might be identified by a print in muck or blood, but to actually match a precise pair of runners seemed unbelievable to him. That's why I think he actually turned up every day for his trial. He didn't try and flee to England like he had done years before when the heat got too much. I think he actually thought he might walk on the murder charge. Like he said to us shortly before being charged, 'You can put the runners there but you can't put me there.' That was his mentality. He was suggesting he had swapped dozens of pairs of runners with other men in Limerick, and someone had given him those runners just before he was arrested in Ennis that time. It was all pie in the sky, but he was trying to create a reasonable doubt in the minds of the jury. But a jury of intelligent people were never going to buy into it, and ultimately they didn't.

A few weeks after finding the unique runner print at Paud Skehan's home, Detective Gilligan travelled back to O'Briensbridge once again. He sprayed the entire landing of Paud's home with the Amido Black chemical dye, and the crime scene effectively came alive once again. There was no doubt but that the footprints in Paud's blood were made at the time of his attack. There were drag marks visible over many of the runner prints, clearly showing that Paud had fallen to the ground after his killers stepped in his blood. Analysing the entire crime scene left the Gardaí in no doubt that whoever had worn the FILA runners had been present when Paud was tortured. This meant that when he was eventually charged with the murder, Campion could not turn around and claim he had merely been passing by and entered the house after the attack, and had panicked and ran away rather than raise the alarm. It would have been a fairly ludicrous suggestion anyway, but it might have created a doubt in the minds of some of the jury. But the crime scene investigation clearly proved that whoever wore the runners that night in April 1998 was a murderer.

The floorboards measuring about 20 feet by 15 feet were later taken to the foyer of the Ballistics Section of Garda Headquarters in Dublin and delicately laid out to re-create the floor space where Paud had been severely beaten and where Campion had stepped in his blood. Each floorboard was labelled and the entire floor space was photographed. The whole floor was now a potential exhibit in the murder trial.

When the FILA runner print was first identified, detectives hoped the second set of runner prints might be matched with Campion's fellow murderer. But despite a detailed examination of Paud's house, no print of these runners was clear enough to get a match that could lead to a prosecution. The scientists who examined the other prints believe the second killer might have worn a particular type of runner, but none of the prints these runners left in Paud's blood had enough identifiable wears or marks that could be matched to anyone. One detective tells me they have their firm suspicions about the identity of the other killer, but that's as far as the investigation has gone.

Once Campion was identified as one of the murderers, we naturally looked at people he would associate with and who he might go out thieving with. Sadly, when we're faced with drawing up a list of suspects capable of gratuitous violence we are never short of names, but we narrowed it down very quickly and focused on two young men as possible accomplices for Campion that night. Both are very dangerous individuals. One would have been a teenager at the time, but the more likely murderer was another man from Limerick who was close enough in age to Campion. But while we have our deep suspicions, that's sadly as far as we have been able to put the matter, and more than likely it will never be solved. I'll put it this way. Once it became common knowledge that a pair of runners had put Willie Campion in the frame for Paud's murder, I'd say another pair of runners met a very sorry and quick end in some part of Limerick. Possibly the only way we'll ever find out for definite who the second killer was, would be for Willie Campion to suddenly 'see the light', make a confession and give up his accomplice who has let him take the rap for the whole thing. But I don't see that happening. The only other way would be to hypnotise Campion and let him 'see the light' without even knowing it. It mightn't be admissible in court, but at least we could visit this other person and let him know we'd be watching him for ever.

When he finally stood trial for murder, Campion chose to take the witness stand to deny he had been one of the killers to tie up and torture Paud. He told the jury that the runners taken from his feet by the Gardaí in Ennis had been given to him by a friend of his cousin, and he said, 'If I was after killing a man I certainly wouldn't have them on my feet.' He said he swapped runners with friends 'hundreds of times', and on being asked what he had to say to the charges of murder and burglary, he said he was 'not guilty' and 'never done any of them'.

Just after 7 p.m. on Friday, 31 March 2000, Willie Campion was found guilty of the murder of Paud Skehan. The jury took less than four hours to reach a majority verdict of 11 to 1, finding Campion both guilty of murder and guilty of committing burglary at Paud's home. Some of Paud's family were actually on their way home to Co. Clare. They hadn't thought the verdict would come so quickly and had intended returning to Dublin the following day. The news of the guilty verdicts was quickly relayed to them and to friends and neighbours in O'Briensbridge. The Gardaí phoned their colleagues back in Clare and Limerick with the news that one of the most vicious criminals was going to prison for a very long time. The detectives had noted that the verdict of the jury was a majority one, and not unanimous. Despite the forensic evidence that the odds were of 'an astronomical nature' that runners other than Campion's had left the identifiable marks in Paud's blood, Campion had managed to raise enough doubt in the mind of one of the members of the jury. By suggesting he had swapped his runners with a friend of his cousin, Campion was trying to create the illusion that he might actually be innocent. However, the jury didn't buy into it, and they returned a verdict which rested easily with their consciences.

During the last week of Campion's murder trial, the case helped make legal history, when for the first time in the history of the State five murder trials were being heard simultaneously. Among the other cases was the trial of Catherine Nevin, who would shortly be convicted of the murder of her husband Tom, shot dead in a contract killing at his pub in Co. Wicklow in March 1997. Another trial was that of Mark Cronin, who was convicted of the murder of Georgina O'Donnell, shot dead with a handgun at a niteclub in Limerick in May 1998. The fourth trial under way at the Central Criminal Court was that of a Co. Cavan man charged with the murder of his mother who was strangled to death at her home; while at the Special Criminal Court, Belfast man Seán Hughes was on trial for the capital murder of Garda Patrick Reynolds who was shot dead in Tallaght, just over 18 years before in February 1982. The three-judge court would later find Hughes not guilty of the garda's murder. Each of the five murder cases served to remind society of the potential for extreme violence that existed in towns and cities and in rural parts of the country.

Right to the very end Campion maintained his swagger and his air of invincibility. Every day the 31-year old attended his murder trial in the company of a young woman, his latest girlfriend. Shortly after he was found guilty of murder he was allowed to spend ten minutes in the company of this woman just outside Court No. 3 at the round hall of the Four Courts, and they kissed and cuddled and said their goodbyes. Then he began his walk towards a prison van handcuffed to a prison officer. Those who had attended the trial and some curious onlookers watched as he was led away to begin his life sentence. As he left the round hall he saw Garda Jarlath Fahy, the man who had taken his FILA runners at Ennis Garda Station in April 1998. Fahy was on his mobile phone when Campion was brought past him. Suddenly Campion put out his hand, looked at Fahy, and without saying a word he shook the garda's hand. It was a most amazing moment, the closest Campion had ever come to making any form of admission in relation to Paud's murder. And then the killer with so many secrets was gone.

Paud Skehan's sister, Margaret Kennedy, didn't attend the murder trial. She remained at her home in Ardnatagle,

O'Briensbridge, close to Paud's old home, and she got the news from her family soon after the verdict. She tells me she is happy her brother got some form of justice.

> It was a terrible shock when Paud was attacked, and it was very sad to see him lying in hospital and suffering. Paud was always working, always tending to his cattle. He wasn't a man for travelling; he worked all his life. Although he never married he had a big family near him. All my children loved him dearly, and he was well known in farming circles and in the village. The Gardaí did a good job in catching one of the killers. I'm glad that at least they got one man for it.

Margaret's daughter-in-law Antoinette, who lives even closer to Paud's old house, says the attack on Paud changed all their lives for ever.

> We were terrified in the weeks after Paud was attacked. I was afraid to walk the lane. You never forget what happened. The first thing I did was get an alarm for the house, but I never thought we should move. We love this part of the country, it is normally so quiet, so rural, so peaceful. Paud's killers came from another place; they brought their violence with them.

In November 2003 Campion failed in his appeal against his conviction for the murder of Paud Skehan. Sporting a tight haircut and wearing a suit, shirt and tie, he remained handcuffed to a prison officer throughout the entire hearing of his appeal. He listened intently as his barrister claimed certain procedures had not been adhered to when his client's clothing had been taken at Ennis Garda Station four days after the attack on Paud. The barrister again repeated the argument that while the forensic evidence clearly put the FILA runners at the scene of the murder, it didn't necessarily follow that Campion had been the one wearing the runners, and that it was still possible that the runner mark had been left after the attack on Paud.

During the murder trial Campion had been surrounded by friends and family, and his young girlfriend had also been a familiar sight in court. Now over two and a half years later, he sat alone in the Court of Criminal Appeal with only prison officers for company. As people walked in and out of the courtroom, he never once turned his head to look for a familiar face. He didn't seem to be expecting anyone.

The three judges of the Appeal Court unanimously dismissed Campion's appeal against his murder conviction. The judges found there was enough evidence showing the runner print had been left in Paud Skehan's blood at the time of the drag marks, showing that the person who wore the runners had been one of the killers. They dismissed all suggestions that procedures had not been followed in seizing Campion's clothing at Ennis Garda Station, and they also said there was no valid reason to interfere with the verdict of the jury. Campion's murder conviction was safe and the life sentence would stand.

Paud's nephew, Paddy Kennedy, says he knows Campion may not spend the rest of his life in prison. He says more should be done to ensure society is protected from such murderers.

The way things are going, life doesn't always mean life. If Campion is released down the line, will he have learned his lesson, will he have changed his ways? Will he just be left out there on his own with the authorities saying 'good luck now' to him, or will there be someone to keep a watch over him?

When Campion's appeal against his murder conviction was dismissed, his barrister tried a different tack by trying to get the nine-year sentence for the burglary of Paud's property reduced. A reduction in that sentence might go some way to convincing the Parole Board in decades to come that Campion might not be such a danger to every man, woman and child. Campion's barrister correctly pointed out that it wasn't clear if anything of value had been taken from the house, and that for the ten years prior to the murder of Paud Skehan, his client had not been in serious trouble. The prosecution barrister countered. While that was technically correct, Campion had spent around seven of those years in prison for aggravated burglary, so it was only true to say he had a 'clean slate' for three years prior to Paud's murder. The three judges of the court, who never had the pleasure of meeting Paud Skehan, didn't attach great weight as to whether or not items of value had been taken from the house. What concerned them was the principle that Paud's home had been violently invaded. Chief Justice Ronan Keane said the attack on Paud Skehan was a 'really appalling crime', and he said the court would not reduce the nine-year sentence for aggravated burglary.

Campion didn't flinch as the appeal against his murder conviction was dismissed. He didn't say a word when the judges refused to reduce the concurrent sentence for robbery. He was a hard man who helped torture and murder a 68-year-old man, and he wasn't going to let anyone know if he was upset.

Just as the three judges of the Appeal Court were about to leave, the Chief Justice chose to make a final comment. He and the other two judges had spent the previous three hours listening to an outline of how Campion had been convicted of murder. They had listened to how the scene of Paud's murder had been preserved from the arrival of the Gardaí on the morning of Good

Friday 1998. They had listened to how a specialist crime scene examiner had spotted the runner print in blood on the wooden floorboard, and how a uniformed garda had the foresight to take clothing from a wet and miserable Willie Campion at Ennis Garda Station while investigating crimes that had occurred hours earlier in Gort, as well as any other crimes. The judges knew that Campion's conviction was unique. It united dogged detective work with that great element of chance. It was purely by chance that Campion was caught acting suspiciously in Ennis four days after attacking Paud, and purely by chance he was still wearing crucial evidence linking him to the murder. But the Gardaí in Ennis, Killaloe, Garda Headquarters and beyond had shown that when they got lucky breaks they could really do something special. As Campion was led back to prison to continue his life sentence, the Chief Justice went out of his way to state: 'In relation to this case, the conduct of the investigation by the Gardaí merits the highest praise. It was excellent police work.'

11

Remembering Brian

Brian Mulvaney ran as fast as he could. The teenager couldn't understand what was happening. Why was he being attacked? He ran out the back entrance of the Orwell shopping centre across a grass verge. It was the early hours of 11 March 2000, and Brian was in the middle of an estate in Templeogue in south Dublin. There were houses all around him, but it was dark. The first punch had stunned Brian, coming out of nowhere. He ran back in the direction of the party, where he had left his jacket. One of his attackers had lured him out of the house-party just a short time before. Brian didn't know that this young man was actually one of the most dangerous thugs that ever walked the streets of Dublin. He didn't know 21-year-old Brian Willoughby had already assaulted three people in separate attacks and that one of his victims had lost an eye. Brian Mulvaney didn't know this seemingly friendly young man was actually out on bail awaiting sentence for the three assaults. And so he had felt safe walking with this man to the nearby shopping centre, where other youths had also gathered. He had never met Willoughby before; Brian was from Firhouse, a few miles away across the River

Dodder. He had come to Templeogue because he was interested in a girl who was at the house-party. But now he was running for his life. Willoughby had suddenly attacked him, punching him viciously. And there was a second attacker, another young man he had never met before, who was also assaulting him for no reason. As he ran from the area of the shopping centre towards a grass verge near a row of houses known as the Watercourse, he was fast getting away from his pursuers. But there was a third person chasing him, someone quicker, someone who stopped Brian's getaway, but someone whom a jury would later find not guilty of murder. Neal Barbour caught up with Brian and within seconds Willoughby and Stephen Ahearne were there too. Over the following moments Willoughby and Ahearne kicked and punched Brian as he lay helpless on the road. Ahearne picked up a stick and beat Brian with the weapon. In another sickening aspect of the assault, Willoughby stamped repeatedly on Brian's head shouting, 'This is carnage. This is deadly.' There was no motive for this attack, no reasoning; it was purely an act of despicable random violence against a decent young man. A short time earlier Brian Mulvaney had been laughing and joking with people at a party and chatting up a girl he fancied. Now he lay dying in the middle of the road.

The murder of Brian Mulvaney is a deeply saddening crime. One particularly distressing aspect of the murder is that the person who led the gang that attacked Brian should have been locked away by the time he committed murder. Willoughby should never have been on the streets of Dublin in March 2000. In late 1999 he had stood at Dublin Circuit Criminal Court and pleaded guilty to three unprovoked and random attacks during which he used either broken bottles or knives to inflict terrible injuries on three men. But despite making full admissions to these crimes, including one where Willoughby told the Gardaí, 'I slashed him, and slashed him, and slashed him', he was actually out on bail awaiting sentence for the three attacks when he attended the same house-party as Brian Mulvaney.

The night before Brian was murdered, he and his Dad Larry went to visit his Mum in St Vincent's Hospital in Dublin. Annie Mulvaney was recovering from an operation and she was delighted to see the two of them. Brian was cracking jokes and had everyone laughing and in great form. That was the type of person he was, always with something to say, full of jokes, full of life. The circumstances of Brian's violent and lonely death are in total contrast to the life he led. His murder has caused unimaginable pain for his parents and his younger sister Aoife, but they also have many good memories of a young man who brought joy and happiness to those around him. Annie Mulvaney tells me her son was full of fun.

When Brian entered the room you knew someone had entered the room. He was extravagant, full of laughter. He spoke loudly and a bit like myself he used his hands to gesture. He was the life and soul of the party; he left people feeling good. He had such a big smile, a smile up to his eyes. My last hour or so with him was very good. It was a good happy night in the hospital.

At the time of his murder, Brian Mulvaney had taken a year out. He was due to start college in Bolton Street the following October. He wanted to be an architect and joked with his sister that when she got a well-paid job she could pay him to design her house. Larry smiles as he remembers how his son was at an exciting period in his life.

Brian wanted to be an architect, but he didn't want to work hard to get there. He was very bright and he just did enough study to get what he wanted. His first year in college would have been a torment for him with all that work, but Brian had just turned a corner. He was coming to understand what life was all about; he was growing from a teenager into a young man. Brian was just a really nice bloke. There was not a bad bone in his body. He was very loud; he'd make so much noise when he was around. He'd sing in the shower; he'd give it loads. He had ideas and opinions about everything, and we had great conversations.

Larry Mulvaney said goodnight to his son at 10.20 p.m. on 11 March 2000. Brian was heading out with friends to Templeogue. With Annie still in hospital and Aoife away at an adventure centre in Co. Mayo, it had just been the two men in the house for the previous few days. As a friend called to collect Brian, Larry jokingly reminded him that he was due to cook dinner the following day. Brian turned to his Dad and smiled saying, 'Don't worry about it. I have it all under control.' He said goodnight to his Dad and then he was gone. Just a few hours after leaving his home in Firhouse, Brian Mulvaney would be attacked and murdered by a gang led by Willoughby.

It was in October 1997 when he was 19 years old that Brian Willoughby committed his first serious random attack. He was on a No. 15 bus in Dublin city centre with a gang of three other youths when they committed an unprovoked attack on another youth. The victim was stabbed in the face and hand with a broken bottle, suffering damage to his right cheek, his arm and his hands. Willoughby was arrested the following month and a file was sent to the Director of Public Prosecutions. But by the time he was charged with assault he had committed two further serious random attacks in Dublin city.

In January 1998 Willoughby and another youth attacked a man who was walking alone on Lower Baggot Street. Willoughby confronted the man and produced a small knife he had concealed in the hood of his jacket. He stabbed the man in the face, neck and hand, as well as punching and kicking him. The second attacker had backed off after punching the man, but Willoughby continued beating his terrified victim. Willoughby then ran away but was arrested by the Gardaí a short distance from the scene of the attack. He readily admitted carrying out the assault, claiming falsely that his victim had made a sexual suggestion to him. The victim of the knife attack needed 100 stitches. As with the attack on the bus, Willoughby was released from custody and a file was sent to the DPP. Willoughby was still out of control and still at liberty, and he was about to commit a third vicious assault.

On 10 February 1998 Willoughby stabbed a man in the face in Dublin's Dame Street in an attack that is shocking both in its depravity and its audacity. It was around 8.30 p.m. and the victim had been approached at random by Willoughby who tried to strike up a conversation with him. Willoughby asked the man if he was gay, and followed him across the road. The man was extremely distressed by this person following him on a public street and talking to him in an aggressive manner. The man tried to get a bus on the Temple Bar side of Dame Street, but when Willoughby said to him, 'I'm coming with you', the man hurried across to the other side of the street. However, Willoughby followed him and began punching him on the pathway. As the man recoiled from the blows, he suddenly realised he was being stabbed as well as punched. The man suffered a number of stab wounds to his face, and all the tendons in his right wrist were severed as he tried to fend off the blows of the knife. The man lost the sight in one of his eyes as a result of the attack. As Willoughby committed this brazen random assault, he shouted something like, 'You're a big fat queer.' He then ran off towards Kevin Street and it wasn't until the next day that he was arrested. Once again Willoughby made a full admission, telling the Gardaí how he had drunk six or seven cans of cider in the city centre in the hours before carrying out the attack. He was charged with the assault but was granted bail. He was also charged with the attacks carried out on the bus in the city centre and on Lower Baggot Street. It would be almost two years before he would be sentenced for these crimes. In the meantime, he was free to roam the streets of Dublin, including his own neighbourhood in Templeogue.

One garda who investigated Willoughby's crimes says it is very frustrating to consider how he was at liberty to commit so many random attacks.

What gets on my nerves is to think of how Willoughby carried out his assaults in public places — on a bus, on two city streets, and finally on a road in the middle of Templeogue. Despite being arrested for each of the three city centre attacks, Willoughby continued to commit random crimes. He simply didn't care. I often think that the killers who are most dangerous are the ones who don't care whether or not they are caught. Brian Willoughby didn't care about covering his tracks. He never thought that far ahead, he simply wanted to hurt people, and because of a slow justice system he found the opportunity to commit four serious attacks, including the murder of Brian Mulvaney.

As Brian Mulvaney was out enjoying the night in a pub with his friends, he got a phone call from a girl inviting him over to a party at a house in Templeogue. He knew three of the girls who would be at the party — Orla, Aileen and Suzanne. Brian was keen on Suzanne and he decided to head over. His friends said that because Brian was going to see one particular girl, there was no need for them to go to the party as well, and one friend said he'd drop Brian over.

For Brian to go to a house-party where he knew only a few girls displayed a good deal of self-confidence. He fitted in wherever he went, he could keep a conversation going and made friends easily. One young person who was at the party described him as 'being like a surfer from *Home and Away*'.

Willoughby was looking at Brian Mulvaney. He was at the house-party too. He had yet to be sentenced for the three city centre attacks carried out over two years before. He didn't know Brian, but he saw how he was fitting in, making people laugh, talking to girls. Willoughby had previously attacked people for no reason other than taking a dislike to them. He was now taking a dislike to Brian Mulvaney for the simple fact that Brian was a likeable person. Willoughby was planning to commit another attack.

To look at Willoughby in a shirt and tie and wearing glasses, he would almost pass for a normal person. But beneath the clothing was someone filled with incredible rage. He has over a dozen tattoos, many of which signify a capacity for extreme violence. The most elaborate design is a machine gun tattooed on his lower right arm. Also on his right arm he has the phrase, 'Rot in Hell', while his left arm features the slogan 'Kill at Will.' Another phrase on this arm is 'Anger is a Gift.' However, none of these tattoos was visible at the house-party that night and he appeared to be like any other young person laughing away, enjoying the music and acting cool.

At some stage Willoughby got talking to Brian and he invited him down to the shopping centre where he was going for cigarette papers. Brian didn't know of Willoughby's violent reputation. He thought he was just being friendly, and so he agreed to head over to the shops.

Brian's other killer, Stephen Ahearne, was also heading for the Orwell Park Shopping Centre. He and fellow teenager Neal Barbour had been out drinking in the Terenure area and had already been involved in two separate unprovoked attacks. They had been walking up Templeogue Road when they attacked a youth walking alone. The youth suffered slight cuts to his head after being struck with a pint glass. Ahearne and Barbour continued walking up towards Templeogue village, where they started to taunt three young men coming out of a pub. They chased after the three men but couldn't catch them. They walked on into the Orwell estate and met another youth who was out driving and showing off. Ahearne and Barbour took a lift towards the shops in Orwell.

Shortly after arriving at the shopping centre, Ahearne met Willoughby. Ahearne knew Willoughby as Willers, while Ahearne was known by the nickname Gookie. Ahearne was only in his mid-teens but he liked to think of himself as a hard man. He knew Willoughby was a dangerous character and he liked that. Brian Mulvaney was standing a short distance away and couldn't hear the conversation between Ahearne and Willoughby. He didn't sense any danger.

Willoughby told Ahearne that Brian Mulvaney was 'from Knocklyon' — an estate near Brian's home in Firhouse — and he said something like 'That fellow there is calling us queers. ... He hates Orwell. ... Let's get him.' Having already committed two random attacks within the previous hour, Ahearne didn't need much persuasion to assist Willoughby in his plan to attack Brian. Two young thugs were about to gang up on an innocent young man for no other reason than to cause hurt.

In the years before Willoughby finally committed murder, he would fantasise about causing pain to other people. He had a severe form of attention deficit hyperactivity disorder for much of his life, and he was extremely homophobic. He would often feel that men who were looking at him were homosexuals. He sometimes harmed himself when he was in a demented state. He would claim he was 'wired up the wrong way', and although he spent time in the Central Mental Hospital, the jury at his murder trial would later accept evidence that he did not have a mental disorder, but rather he had a conduct disorder and that he knew right from wrong. When he decided to organise a gang to attack Brian Mulvaney, Willoughby was in control of his actions. His actions may have been abnormal, but he was not insane. He knew what he was doing.

Willoughby would often record news bulletins on his VCR and look for scenes with any type of violence. He liked to watch news reports where police forces clashed with protestors, or violent incidents at sports events. He would then play back the video and using a hand-held camera he would record the scenes once again, but this time he would put his own voice over the real-life violent scenes, cheering when punches were thrown or when fights became particularly nasty. One detective says Willoughby had clearly planned for an attack such as the one he carried out against Brian Mulvaney.

What I think is interesting is that Willoughby liked to watch real-life violence. It wasn't horror films or action adventure type stuff; this was real news footage. It would certainly make you wonder about the effect of showing such scenes on the news. It's scary to think of what certain people take from watching the news. Willoughby would even get a thrill out of watching dirty tackles in football matches. But although he had all these violent thoughts, he was able to pass himself off to many people as a nice young lad. He was able to control his lust for violence. And he was a coward as well. He always had to either be carrying a weapon or be with a gang of fellow thugs before he'd attack innocent people. In school he would doodle on his copy books and would draw violent scenes. He was once asked to draw his neighbourhood and he drew two scenes: one scene was by day which was all very nice with trees and dogs and the like; and then the night scene had a person lying injured on the street. It was a scene very like what sadly happened to Brian Mulvaney.

At first Brian was too fast for the killers. If Neal Barbour hadn't caught up with him and began to tussle with him, Brian might well be alive today. And when Barbour stood back and witnessed Ahearne and Willoughby attacking Brian, he did nothing to try and stop the assault. Ultimately, a jury found Barbour not guilty of murder. In Barbour's statement to the Gardaí he said he had his back to the group when he heard sounds of a commotion, turned around and saw Brian running away while being chased by Ahearne and Willoughby. Barbour had arrived at the Orwell Park Shopping Centre with Ahearne and he didn't know Brian Mulvaney either. But for some reason he ran after Brian, and after about 100 yards he caught up with him. Brian was six feet one and he was fit, but he was also stunned after Willoughby and Ahearne had begun punching him. As Barbour started pulling at Brian's clothing, preventing his getaway, Brian's brown hooded top and his white T-shirt were pulled off him. As Ahearne and Willoughby began their assault, Brian was left bare-chested in the middle of the road. And then as people slept in their beds near by, Ahearne and Willoughby killed 19-year-old Brian Mulvaney. A jury would later find Ahearne guilty of manslaughter, while Willoughby would be convicted of murder.

Larry Mulvaney opened the front door of his home and saw two Gardaí. Detectives Joe Molloy and Joe McLoughlin were bringing the most upsetting news. It was some time after a young man had been found lying fatally injured in the middle of the road in Templeogue, and the Gardaí believed it might be Brian. The people who had found Brian on the road had called for an ambulance but they hadn't called the Gardaí. It was only when Brian was taken to Tallaght Hospital and when doctors looked at his injuries that they realised Brian had been the victim of an attack. He had suffered repeated blows to the head. The doctors phoned the Gardaí and detectives were sent immediately to the Watercourse and the area around Orwell Park Shopping Centre. The Gardaí sealed off the location where Brian had been found and one garda found a button from Brian's Pepe jeans. His hooded top and T-shirt would later be found thrown into a nearby back garden, and the stick that Stephen Ahearne used to help kill Brian was dumped in undergrowth close by. Some of the girls who had been at the house-party had come down to the scene. One of them held a man's jacket. The girl said it belonged to Brian Mulvaney, who had left it in the house when he went out for a walk with another young man, and he hadn't returned. Brian's passport was inside his jacket pocket, and the detectives feared that the young man who had lost his life was Brian.

Larry Mulvaney didn't immediately recognise his son when he saw Brian's body at the hospital. He had suffered a lot of soft tissue damage to his face. His cheek and his chin were cut and his lip had bled profusely. As Brian lay in the middle of the road, he had fallen unconscious after Ahearne beat him with a wooden stick and Willoughby 'danced' on his head. Because he was concussed, he had a suppressed cough reflex. Brian died after suffocating on his own blood. If any of his attackers had turned him on his side, he might not have inhaled so much blood and might have been saved. But after carrying out their callous and random beating, his attackers left him lying unconscious on the road. They didn't raise the alarm, they didn't make an anonymous emergency call, and they allowed the teenager to die.

Aoife Mulvaney was 15 years old when her only brother was murdered. Over the following three years Aoife's life and that of her parents would be dominated not only by the loss of Brian but by the trial of the three alleged murderers. Aoife has many fond memories of her big brother.

Brian was quite protective of me as his little sister. As kids we fought like cat and dog, and then as we got older we had things in common and we did things together, and we got on really well. He liked my friends and I liked his. He was at the stage that any time our parents were away he'd throw a huge big bash in the house, and if he wasn't on my good side there was no way a party could happen. And then because he was the older brother I was always allowed to bring friends over and it was really cool. Everybody thought he was great. I miss Brian all the time.

When Larry Mulvaney saw his son's injuries, he knew Brian hadn't been knocked down or injured in any type of accident. The Gardaí were still trying to establish what exactly had gone on at the location where Brian had been found lying on the road, but they more or less told Larry that sadly it appeared Brian had been beaten up. Larry had to go to his wife, who was still in St Vincent's Hospital, and tell her their son was dead. Annie was recovering after an operation, and in an effort to protect his wife Larry initially told her that Brian had died in an accident.

Aoife Mulvaney was preparing to travel home from Westport when she got the news. She had been doing a week's work experience at an adventure centre and was getting on the train with three other girls. She heard the news on the radio about a young man being attacked and killed in Templeogue. She told one of the other girls that she lived close to Templeogue and she wondered who that person was. Then she got a call on her mobile from a friend who said that one of 'the lads' might have been killed. She immediately rang home and asked her Dad if Brian had come home. Larry couldn't talk. He dropped the phone, and Aoife found herself talking to her Mum. Aoife knew Annie was supposed to be in hospital and she knew then that something terrible had happened. Annie now knew that Brian's death was not an accident. Aoife still had to travel all the way from Mayo to Dublin before being reunited with her parents. It was the saddest day of their lives.

After killing Brian Mulvaney, Willoughby and Ahearne walked up to the house-party from where Willoughby had earlier lured Brian away to his death. It was Ahearne's first time at the party. He had blood on his clothing and he and Willoughby claimed they had been in a fight with a gang from a local neighbourhood.

Garda Tom Stack sat down with many of the young men and women who had been at the house-party. By this time Willoughby and Ahearne had left the house, parted company and gone home. Stack had previously been a community garda and was known to many of the young people in the area. A number of the group had been drinking heavily and some had taken drugs, but the enormity of what had just happened to Brian Mulvaney was sinking in fast, and the party atmosphere had been replaced by shock and sadness. The Gardaí received a very mature reception from the youths when they started asking who had been in the house and who might know what had happened. The detectives were quickly given the names of Brian Willoughby and Stephen Ahearne.

How Willoughby ever came to attack Brian Mulvaney will forever be a cause of great frustration and upset for the victim's family and indeed for the Gardaí, who consistently caught Willoughby for some of the most horrendous attacks ever witnessed in Dublin, only to see him allowed back out on the streets. In December 1999, three months before he murdered Brian Mulvaney, Willoughby had stood in the Dublin Circuit Criminal Court, having pleaded guilty to carrying out the three random attacks in Dublin city in 1997 and 1998. For stabbing three men in three random attacks, the detectives believed he was facing the prospect of a lengthy sentence. But he wasn't sentenced in December 1999, and instead of being kept in custody and against the strong opinion of the Gardaí, he was released on bail.

In April 2000, one month after the murder of Brian Mulvaney, Willoughby stood in court to be sentenced for the three random attacks over two years before. He was now in custody charged with Brian's murder. The court heard how one of Willoughby's victims from 1998 had lost the sight of one eye. Judge Elizabeth Dunne heard that Willoughby had been in a motorbike accident shortly after committing the three attacks and had spent a week on a life-support machine. The judge read psychiatric reports describing how Willoughby was an extremely disturbed young man but was not suffering mental illness. She sentenced him to a total of five years in prison for the bus attack and the attacks carried out at Lower Baggot Street and Dame Street. The sentence was to start immediately. The court was told that he was now also facing a murder charge — for an offence committed while on bail.

As Willoughby began his five-year sentence, the justice system was finally starting to deal effectively with an incredibly dangerous person. However, this action came one month too late for 19-year-old Brian Mulvaney, a decent young man whose life could have been saved if the justice system had previously listened to the Gardaí, kept Willoughby off the streets and dealt with his other admitted crimes more speedily.

Brian Mulvaney's parents are deeply upset at the fact that their son was murdered by a man who was out on bail despite pleading guilty to three other violent assaults. To Larry and Annie, and to many others, it simply defies logic that Willoughby could have found himself free to commit murder, having already admitted carrying out those other attacks. Annie says the problems with the bail laws in this country must be addressed.

> In relation to the bail issue, I will keep fighting for changes. I think the bail laws are wrong. People out on bail commit so much of the crime in this country. Our son met a criminal that night that he shouldn't have met because that criminal should have been in prison. I don't know why it takes so long for a person to be sentenced when they admit a crime. What is the problem? If they need psychiatric reports, why aren't they ready already? If the same crimes were committed in France, for example, Willoughby would not have been out on bail when he murdered Brian. If you plead guilty to a crime in France, you are sentenced on the same day. Why didn't that happen for Willoughby at the Circuit Criminal Court?

Larry Mulvaney agrees and continues:

> When someone pleads guilty to random assaults, why not put them into custody immediately? Even if the judge is not able to sentence them on the day, if they've pleaded guilty they are convicted criminals and should be held in prison until they are sentenced. How can someone like Willoughby, who admits random crimes, be granted bail? It wasn't like he robbed sweets from a shop; he committed serious crimes against three different people, and yet he was allowed out on bail, and during that time he murdered Brian. If you are out on bail you should wear a tag that can alert the Gardaí if you leave your house, but Willoughby shouldn't have been out on bail in the first place.

A short time before his murder, Brian went to visit his relatives in France. His mother had come to Ireland when she was 19, and now at around the same age Brian was visiting his mother's homeland. Larry Mulvaney had met his future wife while attending a Celtic festival in France. He and Annie were married in a village south of Paris in 1980, and Brian was born in Dublin the following year. He loved to visit his mother's side of the family. He loved practising his French with an Irish accent. While he was there a cousin taught him how to cook spaghetti carbonara, and he was really proud of himself.

Brian loved being around people and he loved children. He used to tell his family he wanted to have loads of children. His family would laugh when he said this, and they'd ask who he thought he'd find who would have all these children with him. And Brian would smile and say it was grand, he'd find someone.

Shortly after Brian's family received the news that he had been

killed, the Gardaí were also bringing news that the people believed
to be responsible were being charged with murder. And so began a
long and upsetting process which would take three years before a
jury would finally give verdicts in the cases of the three accused.
Aoife Mulvaney had turned 18 by the time the trial finally began.
She remembers how her family were simply drained by the court
experience.

> You come home from court and you don't know what to do.
> You're just so anxious all the time. About a month before the
> trial in 2003, I got a sick feeling, and you never get rid of that
> horrible feeling, and you end up so tired. It took so much out of
> us all. For weeks after the trial, all you want to do is sleep. And
> we were so angry as well that we had to go through this.

In March 2003 Brian Willoughby, Stephen Ahearne and Neal
Barbour stood trial for the murder of Brian Mulvaney. The jury
listened carefully to the evidence of how Willoughby had lured
Brian to the Orwell Park Shopping Centre and had then enlisted
the assistance of Ahearne in attacking Brian without warning. The
jury also heard how Barbour was the one who caught up with Brian
as he tried to flee his attackers, and how Barbour had then backed
off and didn't intervene to stop the attack. The jury found
Willoughby guilty of murder, Ahearne guilty of manslaughter, and
Barbour not guilty. Willoughby was given an automatic life
sentence; Ahearne was remanded in custody for sentence; and
Barbour walked free from the court. As the members of the jury
were thanked for their great attention to the case, many of them
were visibly stunned to learn that Aherne and Barbour still faced
charges relating to violent attacks carried out on the same night
Brian was beaten to death. Meanwhile, Aoife Mulvaney had run

from the court distraught. She remembers the mixed emotions of that day.

When I jumped up and left, I think it was the shock, you know. You wait for something to happen and then they come out and it's so flippantly said, and all of a sudden it's done and that's it. When you're told to come back into court, you're not told there is a verdict. It could be that the jury is checking something. But they just said they had reached a verdict and that was it. It's so strange to be in two minds, because you are so happy about the murder verdict and the manslaughter verdict, but there is someone else that the State felt there was enough evidence against, but he's found not guilty. It's very difficult to be happy, and very difficult to be upset. And then at the end of it you realise that Brian still isn't coming back, and that's even a bigger shock because it all comes to an end, but it doesn't really come to an end.

As Willoughby was given his automatic life sentence and quickly led out of the court, the Mulvaneys were not given the opportunity to address the court about the impact the murder of their teenage son had on their lives. When Ahearne came to be sentenced for manslaughter six months later, Larry Mulvaney took the witness stand to outline some of the trauma Brian's violent death had caused to himself, Annie, Aoife and all Brian's family and friends. Mr Justice Barry White also heard evidence of the other attacks Ahearne had carried out in the Terenure/Templeogue area in the hour before he killed Brian. Ahearne's family had told him to tell the truth to the detectives, and the judge took his co-operation with the Gardaí into account. He was jailed for ten years.

In June 2004 Neal Barbour returned to the Central Criminal Court where he had been found not guilty of Brian's murder. He pleaded guilty to the two random assaults on young men which occurred in the hours before he had chased Brian in Templeogue. Barbour was jailed for 18 months.

Larry Mulvaney tells me how it was difficult to adapt to life after the trial.

It was three years after Brian's murder before the trial was heard and the verdicts reached, and then we had to wait six months for the sentencing of Ahearne. And then when all that was finished, it was like someone had robbed your crutch. You focus so much for three and a half years of your life on a court case, waiting for something to happen, and then for that to be over, and you're left with total emptiness. All of the things that have been hidden way for three years all of a sudden explode on top of you and it's very difficult to deal with. I think the trial process went on far too long; they had the people that did it, yet it took so long. It shouldn't take three and a half years for a criminal case to be concluded. After the trial we were trying to get back to some type of normality and it was very difficult. We were trying to get to the stage in our lives where we were before Brian was murdered, but you never get to that stage because it doesn't exist any more.

The securing of a murder conviction against Willoughby reflected the fact that the killer had plotted to attack Brian. It wasn't a spur of the moment assault; it was a planned murder. His murder is one of a number of random killings of young men attacked late at night in Ireland in recent years. One such crime was the gang attack on Brian Murphy on the roadside outside

Annabel's Niteclub in Dublin in August of 2000. Like Brian Mulvaney, Brian Murphy was repeatedly kicked and punched as he lay on the ground. The Director of Public Prosecutions directed that four young men face trial for manslaughter — one was later convicted, two were convicted of violent disorder, and one young man walked free. The Mulvaneys were among those providing comfort and support to the Murphy family during the trial at the Dublin Circuit Criminal Court in 2004.

In late 2004 the Mulvaney family joined with a number of families of murder victims and formed a group to campaign for changes within the justice system so as to greater protect society. AdVic (Advocates for Victims of Murder) will highlight many issues that need urgent attention, including the need to give a true and proper meaning to the term 'life imprisonment'.

As well as seeking to highlight the problems with the bail laws and with the delays in the justice system, the Mulvaneys are understandably concerned about the lack of a proper sentencing policy for convicted murderers. Willoughby was 24 years old when he was jailed for life for the murder of Brian Mulvaney. He has spent much of his sentence at Mountjoy Prison and has occasionally spent time at the Central Mental Hospital. Under the current policy of treating all murderers in the same manner, Willoughby will be allowed to start applying for parole by the time he is in his mid-thirties. It is highly unlikely that he will be granted any form of parole for a very long time to come, but on the other hand there is the sad reality that even after stabbing men at random, he still found himself walking the streets of Dublin until he murdered Brian Mulvaney. The prospect of Willoughby ever being released would instil immense fear in the community of Templeogue, and would horrify both the Gardaí and Brian's family. One detective says he will be watching

Willoughby's progress through the prison system for as long as he's alive.

Basically it is killers like Willoughby that are a danger to every man, woman and child. Willoughby killed without reason, without motive, and he was legally sane when he did it. Given a chance, I believe he would randomly kill again. The whole ethos of the prison system is to try and rehabilitate prisoners. Well, I can tell you I don't care if he is a pensioner when he gets release, he would still be a danger to every man, woman and child. But as time goes on, the problem with these killers is that their crime becomes forgotten, certainly not by the victim's family but by the authorities. My fear is that in 15, 20 or 30 years' time Willoughby will apply for parole, and it will fall to someone who is currently a child to make the decision, and they may consider giving him a chance. And Willoughby has this 'butter wouldn't melt in his mouth' look about him. It must never be forgotten that he has claimed the life of one innocent young man and has left three others scarred for life.

Larry Mulvaney agrees that his son's murderer should remain in prison for the rest of his life.

I think it's especially important that people focus on these criminals, killers like Willoughby who are intent on hurting others. And whether it's 20 years or 40 years' time or whenever, the intent is still going to be there. If Willoughby was ever let out, his brain won't have changed. There are not many murderers like that. There are only a few, but unfortunately our son met one of them. Willoughby knows right from wrong, he is a very cunning person, and I personally believe that if he was ever let out, he would commit murder again. I think when society looks at someone who is a bad egg, society needs to say, 'That is a bad egg and that bad egg is never ever going to change.'

Larry and Annie have many treasured photographs of their son — Brian playing the guitar, laughing with his sister, play-acting with friends, smiling with his parents. He was a charmer, the type who would never be refused entry anywhere because he'd charm his way in. He loved to liven up parties by singing songs. The Mulvaneys have many happy memories of a son who was just becoming a man, and who was full of life. Aoife Mulvaney tells me how she misses her brother.

I'll always miss him. I do try and get on with my life, but I miss him. Sometimes I forget what has happened, and I see guys who look like him and for a second I think it's Brian. That sounds crazy because it's such a huge thing that has happened. But there are even times that I wake up in the middle of the night and hear a sound and I think, 'That's Brian coming home. It's OK.' It was always the two of us growing up and then to suddenly have a life without my older brother is very strange. Sometimes I'd still say things like 'Brian does that', and then I'd say 'Sorry, Brian did that.' I go into his room and it still smells of him. Even now you walk in and it's like he was in there yesterday. People always say to me do you have any brothers or sisters, and I always say I have a brother. I mean he mightn't be here, but I have a brother.

12

Fifteen plus Life

Peter Whelan didn't speak a word as he repeatedly stabbed 19-year-old Sinéad O'Leary and 20-year-old Nichola Sweeney. Having broken into Nichola's home and crept up the stairs, turning off lights as he went, he didn't make a sound as he approached her bedroom. Removing one knife from his belt, and then another, an evil grin enveloped the teenager's face as he confronted the young women and carried out the random attack. He first attacked Sinéad, standing over her as she lay on the floor and stabbing her repeatedly in her arms, chest and stomach. When one knife broke in Sinéad's arm, he took a second knife from his belt and went towards Nichola, who ran towards her en-suite bathroom. Thinking her friend had managed to get to the safety of the bathroom, Sinéad, bleeding from her arms and stomach, managed to drag herself downstairs and hid in another bathroom. But upstairs, Nichola hadn't been able to get the bathroom door locked and Whelan kicked the door in, putting his boot right through. Over the following harrowing moments Nichola suffered 11 stab wounds, including one that pierced her heart, and she died on her bedroom floor. The life of one young woman had just been ended in the most vicious and cruel of circumstances, and the life of another was changed for ever. The attack lasted just a matter of minutes, and then 19-year-old random murderer Peter Whelan was gone, walking the short distance to his own house. There was no logic, no reason and no motive. There was only silence.

Just minutes before the attack, Nichola and Sinéad had been putting the last touches to their make-up before heading out for the night in Cork city. Sinéad sat on the end of Nichola's bed, while Nichola was looking in a mirror in her bathroom. It was 10.55 p.m. on the night of 27 April 2002. The teenagers had the house to themselves as Nichola's brother Seán had just headed over to a friend across the city. Nichola's parents, John and Josephine, and her little 4-year-old brother, Christopher, were in London for the weekend. So Nichola and Sinéad were alone, chatting and laughing, preparing for a Saturday night on the town. And they had much to talk about; the two friends hadn't seen much of each other in a while, as Sinéad was in college in Dublin. But now she was back in Cork for the Easter break and really taking it easy. The pair had originally planned to stay in and watch a film; Sinéad was cooking chicken and mushroom pasta. But their friends had phoned a couple of times to entice them into town, and although it was late enough it didn't take much persuading to get Nichola and Sinéad to change their plans. The taxi was ordered and the two prepared to head into the city.

Nichola's bedroom window was open, and as Peter Whelan sneaked around the back of the house, he heard the voices of both women. He didn't know Sinéad, and he barely knew Nichola as a neighbour. They had never spoken. But now he was breaking into his neighbour's house intent on killing someone. He tried the front door but it was locked. When he tried the back door he found it was open.

The taxi was due to collect Nichola and Sinéad at around a quarter past eleven. But the two were ready with 20 minutes to spare. As Sinéad finished her make-up she called out to Nichola, asking if she should ring the taxi to come that little bit earlier. It was to be the last conversation the teenagers would have. From her position at the end of Nichola's bed, Sinéad could see down the landing. All of a sudden she saw a figure coming towards the bedroom. Before she could register what was happening, Whelan was in the room.

Sinéad O'Leary is a remarkable woman. She's a survivor who, in the face of terror that most of us will never experience, displayed an incredible presence of mind that helped catch her friend's killer. When the Gardaí later arrived at the scene of the attack Sinéad, bleeding, exhausted and distraught, was able to mumble the crucial description: '... grey top, goatee beard ... shaved head ... blue jeans'. Sinéad's physical scars will heal to some degree in time, but the memory of sitting with her friend who lay dying will remain with her. Sinéad tells me her clear memory of the attack.

When Whelan came into the bedroom, the only part I can't remember at all is that first second or two. I do know I was on the floor within seconds. I either fell or was pushed and he was stamping on me and punching me. I was calling out to Nichola and she came out of her en-suite. Then he pulled up his shirt and looked over at her, showing her the knives. And then he just started lashing down on me with one of the knives. The attack on me lasted about 60 seconds.

As Nichola looked on both stunned and horrified, Whelan stabbed Sinéad four times in the chest, three times in the stomach, once in the back and a number of times on her arms. Standing over his victim, he was intent on committing murder. He aimed the knife at Sinéad's chest and stomach, but he wasn't looking down at his victim; he was looking towards Nichola, who was screaming at him to stop. With Whelan distracted by Nichola, Sinéad was able to use her arms to protect herself from certain death. Her right arm suffered most of the damage as the knife broke in her arm. Still not saying a word or making a sound, Whelan took out a second knife from his belt, a larger knife, and lunged towards Nichola.

Just months before he murdered Nichola Sweeney, the Gardaí became aware of just how violent Whelan was. The most extreme example of his dangerous behaviour before that terrible night was an attack on a group of young people just moments into the New Year of 2002, after earlier trying to gatecrash their house-party. As a group of teenagers came out of the house to celebrate the turn of the New Year on the green outside, Whelan and another thug attacked the group. He used a hurley and a bottle during the attack, and he would later receive a nine-month jail term for the incident. But he was only sentenced for this attack in January 2003, nine months after he murdered Nichola and attempted to murder Sinéad. By the time he broke into the Sweeney home that night, he was known to the Gardaí as a dangerous character, but the teenager had not yet seen the inside of a prison cell.

Less than an hour before he murdered Nichola, Whelan had been involved in a confrontation with a barman at the nearby Rochestown Inn. He had gone there with his friends, Barry Dolan and Stacy McCarthy. Whelan was trying to catch the attention of a girl who was sitting with her friends close by, but the girl wasn't interested. At some stage the barman said he would not serve one of Whelan's friends because he was under age. Moments later, when the barman had his back turned, Whelan picked up an ashtray and went towards him. Someone shouted out a warning and the barman's quick reflexes enabled him to take the ashtray off Whelan. An incident like this happens every weekend in some pub in some part of Ireland, but there was something deeply sinister lurking within Whelan, some unexplained rage, some type of murderous intent.

Whelan hadn't been in any trouble for the four months before that Saturday night for the simple reason that he had been off the streets of Cork. He had spent most of this time on a three-month programme from mid-January to April 2002 at a treatment centre in Co. Limerick for alcohol-related and behavioural problems. His parents had placed him there less than two weeks after he attacked the group of youths celebrating the New Year. After showing exemplary behaviour, keeping his violent tendencies suppressed, he came out of the centre on Sunday, 14 April. On the night he murdered Nichola Sweeney he was drinking Cidona. Someone may have bought a round of beer as well, but one fact not in dispute is that on the night he committed a random murder Whelan was sober.

While Nichola and Sinéad were getting ready to go out, booking the taxi and happily chatting in Nichola's bedroom, a quarter of a mile away Whelan had murder on his mind. He had left the Rochestown Inn and walked with his friends, Dolan and McCarthy, to Dolan's house. By the time the Gardaí had arrived at the pub in response to the reported disturbance, Whelan and his friends were already outside the pub. The Gardaí advised Whelan to go on home, where there were court summonses waiting for him, directing that he attend the District Court to answer charges relating to the New Year's attack. Whelan knew the summonses would come sooner or later, and he knew that his spell in the treatment centre in Co. Limerick would go in his favour if a court case came around. Nevertheless, it was infuriating to hear he had got the summonses, especially after his 'good behaviour efforts' at the centre. As he walked away from the pub, Whelan didn't plan on going home just yet. He was out with his friends and it was early. After being directed by the Gardaí to move on, Whelan, McCarthy and Barry Dolan went to Dolan's house, but Dolan's parents would not allow his friends to stay. So McCarthy and Whelan began walking back up the Rochestown Road towards Whelan's home and towards the Sweeney house.

As the two teenagers walked along the roadside, Whelan continued to display more violent behaviour. He picked up a rock, held it waist high and then held it above his head, saying, 'I'm going to kill someone tonight.' A car pulled up and McCarthy accepted the offer of a lift back to Passage West some miles on. As he arrived at his family home at Underwood off the Rochestown Road, Whelan was now alone and violent intent was brewing within him. He was given the summonses that had been delivered to the house earlier that evening. Shortly afterwards, he secretly armed himself with two knives and then left the house. He turned right and walked the short distance to the large front gates of the Sweeney house. It was now 10.50 p.m.

It was Nichola Sweeney who chose Underwood House as the new family home five years before she was murdered there. The impressive house is set up on a hill, east of Douglas on the south side of Cork city. The house faces northwards, looking out on to the tip of Lough Mahon and nearby Hop Island, where Nichola indulged her love of horse riding at the local equestrian centre. The driveway to the Sweeney house is a curving slope upwards and the alternate pathway is steep. High walls and an eight-foot high electronic gate protect the house. When Whelan broke into these grounds, he scaled the wall beside the gate before sneaking around the back to enter the house.

When I meet Nichola's parents at their home the sadness is palpable — such a beautiful setting, such a dreadful event. Nichola's parents, John and Josephine, worked hard in London for 19 years building up a thriving pub business and rearing Nichola and her brother Seán, three years younger. Nichola's little brother, Christopher, was born in Cork in 1997, three months after the family moved back to Ireland. John and Josephine are both from Co. Kerry, John from Glenbeigh on the Ring of Kerry and Josephine from the village of Beaufort. The Sweeneys built up a happy and rewarding life in London but they always missed their homeland. Their two eldest children loved coming to Ireland to visit their relations, and they were always keen to return and live here. So when friends passed on information in 1997 about a beautiful house coming on the market just outside Cork city, the Sweeneys were sold on the idea. John said his family returned to Ireland full of expectation and excitement.

I remember Nichola just loved this house when she saw it, and she loved the location, just outside Cork. We all did. We had moved to England in 1978 but returned for a time in 1981 and Nichola was born in Cork. We moved back to London in 1982 and remained there until 1997. Nichola and Seán always wanted to come home to Ireland, as did Josephine and myself. We came back to Ireland when the Celtic Tiger was beginning to show, but we had seen other families come home and not settle. We took a conscious decision not to sell up our businesses in London just in case. Our youngest son Christopher was born shortly after we moved back to Ireland, and we were all very happy with the move. I continued to spend a good deal of time minding the pub business in London, and commuted between Cork and London whenever I could. On the weekend Nichola was murdered, myself and my wife Josephine were over in London with Christopher.

Nichola had managed to get the bathroom door closed. She tried to lock the door but couldn't. Whelan kicked the door in; such was the force he used that his foot went through the door. Inside the bathroom he stabbed Nichola a number of times. Somehow Nichola managed to run from the en-suite back into her bedroom. She ran towards the dormer window in a desperate effort to get out, but Whelan chased after her and stabbed her again. One of the knife wounds pierced the left ventricle of Nichola's heart. As Nichola lay on her bedroom floor, Whelan left the room without a word. He noticed Sinéad was missing from the spot where he thought he had killed her. He walked downstairs; it was still in total darkness. He paused but heard nothing, and then without a word he was gone.

Meanwhile Sinéad was hiding in the downstairs bathroom. She thought Nichola had made it to safety in the en-suite upstairs, and Sinéad now stood trembling in the darkness, listening for sounds to indicate where the attacker had gone. It was pitch dark downstairs, where Whelan had turned out all the lights. Sinéad remembers those moments hiding in the bathroom.

I had managed to get downstairs, but I knew our two mobiles were still upstairs. It was dark. I couldn't see very much, but I managed to get into the downstairs bathroom and locked myself in. I can still remember looking at myself in the big mirror there. I didn't see the blood at all. My feet were covered in blood, and it was all over the floor. But when I was looking at myself I couldn't see it. It didn't register. I was there two or three minutes thinking what to do next. And then I could hear him walking around the house. I heard him walk past as if to go around the back of the house. I thought he was going to break in through the window of the bathroom I was in. I opened the door and called out for Nichola. There was no answer.

Sinéad O'Leary was now faced with the terrifying prospect of leaving the locked bathroom. But she knew she had no real choice. She had called out to Nichola and there was no reply. She knew their attacker could come back into the house at any second. She had to get to Nichola; she had to get to one of the mobile phones. She opened the door again and ran up the stairs, still bleeding badly, but alive. She thought Nichola might be OK because she had made it to the en-suite. She ran into the bedroom and saw her friend lying face down on the floor next to the bed. She turned Nichola over and sat beside her. Nichola was groaning, but she was fading. She died a short time later lying beside Sinéad.

Less than ten minutes after Whelan first appeared at Nichola's bedroom door to begin his horrific attack, Sinéad O'Leary was sitting slumped beside her friend, with her own arm split open and the nerves in her arms almost numb. She managed to get one of the mobile phones down beside her and she dialled 112, the European standard emergency dialling number. She tried to tell the operator what had happened, but she was put on hold. She eventually got through to someone and gave the address of the house and both her own mobile number and Nichola's, and she then rang her Mum and Dad. Noreen and Nollaig O'Leary were at home in Montenotte on the other side of Cork when they got a call that would change all their lives for ever. Sinéad told her parents how she and Nichola had been attacked with a knife only moments before and that she was lying injured with her friend. As Sinéad's parents ran to their car to drive to Rochestown, Sinéad rang the emergency services again. Sinéad lost a lot of blood that night, but she managed to 'keep herself together'. In an amazing display of mental composure, she was able to give the emergency services the codes for the gates which would let them into the grounds. This was to prove essential in allowing the Gardaí and medical personnel quick access to the house. Having made the phone calls and knowing that help was on the way, she sat beside Nichola. She was trembling and hysterical, knowing their attacker could reappear at any moment. But help was on the way, help for Nichola. And then Nichola's mobile rang. It was her mother Josephine.

Josephine Sweeney had spoken to her daughter earlier that night. They had both been watching the *Stars In Their Eyes* programme and were rooting for a Cork girl to do well. Josephine had told Nichola she'd ring back later. And so, shortly after eleven o'clock, having put Christopher to bed, Josephine rang again from London. Sinéad answered the phone and recognised the voice of Nichola's Mum, calling to wish her daughter goodnight. In a distressed voice Sinéad told Josephine there had been a break-in and that she and Nichola had been attacked. Naturally, Josephine was shocked and said she wanted to speak to Nichola. Sinéad had to tell her Nichola couldn't talk to her. It was an incredibly upsetting call for both women — Sinéad, suffering multiple stab wounds and now in shock, fearing her friend might be dead, and Nichola's mother ringing from London to say goodnight to her eldest child, only to hear that she was injured in some way and couldn't come to the phone. The call was somehow disconnected. Sinéad heard the sirens of the emergency services and garda cars were already speeding up the driveway. Less than half an hour after the attack, the Gardaí entered the house. Sinéad dragged herself to the top of the hallway and saw the officers at the foot of the stairs. She knew she had to stay alert until help came. A garda came up the stairs and sat down beside her, cradling her. She gave a description of the attacker and then finally passed out.

Over in London, Josephine Sweeney was distraught. After the very brief conversation with Sinéad she knew something terrible had happened at home. She rang Nichola's mobile a second time and she now found herself talking to a man who identified himself as a garda. She asked where her daughter was and why could she not talk to her? The garda seemed very distracted and the tone of his voice indicated something bad had happened. The officer had just arrived at the house and was trying to make sense of what had gone on. The first priority was to ensure the attacker was no longer in the house. He told Josephine he would call her back, and then he hung up.

John Sweeney was working at one of their pubs in London, the Archway Tavern, when his wife called. He knew from her voice that something awful had happened. She wanted him home straightaway. It took him five minutes to get back to the apartment. Over the following hours, amid numerous phone calls to Cork, their apartment would be a scene of confusion, disbelief and untold grief, as the word finally came that their eldest child had been murdered.

Gardaí Tim McSweeney and Denis Moynihan were in the first patrol car to speed up to the front gates of the Sweeney home at 11.20 p.m. Detective Garda John Riordan followed in an unmarked car. Moynihan punched in the code for the gates to gain access to the driveway, and he then walked up to the house while the other Gardaí drove up. As Riordan jumped out of his car he heard a female voice calling out, 'Help! I'm upstairs.' McSweeney came around from the other side of the house, and both of them entered by the front door. They had only gone a short distance when they knew something dreadful had taken place.

The Gardaí saw blood all along the hallway leading to the stairs, blood on the sink in the downstairs toilet, and blood along the staircase. As the Gardaí arrived at the foot of the stairs they looked up and saw Sinéad. She was bleeding profusely, shaking and had gone very pale. Riordan sat down beside her and held her close while the other Gardaí drew their batons and began looking around the rooms upstairs. Sinéad said, 'I'm dying. Am I going to die?' Riordan reassured her and told her to hang on and that an ambulance was on the way. She asked about Nichola, and just then the mobile phone rang again. Sinéad had kept Nichola's phone with her after answering Nichola's Mum in the bedroom. Sinéad answered. Again it was Josephine Sweeney calling from London. Sinéad could hardly talk and she passed the phone over to John Riordan. Having just arrived at the house, the garda didn't know who he was talking to. Josephine told him she wanted to talk to her daughter Nichola, and that Sinéad was not her daughter. She informed him that this was Nichola's phone, and why was a garda on the end of Nichola's phone? It was a deeply distressing conversation for all involved. As the garda was talking to Josephine, another officer whispered to him that they had found a young woman in one of the bedrooms and they couldn't detect a pulse. Riordan told Josephine he would have to call her back and reluctantly he hung up.

By this time ambulance crews were already in the house, and the Gardaí had searched every room in the house and established that the attacker had fled the scene. John Riordan stood up from the floor of the stairs to allow Sinéad receive urgent medical treatment. Gardaí Linda Conway and Peter Moran had also arrived at the house. Riordan borrowed Linda Conway's notebook and asked Sinéad if she could describe the attacker. Sinéad was utterly exhausted, she had suffered over a dozen stab wounds to her upper body, she was physically drained and was now suffering extreme shock. But somehow she managed to give a brief description of the young man who had stood in Nichola's bedroom less than an hour before. Then she was taken away in an ambulance. She remembers finding out that Nichola was dead.

When I had found Nichola on the floor next to her bed, I turned her over and sat beside her. I first thought she was unconscious. She was groaning. But I know now she died while I was there with her. I didn't actually find out Nichola was dead until about three or four in the morning, when one of the nurses told me Nichola had passed away. I know I was really angry at the time because I was asking everybody how she was, and no one would tell me. I was told she had been put in a different hospital, and I was asking about her all night. I think the nurse told me because I just wouldn't shut up at all about it. I wanted to know how she was. But I think deep down I knew she was dead. That was the worst part, because I first thought that night that Nichola would survive, that she'd pull through. But one of her wounds was fatal.

Nichola Sweeney and Sinéad O'Leary first met in the library of their secondary school in Cork. Just like the Sweeneys, the O'Learys had spent many years in England before returning to live in Ireland. Sinéad and her brothers, Tadhg and Barra, spent their early years in Pinner, just outside London. When Sinéad was in her mid-teens the O'Learys returned to Cork. She was exempt from studying Irish for her Leaving Cert and that's how she made friends with Nichola. The two girls were always put together in the library with another girl while everyone else was attending Irish classes. Nichola and Sinéad were part of a gang of six or seven girls who hung out together in school and after school. Once they all completed their Leaving Cert, the teenagers saw less of each other as they began studying at different colleges. Nichola opted to study Travel and Tourism at Skerry's College in Cork, while Sinéad moved to Clontarf in Dublin to study Business at Trinity College. But whenever they got a chance all the girls would still meet up in Cork. Sinéad never really settled in Dublin and always looked forward to getting home and seeing her family and friends. On the night they were attacked, Nichola and Sinéad were looking forward to meeting some more of their friends in town. They had been to Fast Eddie's Niteclub a few nights before, and were probably going to head for the Savoy Niteclub this time. They were also looking forward to Sinéad's 20th birthday the following week. Nichola already had her outfit picked out to wear for the birthday party.

Seán Sweeney answered his mobile. It was his Dad calling from London. At the time of his sister's murder Seán was 17 years old. That Saturday he had been working in a hotel until 8 p.m. and had then gone home. He had left Nichola and Sinéad shortly after 10.30 p.m. when a friend called, and he was now over in Bishopstown. The moment he answered the phone Seán could tell his Dad was very distressed. Something had happened at home in Rochestown, someone had broken into the house, Gardaí were there, and Nichola and Sinéad had been hurt. No one could reach Nichola on her mobile phone. Seán immediately tried to find a way back across Cork city. He tried to get a taxi, and rang the Gardaí to see if they could help, but he then made contact with a friend who gave him a lift to Rochestown.

John Sweeney remembers the frustration he and Josephine felt in London that night, not knowing what had happened to their daughter.

When I arrived back at the apartment in London, Josephine told me about the conversation she had had with Sinéad and with the garda. Josephine's understanding from that call was that someone had broken into the house, a burglar, and that Nichola was hurt. There was no suggestion from the conversation at that time that Nichola or Sinéad had been stabbed. We later learned that at that time Sinéad was very badly stabbed and Nichola was lying fatally injured in her bedroom. But our initial understanding was that maybe Nichola was hurt because the burglar hurt her. The mental picture I had was that some thug had given Nichola a belt and that she had broken her leg at the worst, or her arm was twisted, or something like that. Not for one moment were we contemplating any type of knife injury.

By the time Seán arrived at the bottom of the driveway of his home, Sinéad was already *en route* to Cork University Hospital. At midnight, just over an hour after the attack, a local doctor, Mehboob Kukaswadia, had declared Nichola dead at the scene. Gardaí were in the process of sealing off the house and grounds, pending a full forensic examination of the scene. A crowd of onlookers had gathered down at the front gates.

The manner in which Seán Sweeney learned about his sister's murder is incredibly sad. After arriving at the scene, Seán approached two Gardaí and told them who he was and that he wanted to get up to his house. He wanted to see his sister. One garda told him he couldn't go up there as it was a crime scene.

Seán told him his sister was up there with her friend and he needed to get in. His Dad had called from London. The garda told Seán that a girl had been murdered in the house. Seán learned that one girl had been taken to Cork University Hospital, and that the other was still in the house. And so Seán raced to the hospital, knowing that whoever was in hospital had survived the attack. He arrived into casualty and told the two nurses there what had happened. The nurses looked up the name of the girl who had just arrived. They told him the name was Sinéad. Seán rang his father in a very distressed state — Nichola was dead.

Gardaí were looking at the crowd of onlookers. The description that Sinéad had given before being rushed to hospital was a very good one. John Riordan had spoken to other detectives including Mick Cummins and Jason Lynch. One garda said there was someone down outside the main gates who had a shaved head and a goatee. Riordan walked down the driveway and saw Peter Whelan. The detective borrowed a torch from someone and shone the light on him. The garda couldn't see any blood on Whelan and he wasn't wearing the clothes that Sinéad had described. However, Detective Riordan still called Whelan aside to talk to him and ask him some questions.

Having murdered one young woman and having attempted to murder another, Whelan didn't want to run away. After committing the attacks he had walked home and washed his hands. He had left one knife in the house when it broke in Sinéad's arm and he had thrown the other one away in the undergrowth as he left the house. After washing the blood from his hands and changing his clothes, Whelan waited. He knew the first young woman he had stabbed had fled somewhere, but was she dead or had she raised the alarm? He didn't have to wait long to find out. The sirens and lights came quickly. Whelan watched and came out of his house. He called in on his uncle who lived next door, asking him what was going on outside. They walked the short distance up to the Sweeney drive. What was all the commotion about?

Within seconds of being called over by John Riordan, Whelan was freely admitting carrying out the attack on Nichola and Sinéad. He had first asked the garda what the scene was like inside the house. And then without showing any remorse he suddenly admitted he had been in the Sweeney house. Riordan immediately called another garda, Chris Cronin, to come over and witness everything. One garda says Whelan's confession was almost surreal.

There is no accounting for Peter Whelan's mind. He is vicious and a danger to every single person. The degree of violence he used against Nichola and Sinéad was sickening. But initially we thought that if the attacker had fled the house he might have fled the locality as well. It's not very often that a murderer hangs around and then stands at the garda cordon acting like a concerned citizen. It's just another example of Peter Whelan's warped mind, a young man capable of incredible violence, but also capable of the presence of mind to stand there as if he's a normal person. And before we caught him he was asking the Gardaí what had happened. But there was also a part of Whelan that was craving attention, craving notoriety. After changing his clothes and washing the blood from his hands, he then freely admits to being the murderer. He effectively hands himself up, but he was gloating. It took Sinéad's description for us to single him out, but once he had an inkling we believed him to be a suspect, Whelan just couldn't shut up.

Shortly after telling the Gardaí he had been in the Sweeney house that night, Whelan brought half a dozen officers to his home a short distance away. He brought the Gardaí to his room where he had hidden the bloodstained clothes under his wardrobe. The Gardaí put the clothes into evidence bags. One garda remembers how they feared Whelan was about to commit another attack.

As we were standing in Whelan's bedroom he went to take down an object from the wardrobe. We saw he was trying to take down a knife. We immediately dived on him. At this stage he was being fully co-operative, and in hindsight perhaps he was just going to hand the knife to us, but we were taking no chances. I always remember that after we dived on him he said to us, 'Cool it, man.' It was just another example of how skewed his thinking was.

At 12.25 a.m. Peter Whelan was arrested on suspicion of the murder of Nichola Sweeney and the attack on Sinéad O'Leary. It was just over an hour and a half since he had attacked the two friends, and it was just over an hour since the Gardaí first arrived at the scene.

Over in London, John, Josephine and Christopher were being comforted by family and friends. At around 1 a.m. Seán phoned his parents with the news that Nichola was dead at the house in Rochestown. His parents were already fearing the worst. During telephone conversations with the Gardaí over the previous two hours, John had asked the officers straight out if his daughter was dead or alive, but the officers had avoided answering the question. He remembers how he moved from thinking his daughter was simply injured to fearing she was dead.

The garda who had hung up on Josephine had said he would ring back. In the meantime, I rang Nichola's mobile again and got no answer. Even though I was worried, I wasn't unduly concerned because I got it into my head that Nichola was out in an ambulance where they were giving her comfort, and that no one could hear the phone. But after about 20 minutes waiting I rang Directory Enquiries and eventually got through to Douglas Garda Station, where I left my mobile number and our landline number. Just then the mobile rang and it was a garda at the scene who was phoning Josephine back. I asked him how my daughter was and he kept saying, 'I'm sorry, I'm sorry. You'll have to ring Cork University Hospital.' I could tell this was the language of someone in a very distressed state and conveying a distressed message. I was getting hugely alarmed and said, 'Garda, could you answer a simple question? Is my daughter dead or alive?' And he kept saying, 'I'm sorry. Ring the hospital.' And at that point I said, 'Oh my God, my daughter is dead', and the garda didn't deny it. Then the other phone rang and it was a senior officer calling on foot of my call to Douglas Garda Station. As I approached the phone I was going into denial, pretending to myself that the first conversation hadn't happened. I immediately asked this man the extent of my daughter's injuries, and he said, 'Mr Sweeney, your priority is to get home as quickly as possible.' The officer qualified this by adding something like Nichola was still at Underwood House and the Gardaí were with her, looking after her. I then thought to myself that it's an hour after whatever incident had happened and Nichola wasn't in hospital, but I was being told to get home as soon as possible. I think it was as coded a message as you could get to tell me Nichola was dead. And then we got the verbal confirmation very very sadly from my son, Seán.

Over the following hours, John and Josephine learned that their daughter had died after suffering a stab wound. Some of their close relatives had learned that Nichola had suffered a number of injuries, but in an effort to spare them the horror, they told John and Josephine that Nichola had been stabbed once. The Sweeneys thought their daughter might have been stabbed by someone who had broken in looking for money, and that maybe Nichola had disturbed him and he had caught her with the knife as he fled. But slowly the full horror of Nichola's death was becoming apparent.

John and Josephine Sweeney arrived at Cork Airport in the early hours of Sunday, 28 April 2002, and were reunited with Seán. In a haze of grief, the Sweeneys had taken in the fact that Nichola had been stabbed, but they now learned that a suspect who had been arrested was a neighbour. John Sweeney says they were stunned.

It just didn't make any sense. This was a neighbour we hardly knew. I would see him occasionally walking his family's spaniel. I had thought he was a polite young fellow. I had no inkling about his violent nature, the real character he was. When I heard he was arrested for Nichola's murder, I thought he was mentally disturbed and we didn't know it. But we've since learned just what a nasty young man he is, causing so much grief for so many people over many years. He was cunning enough to carry out his violent actions away from his own doorstep until that night. He was causing trouble in Passage, Douglas and Carrigaline. He caused trouble in lots of pubs. It was known to the Gardaí that he was violent, but we didn't know it. I often think if we had known of the danger this neighbour posed, then things might have been different. If anything is to be learned from Nichola's murder, I think it is that the Gardaí should get out of their cars and get in more amongst the community, the law abiding community, and let people know if a person has violent tendencies. Too much policing is done from a patrol car and the end of a telephone. It was only after Nichola's murder that we learned about Whelan's capacity for evil.

As Whelan was charged with the murder of Nichola Sweeney and remanded in custody, the Sweeney family began a lifetime of suffering. John Sweeney says they can never fully come to terms with what happened.

If Nichola died in a traffic accident or from an illness we would naturally be heart-broken, but we could at least make some sense of it and come to accept it in some way. But a murder is just a totally unnatural event, and we find it impossible to accept it. The violence that Nichola was subjected to that night was cold and calculated and was pure evil. Nichola was a beautiful child, and I'm sure every proud Dad talks like that, but Nichola was a beautiful person. She would never let you hurt an insect. She was frightened of spiders, but wouldn't let you hurt them and would ask you to put them outside. Nichola was truly a wonderful, special human being, and she died at the hands of a truly horrendously evil person. If only we'd known what a real danger this neighbour was. It is just so unfair and we have to live with that for the rest of our lives.

As Nichola Sweeney was laid to rest amid harrowing scenes in Co. Kerry, her friend, Sinéad O'Leary, was recovering in hospital from her injuries. In time most of her injuries would heal well, although she would suffer long-term nerve damage in her right arm. Sinéad spent almost a week in hospital before returning home. She travelled to Co. Kerry for Nichola's Month's Mind Mass, where she sang a song for her friend. Sinéad tells me how she copes with what happened that awful night.

The way I look at what happened is that I was lucky to be there with Nichola. Because if I wasn't there, she would have been there on her own, and with one girl on her own, she might have suffered a lot. I like to think Nichola didn't suffer much pain because I didn't feel anything for about ten minutes, so I think Nichola wouldn't have felt pain. That's why I can deal with it. I feel that at least I was there with her, that she wasn't alone, that I was with her when she died.

When Whelan had been approached by Detective Riordan near the front gates of the Sweeney home, he had quickly admitted using two knives to attack Nichola and Sinéad. The Gardaí had found one knife in the house, but the second knife wasn't found until the next day. Superintendent Brian Calnan, who led the investigation, says a crucial factor in the case was ensuring a thorough forensic examination of the crime scene.

The first priority we had was the preservation of life and ensuring medical attention got to Nichola and Sinéad. At the same time the Gardaí were deployed to stop anyone other than medical personnel entering on to the property. It was extremely important that the scene was sealed off as soon as possible. One knife was left at the scene of the murder, but it turned out this was the knife used to attempt to murder Sinéad. The knife used to murder Nichola was lying hidden in the long grass on the property. We found this knife the following day after getting information from Peter Whelan.

If Whelan had opted to contest the charges of murder and attempted murder, the Gardaí now had both weapons as well as Whelan's bloodstained clothing. The only way he could conceivably have fought the charges was by pleading insanity. But one garda says this wasn't an option for Whelan.

Peter Whelan was assessed by a number of psychologists, and they all concluded that he is not and was not insane. There is no doubt he is warped, he is evil, but he is in control of his faculties. Consider how he didn't speak a word as he attacked Nichola and Sinéad. He wasn't out of control, screaming and roaring; he was cold and clinical, in full control of his mind and his movements. It was as if he had planned such a murder. He was acting out a fantasy. When he confessed to the attack he actually told officers he was 'sorry he didn't do more'. What Whelan did was sick, but he is not sick, he is not ill. He is simply a very bad young man and that's why we hope he will spend the rest of his life in prison.

Peter Whelan is the youngest of four children. He attended primary and secondary school in Passage West, but did not sit his Leaving Cert. At the time he carried out the attack on Nichola and Sinéad, he was serving his time as an apprentice with an engineering company in Carrigaline, and he had been in work as usual on the day before the attack. He had convictions for public order offences dating back to 2001. He had a conviction for drunkenness, for which he received a fine of £100. Whelan also carried out a number of serious attacks on property, including a public house. But to his close neighbours in Rochestown, until the night of 27 April 2002, he had passed himself off as a pleasant and responsible young man.

Nichola Sweeney should have celebrated her 21st birthday in October 2002. Instead, her family were preparing for the murder trial which was listed to begin the following January at the Central Criminal Court. In the meantime, John and Josephine and their sons, Seán and Christopher, were facing their first Christmas without Nichola. John Sweeney wanted to address the judge if Whelan was convicted of Nichola's murder, but he was trying to put all thoughts of the court case out of his mind until after the Christmas period. But then on 13 December John got a call from Brian Calnan. Whelan wanted to plead guilty to Nichola's murder and he wanted to do it before Christmas.

On Friday, 20 December 2002, Whelan stood in a packed courtroom at Court No. 2 at the Central Criminal Court. As the Sweeney and O'Leary families looked on from the back of the courtroom, Whelan pleaded guilty to the murder of Nichola Sweeney and the attempted murder of Sinéad O'Leary. Mr Justice Paul Carney listened as Sinéad bravely took the witness stand to outline the injuries and emotional trauma she suffered from the knife attack. The way the courtroom is arranged meant that Sinéad had to walk within a few feet of Whelan when she was going to and from the witness stand. Although Whelan was under heavy security it was still an added trauma for Sinéad, but one she came through admirably. John Sweeney also walked by Whelan as he took the witness stand to plead with the judge to impose a sentence that would give a true and proper meaning to a life sentence for his daughter's killer.

John Sweeney knew that Judge Carney had no discretion in imposing a sentence for the murder of Nichola. The sentence for murder was mandatory, and everyone knew that life imprisonment rarely meant what it said. But the fact that Whelan had pleaded guilty to the attempted murder of Sinéad gave Judge Carney an opportunity to ensure that Whelan would be locked up for the rest of his life. There is no mandatory sentence for the crime of attempted murder, so John Sweeney asked the judge to consider imposing a sentence of 70 years on Whelan for the attempted murder charge. John said this would ensure that this dangerous man would not be allowed to commit further random murders, and would make sure his daughter's killer, and Sinéad's attacker, would be properly punished. Although Judge Carney did not impose a 70-year sentence as John Sweeney urged, the judge did impose a sentence that is unique in the Irish justice system.

For the crime of murdering Nichola Sweeney, the judge imposed mandatory life imprisonment. For the crime of attempting to murder Sinéad O'Leary, the judge imposed a sentence of 15 years, but he directed that this sentence be consecutive to the life sentence. Such a sentence had never been imposed before, and it reflected a realisation that a life sentence did not mean what it implied. There had been other cases where a similar sentence could have been imposed but wasn't. When Mark Nash was convicted of the double murder of Carl and Catherine Doyle in 1997, he also received a concurrent eight-year sentence for beating Catherine's sister Sarah Jane. When Derek Hickey was jailed for life for the murder of his six-month-old daughter Leilah Smullen in 2000, he was given a four-year concurrent sentence for stabbing Leilah's mother, Sinéad. And there were many other cases where a life sentence prisoner was serving another sentence at the same time, rather than before or after the life sentence. Judge Carney's sentencing of Whelan was a new departure, ensuring that at least one young random murderer would remain in prison for a very long time.

When Whelan's legal team challenged the consecutive sentences at the Court of Criminal Appeal, they argued that it was not practical to have a sentence consecutive to a life sentence. Judges, like everyone else, recognise that a life sentence might have a particular meaning in law but has a different reality when put into practice by the authorities. The three Appeal Court judges simply turned the sentences around, directing that Whelan would serve the 15-year sentence for attempted murder before beginning his life sentence.

Whelan is currently serving his 15-year sentence at Cork Prison for trying to murder Sinéad O'Leary. His life sentence will not begin until 2017. It will be into the 2030s before he will have even the slightest chance of parole, by which stage he will only be in his late forties. But it is that very uncertainty over whether or not Whelan will spend his entire life in prison that has led the Sweeney family to establish an extensive campaign to ensure that 'life' really does mean life. Through a special website — www.nicholasweeneyfoundation.org — John and Josephine are reaching out to other families bereaved by murder. The website reflects the extreme disquiet among many people that only a handful of murderers sentenced to life imprisonment will actually spend the rest of their lives in prison. The Sweeneys also firmly believe that the family of a murder victim should be consulted before any decision is taken to release a killer. John Sweeney says the foundation is a way of honouring Nichola's memory.

I think judges are often very frustrated at the fact that they have no discretion in dealing with murderers. When it comes to murder cases, an Irish judge is just a rubber stamp, imposing a mandatory sentence that the State will often not honour. And some of these prisoners applying for parole are very cunning and very devious, behaving themselves in prison. Remorse shown by prisoners should be disregarded. It's just words. There is no one on this earth who can say a prisoner won't reoffend. That is the key to this issue. In the interest of society, and certainly in the interest and humanity of the victim's family, the State should respect that. And whoever is charged with considering murderers for release should ask themselves, 'If it were one of us, would we feel happy that someone was coming back into society who had killed our son or daughter?'

John Sweeney believes that murderers should not only be kept incarcerated, but should be forced to give something back to society.

Murderers are paying a very small price for what they have done, bearing in mind all the comforts they have in prison, with DVDs and pool tables. I honestly think that people who have committed crimes as heinous as Peter Whelan should be in a prison reminiscent of something from the turn of the century, where they actually go out and work in fields, to justify their keep, so to speak. There really should be some type of punishment involving labour, if for no other reason than its deterrent value. I'm absolutely certain that some people who experience prison in the shorter term have no qualms about going back there because it's an easy life. I don't want to see a situation where prisoners are breaking stones with pick axes and with a fellow standing over them with a whip bleeding them to a pulp. That is not humane. But they should be made to go out and do something purposeful, like plant vegetables, something that has a punishment value while still providing something to society.

Sinéad O'Leary says the 15-year sentence Whelan is currently serving for trying to murder her is not enough.

My life has completely changed because of what happened. I'm a completely different person. I am managing to cope, but it is very difficult. I do get nervous if it's night-time and I'm on my own walking. I don't like being on my own. A 15-year sentence for what he did to me alone is not enough. This person tried to take my life, but I'm not going to let him win. His aim that night was to take Nichola's life and my life. Since it happened, I've been fighting to survive, to get on with my life. I'm just one of those stubborn people. I will not let him win. I've been very open about it and talk to my friends and family about it. I knew if I shut it away it would affect me in later years.

Nichola Sweeney had so much ahead of her when her life was so brutally cut short. She loved working with people, she was very interested in the pub business and also in public relations. At the time of her murder she was working part-time at the café in Brown Thomas in Cork city as well as studying full-time in college. Her great people skills might one day have seen her working in her own pub in Cork. She just loved to chat to people, and on the night of her murder it is no surprise that she and Sinéad were talking loudly and happily as they got ready for a night out in town. It's an image of two young women full of fun, full of warmth, full of life.

Sinéad O'Leary dropped out of Trinity College shortly after Whelan tried to murder her. She never really settled in Dublin anyway; she had put the course in Trinity down just to fill up her CAO form. She returned to live full-time in Cork and eventually decided to study psychology at University College Cork. Her parents, Nollaig and Noreen, her two brothers and her friends have all been a great support to her. She knows she is a unique survivor of a violent crime. There are few people who have come face to face with a murderer and lived. She tells me how she went for counselling, but it didn't help.

When I'm older I want to work with families of victims, because I think I can help them. From what happened to me, there wasn't anyone around who had suffered what I have, and survived it. So I had no one I could relate to from that point of view. So I was thinking that maybe because I was able to cope with what happened and tried to get on with my life, maybe I can be a help to other people with counselling and things like that, because I went for one counselling session after I was attacked, and I felt that they really didn't know what they were talking about. I felt there was absolutely no point in talking to people who didn't know where you are coming from. I think about Nichola every day. I'm just happy she wasn't alone and that's what keeps me going when I'm feeling down. When I think about Nichola I think about all the good times we had, and myself and the rest of her friends are always talking about the laughs we had with her, all the nights out and the laughs. I'm able to separate Whelan and Nichola in my mind, and when I think of Nichola I don't think of him.

Sinéad doesn't like being on her own. She couldn't cope with being in her house without a dog. When one dog, Cassie, passed away, Sinéad got another dog, Locky, who stands guard in her family home, providing protection and peace of mind. From the back of Sinéad's home in Montenotte she looks south-east across the River Lee to Nichola's home in Rochestown in the far distance. Sinéad tells me she may well stay living locally.

I do see myself staying around Cork. I love Cork. I didn't really like London or Dublin. It's kind of strange with everything that has happened here, but I actually still really like Cork. I went back to Nichola's house a few months after the attack, and I went up to Nichola's room. I don't know what it was, but I had to do it. Her Mam showed me the outfit Nichola had got for going out on my 20th birthday.

Whelan's knife attack on Nichola and Sinéad lasted only a matter of minutes, but its effect will last a lifetime. Nichola's family are completely devastated by the incredible evil that occurred shortly before 11 p.m. on 27 April 2002. In the aftermath of Nichola's murder, the Sweeneys sold two of their pubs in London. They simply didn't have the willpower to continue the businesses. John and Josephine now dedicate much of their time to preserving their daughter's memory and fighting for justice for all murder victims and their families. As well as being a cherished daughter, Nichola was a much-loved older sister to Seán and Christopher. Through the Nichola Sweeney Foundation, the Sweeneys have ensured that their daughter's murder will never be forgotten, but also that her full and happy life will forever be remembered and honoured.

John Sweeney says his daughter's loss is indescribable.

The reality that people can die young does flick through everyone's mind I'm sure from time to time. But you think this will never happen. But when someone is murdered, and the murder is in such appalling and horrific circumstances, without any motive or reason, it is very hard to understand that. It's very hard to understand that a human being can do something so dreadful to another human being. There is not an hour of the day where Nichola doesn't come into your mind one way or another, and very often it will culminate in thinking of the horrendous way she died. There are times when these visions come into my mind and I try to deal with it by trying to totally shut her from my mind, and this causes further mental anguish as I can never allow my mind to forget Nichola, no matter how much the pain. Josephine is just so devastated, and when we go to Kerry she always insists on going to Nichola's grave, even if it is the early hours of the morning. And Seán and Christopher miss Nichola so much too. They both had a very close bond with their big sister. Christopher used to go into Nichola's room to wake her up in the mornings. After her murder he was asking where Nichola was, and we had to tell him she had gone to heaven. And he would ask many awkward questions about her death, and how it is that she is up in heaven and also lying in a grave.

13

Lifers and Survivors

In the early hours of 30 April 2000, 18-year-old Sinéad Smullen was found collapsed on a road in the centre of Newbridge town. The teenager had staggered from a nearby flat after her boyfriend had stabbed her in the neck without warning. The Gardaí arrived on the scene within minutes and rushed Sinéad to the local garda station, where a doctor gave her immediate medical attention. In the meantime, other officers went to the flat Sinéad shared with her boyfriend, Derek Hickey. He was standing outside the flat and told one officer, 'I was just on my way down to you to give myself up.' While some Gardaí arrested Hickey, others went to the front door of the flat but it was locked. They forced open the door and walked inside. In a cot in the bedroom of the small one-bedroom flat they found Leilah's body.

Leilah Smullen was born on 18 January 2000; she was almost three and a half months old when her father stabbed her to death.

When a person pleads guilty to a murder, the registrar of the Central Criminal Court reads out the specific charge the accused faces. When Hickey pleaded guilty to the murder of Leilah, nothing on the charge sheet said the victim of the crime was a baby. Nothing on the charge sheet indicated that he stabbed his little daughter six times.

Sinéad Smullen is one of the few people who have come face to face with a murderer and lived. Having lost her little baby, this remarkable young woman has displayed great courage in attempting to get on with her life while also keeping Leilah's memory alive. She has treasured photographs of her first-born child looking straight at the camera with big blue eyes, smiling, reaching out. Sinéad will never forget how Leilah lost her life, but she tells me how in Leilah's short life she brought much joy.

Leilah was beautiful, she was like a little flower. I named her Leilah because I happened to be looking at Lilies and I was thinking of names and Leilah just came into my head. She looked like a Leilah, she had the face for it, and I always loved the name Sophie so that was her middle name. We had only started to spoon-feed her that week. I was terrified doing it, afraid she would choke, but she loved it, sitting up on the couch, smiling away.

Sinéad and Hickey had been going out for just over a year before he turned on her and their baby. They met when she was 17 years old. Hickey was 24. When Sinéad later became pregnant the couple moved in together in a flat in the centre of Newbridge.

Just hours before he murdered his daughter, Hickey had travelled with Sinéad on the train from Newbridge to Dublin to buy a christening gown. Leilah was due to be christened shortly, and everyone was looking forward to a special day. The couple arrived home in the early evening and met with friends and family, but later when they were alone a row developed.

Sinéad remembers how Hickey began to stab her.

There was nothing but rows throughout the whole relationship, so I was deciding that night that I wanted to end it. I was planning to head back to my parents, and was taking Leilah with me. I told him he could come over and visit her anytime he wanted. The next thing I knew he came back into the bedroom with a knife from the kitchen. All I could see was this hand coming towards my face. I jerked back, and next thing I held my neck with my right hand. I could feel the blood, and I realised then that he was trying to kill me. I started screaming and screaming, screaming for help. I turned my back to him, and he stabbed me in the back. I flung myself on to the bed. He climbed up on top of me and was aiming to stab me in the throat. I don't know where the strength came from, but I kicked him off. As he went to get back up I could hear Leilah crying. She had woken up with all the commotion. I went to get her out of the Moses basket, but he made a swipe for me again. The only thing I could think of was to get a mobile phone, call the Guards, call 999, get help.

There was only one way in or out of the flat, so Sinéad ran to the front door and ran out crying for help. Hickey didn't follow her.

The State Pathologist, Dr Marie Cassidy, later concluded that Leilah would have fallen unconscious immediately she was stabbed and would have died quickly.

Once arrested, Hickey was brought to Newbridge Garda Station where Sinéad was already lying on the floor being treated for her neck wounds. Sinéad could see Hickey in another room. He called over to her: 'There's no point in getting Leilah. She's dead. I killed her. You're not going to get her. Neither am I.'

Sinéad was rushed to Naas General Hospital and later to St James's in Dublin. It was there that her parents, Mags and Seán, had to break the news to her that Leilah was dead. Sinéad remembers.

I couldn't take it. I literally couldn't take it. I was thinking in my head, that's the end of me. I can't live without her. She was my baby and I just didn't think I could go on without her. I thought if she's dead, I go. She was my whole life.

In June 2001 Hickey was jailed for life after pleading guilty to the murder of Leilah Sophie Smullen. He also admitted stabbing Sinéad and he received a four-year sentence for that attack, to be served at the same time as the life sentence. Hickey had previous convictions for public order offences and criminal damage and he was known to harm himself.

Hickey is serving his life sentence in Arbour Hill Prison and works in the Fabric Shop, helping to provide blankets and duvets for inmates in Irish prisons. In 2000, while on remand at Cloverhill Prison, he wrote letters to Sinéad that he somehow managed to have delivered to her. The letters contain disturbing ramblings, with sentences running continuously without full stops. Part of one letter refers to a world with 'no dogs or babies allowed'. The letters caused great distress to Sinéad who wondered how Hickey could still terrorise her from prison. Although he had never harmed his baby daughter before that night in April 2000, he had physically assaulted Sinéad a number of times.

Considering that temporary release has previously been given to parents who killed their children, it is likely that at some stage in the future, decades from now, Hickey might be granted parole. Understandably, such a prospect causes grave concern for Sinéad Smullen.

I fear that sometime in the future he is going to be released. I'll be watching over my back and Leilah will still be dead. I'll never get her back. I'm never going to see her smile, hear her cry or gurgle. I'll never hold her again or feed her, play with her, bath her, see her walk. I still have nightmares about the attack. I don't really mind that he only got four years for attacking me. I just want to see him serve a full life sentence for murdering Leilah.

There are around 200 people in Irish prisons serving a life sentence for murder. Of these convicted murderers only a handful will remain in prison for the rest of their lives. As part of the State's policy of trying to rehabilitate offenders, most murderers will be granted some form of temporary release long before they have spent even 20 years in prison. It is worth considering that over one-fifth of all convicted murderers in Ireland are already out of prison on temporary release.

Apart from Jimmy Ennis, who is content to see out his days as a guest of the Irish Prison Service, the longest serving prisoners are English serial killers, John Shaw and Geoffrey Evans. In 1976 they abducted, raped and murdered women in Counties Wicklow and Mayo. Both had a long list of convictions in England before they ever set foot in Ireland, yet these extremely dangerous men still found the opportunity to bring terror to our shores.

Shaw was just 10 years old when he was given a two-year suspended sentence for house-breaking in 1955. During his teenage years he racked up numerous convictions for breaking and entering, and spent two years in juvenile detention. In August 1966, when he was 21 years old, he was given a four-month sentence in England for indecent assault. His potential for extreme random violence was further exposed in February 1971 when he was given four years for charges of attempted rape and burglary. He soon linked up with Geoffrey Evans who was a year older and every bit as dangerous. Evans also had a long list of convictions before he came to Ireland in the mid-1970s. His most notable sentence was one of five years for robbery, which was imposed in March 1970.

By the time they came to Ireland both Shaw and Evans had spent over seven years of their lives in prison in England. Today they are two of Ireland's most notorious lifers. They now lead quiet and contented lives in Arbour Hill Prison, and although they have recently applied for parole, they are resigned to the possibility of dying in prison. Evans works in the kitchen of Arbour Hill, where he has free interaction with other prisoners. He is a small man who looks his age. He was regarded as 'the brains' of the murderous duo. He previously worked in the Carpentry Shop in Arbour Hill, where he made lamps and other ornaments that he would sell to other prisoners.

John Shaw also enjoys a very relaxed regime at Arbour Hill, where he is in charge of the video library. He gets on well with the other prisoners, he has access to books and papers, and has his own television and video games. When Shaw was moved for a short time to Castlerea Prison at his own request 'for a change of scenery', a second prison van was needed to transport all his belongings that he had built up over the past 30 years in prison. However, he couldn't settle in the lower-security prison and he soon returned to the comfort of Arbour Hill. The only visitors he and Evans get are from members of the British Embassy, who check that the two prisoners have no complaints about their surroundings. Both Shaw and Evans know that in their case 'life' will most likely mean exactly that. Even if they were ever to be granted temporary release, there is a note on their files that the English police are to be notified immediately — the serial killers are wanted for questioning in connection with a number of serious unsolved crimes in England dating from the early 1970s.

While Shaw and Evans have chosen not to seek a transfer to a prison outside the Irish Republic, another long-serving and dangerous killer did avail of legislation for the transfer of prisoners so he could move closer to home. In March 1982 Richard O'Hara from Belfast was jailed for life for the murder of 19-year-old Deborah Robinson, who was strangled to death in a Dublin factory in September 1980. Deborah had travelled from Belfast to Dublin early on a Saturday morning for a blind date, and after meeting her date in Swords, Co. Dublin, she later travelled to the city centre to get the bus back to Belfast. By chance she met O'Hara, who told her he was from Belfast too, and he tricked her into walking with him towards where he worked. After murdering Deborah he brought her body to Clane in Co. Kildare where he callously threw her body into a ditch. After serving 16 years of a life sentence, he was transferred in 1998 to Maghaberry Prison in Co. Antrim. Such a move is seen as a clear indication of the possibility that O'Hara, who is now in his fifties, might be given parole in the future.

One other long-term prisoner who has sought a transfer out of the Irish prison system is Scottish national, Ian Watson. In 1984 he was 30 years old when he pleaded guilty to the murder of a young boy in a town in Leinster. Watson had been living in the town for a number of months in late 1983 and early 1984. He was arrested a short time after the child's body was found in the town and he immediately admitted the murder to detectives. Because he pleaded guilty to the murder, no evidence emerged of how Watson had a number of previous convictions for theft and drugs offences in Scotland. He was just 12 years old when he was first convicted of a minor offence, and over the following years he was given short prison sentences for burglaries committed in Edinburgh. Just like

Shaw and Evans, Watson was able to come to Ireland and invent a new life without the Irish authorities being aware of his criminal past. After being jailed for life in 1984, he found it very difficult to adapt to long-term prison life and he spent time in a padded cell. He is described as moody and unpredictable. In October 2001 he applied to be repatriated to Scotland but his request was turned down. One garda who investigated Watson's crime puts it succinctly: 'This was a savage murder of a young boy. Anyone who commits such a crime should never be let out of prison.'

Teenage killer Brian Fortune also avoided much media attention by pleading guilty to murder. He was originally charged with the double murder of 62-year-old Margaret Nolan and her 24-year-old daughter, Ann, who were strangled to death at their Wicklow farmhouse in 1985, but Fortune only pleaded guilty to the murder of Margaret Nolan. The 18-year old was given a life sentence, but just like the sentencing of murderers such as Michael Holohan, Frank Daly and Ian Watson, no evidence of Fortune's crime was heard in court. One month later the State announced that it was effectively dropping the second murder charge. Fortune was not acquitted of the murder of Ann Nolan, but the prosecution team said it did not intend producing evidence of the crime, and the murder charge would simply remain on file. No reason has ever been given as to why the second murder charge was not put before a jury. This legal limbo has caused anguish for Ann's extended family and immense frustration for the Gardaí. No matter what the authorities might say to the contrary, officially the murder of Ann Nolan remains unsolved, and Fortune is serving just one life sentence — for the murder of Ann's mother.

A similar situation exists in the case of Malcolm MacArthur who is serving a life sentence for the random murder of Nurse Bridie Gargan, whom he beat to death with a hammer while stealing her car in the Phoenix Park in 1982. MacArthur also faced a charge of murdering Co. Offaly farmer Donal Dunne, who was shot dead by a person answering an ad to buy a gun just a few days after Bridie's murder. But after MacArthur pleaded guilty to the murder of Bridie Gargan, the Director of Public Prosecutions entered a *nolle prosequi*, whereby the charge of murdering Donal Dunne was not proceeded with in court and would simply remain on file. Therefore, MacArthur is officially guilty of only one murder. In 2003 he was moved to the low-security Shelton Abbey Prison in Co. Wicklow to prepare him for eventual release into the community.

While MacArthur is considered a lower security risk, another murderer who has been in prison for over 20 years is still considered a high-security prisoner. John Cullen was 33 years old when in November 1983 he was jailed for life for the murder of Dolores Lynch by setting fire to her home at Hammond Street in Dublin the previous January. Dolores's mother and aunt also died in the fire. Cullen has spent much of his life sentence in Portlaoise and Wheatfield Prisons and is still considered a very dangerous character.

For the protection of every person, more action must be taken to ensure greater monitoring of life sentence prisoners who are granted temporary release. While the case of random killer Thomas Murray is the clearest example of the effects of failing to keep track of murderers who are on temporary release, he is not the only one to commit further gratuitous violence.

Dominic Burke was just 19 years old when he and an accomplice attacked a bachelor farmer in Ballinhassig, Co. Cork, in 1984. The farmer died after being severely beaten, and Burke was found guilty of murder and was given a life sentence. However, just nine years later in 1993 Burke was given periods of temporary release and for three years he appeared to have turned a corner in his life, working as a forester and on building sites. However, around this time he also developed a gambling problem, and when he got into debt he became involved with a gang that in October 1996 broke into a cottage in Co. Cork and terrorised a 74-year-old man and his 73-year-old brother-in-law during the course of a robbery. At the time he took part in the attack Burke was actually at large, having failed to return to prison over four weeks before. He was later jailed for seven years for the attack, with the sentence to run concurrent with his life sentence.

Another life sentence prisoner was alleged to have tried to entice children into his car while out on temporary release. This man was 26 years old when in 1986 he was convicted of murdering his wife in Dublin by beating her with an iron bar. However, he was later given temporary release from prison, and a jury at the Dublin Circuit Criminal Court later heard evidence of how in 1999 the man had allegedly approached four children in Dublin's inner city under the pretence of 'looking for directions'. The man was found not guilty of the charge by direction of the judge. However, he was taken back into custody and put on East 2 landing in Arbour Hill Prison to continue his life sentence.

Because of the fact that anyone who is convicted of the murder of a garda or prison officer will only serve a maximum of 40 years in prison, it is very likely that if any regular lifer ever ends up spending 40 years in prison (and unlike Jimmy Ennis they actually want to get out), such killers will bring a court case challenging their continued incarceration.

One man who will likely remain in prison for a very long time is convicted double rapist, Philip Colgan. He was just 19 years old when he was given an eight-year sentence for raping a 79-year-old woman after breaking into her home in north Dublin in 1992. He was also given a concurrent six-year sentence for sexually assaulting a Spanish student on the same night. While in Mountjoy Jail, he became a model prisoner and he secured early release from his eight-year sentence. In March 1999 he found himself back on the streets and, in another random attack, he abducted and murdered 24-year-old Layla Brennan shortly after she got into his car in Dublin. He brought Layla's body to the Dublin Mountains and hid her remains in undergrowth. He later confessed to his wife what he had done and he is now serving a life sentence for Layla Brennan's murder. The Brennan family cannot comprehend how a double rapist could be allowed to walk the streets unchecked. Layla was an adored daughter and sister, and the circumstances of her murder highlight what happens when the State fails to keep track of the most dangerous people in this country.

One serious anomaly that exists with a life sentence is where a murderer is also convicted of raping his victim. It is simply not right that a person who is convicted of two such separate crimes receives concurrent sentences. In one particularly disturbing case a murderer was not only given a life sentence for murdering a teenage girl, but was also given a ten-year concurrent sentence for raping his murder victim. The feeling of the girl's family, and indeed the Gardaí who investigated the case, is that the sentence does not reflect the depravity of the crime. They rightly argue that the crime of rape is a horrendous physical attack in itself, and as such it should be treated as a separate crime. Detectives believed the murderer should have first been made to serve the sentence for rape and when this ten-year sentence was completed, he should have then begun his life sentence.

There are only a small number of women who are serving life sentences for murder, the most high profile of which is Catherine Nevin. She was convicted of murdering her husband, Tom Nevin, who was shot dead at their pub, Jack White's, in Co. Wicklow in March 1996. Nevin did not pull the trigger herself and a jury accepted the prosecution case that she had hired a hitman to murder Tom and to tie her up to make it look like a robbery. She is a model prisoner, and like possibly every female murderer at the Mountjoy Women's Prison, she is likely to get parole at some stage in the future. It is worth noting that Nevin was not given the maximum ten-year sentence for soliciting three men to murder her husband, even though she had obviously solicited someone else who was prepared to commit the murder. Instead, she was given a seven-year sentence to run concurrently with her life sentence for murder. It is likely that when the Parole Board comes to consider Nevin's case they will attach some weight to the fact that the judge who heard the case did not give her the maximum sentence for soliciting to kill.

Of the lifers in Irish prisons, a handful are suspected of being responsible for other murders. Some men are considered suspects for the random murders of women, while others are suspects for unsolved gangland murders, and a small number of other lifers are suspects for murders in other jurisdictions. One long-serving prisoner was asked to submit a DNA sample as part of an investigation in Britain into an unsolved murder of a young woman. Through the PCR technique, the police in Derbyshire hope evidence left at the scene of a murder in 1970 can now be matched with the killer. The suspect in an Irish prison, however, declined to give a DNA sample.

There are many issues that need to be addressed in relation to life sentence prisoners: the need to tag repeat offenders; the need for powers to compel the giving of DNA samples; the prospect of re-interviewing or even hypnotising murderers who may have killed others; the need to keep proper track of every lifer given temporary release; the need for the authorities to treat the families of murder victims with dignity and respect; and the need to give a true and proper meaning to the term, 'life imprisonment'. In every town and village in Ireland there is a family which has not only been affected by murder, but also by the added trauma of uncertainty about when a convicted murderer might be released from prison.

Donal Kealy often rings the Training Unit at Mountjoy Jail to ask about his daughter's killer. Catherine was strangled to death in a car park in Thurles in April 1992 by Anthony Kiely. He was convicted of Catherine's murder and jailed for life, but more recently has been given temporary release to attend work courses. Donal Kealy says the justice system is on the side of the murderer.

I had thought that life meant life, but I soon learned that life means seven years plus. I am not a cruel person, but I cannot fully grieve for my daughter, knowing her killer is getting day release to attend classes and going back to prison at night. It's a disgrace. The reason there are so many murders in this country is because killers know they can get out of prison after a relatively short time. This killer has destroyed all our lives. The whole system is a pure joke.

One prison officer tells me how long-term lifers are essential in prisons.

Lifers are the backbone of the prison population. Prison is their long-term 'home' and naturally they want to keep their house clean, and many of the older lifers tend to help prison officers keep the prison orderly. And they know there will be a fair payback for them at some stage with parole or more relaxed prison visits. One prison now has a family room, where a murderer's family can come and visit for a whole day with the lifer. There is a TV in the room and flowers and it doesn't look like a prison cell.

Some of the convicted murderers who will one day qualify for parole are parents who have killed their own children. Some are declared insane and placed in the Central Mental Hospital, while others are now serving life sentences among the mainstream prison population. It is imperative that these people are tagged or monitored for the rest of their lives, just as much as any random killers who may convince the authorities they are reformed and rehabilitated.

Over 50 years ago Nurse Katie Cooper wrote of her desire to see a safe and peaceful world. Katie witnessed the suffering of many people and yearned for a better world for future generations. Her murder in 1953 and the subsequent execution of her killer marked a dark period in Irish life. And since that time hundreds of Irish citizens have been murdered, yet only a handful of killers have served anything near a life sentence. It is the families of murder victims who are really serving life sentences today.

In Newbridge, Sinéad Smullen has tried to get on with her life after the murder of Leilah. She tells me her baby girl was 8 lb 11 oz. Sinéad didn't think she could ever recover from losing her. Yet somehow she struggled through and found the strength to attend the Central Criminal Court and see her former boyfriend jailed for life for his daughter's murder. She later formed another relationship and has a little boy named Shane. She says she will always remember Leilah.

She was loved so much and she is still loved. She was my first-born child and I'll never forget her, my first baby, my first girl. Half my heart is still with her, and half is here with little Shane now. Shane is my pride and joy.

The covering of the cot where Leilah's life was taken was light blue. It featured little teddy bears wearing pyjamas and hugging the moon.